This is a collection of newly commissioned essays by established scholars, responding to recent debate on political theatre of the turbulent early years of the seventeenth century. Theatre is widely interpreted, to take in masques and civic pageantry as well as plays for the public and private stages.

The authors attend to the workings of censorship, the social implications of pageantry, Reformation ideals and popular theatre and to the politics of the masque throughout the period. An early chapter discusses the work of revisionist and post-revisionist historians. The drama of Jonson, Dekker, Middleton, Massinger, Chapman, Heywood and Rowley is given detailed attention, while Shakespeare's plays are considered in the introductory chapter in relation to recent trends in political criticism.

THEATRE AND GOVERNMENT UNDER THE EARLY STUARTS

THEATRE AND GOVERNMENT UNDER THE EARLY STUARTS

EDITED BY

J. R. MULRYNE

Professor of English, University of Warwick

and

MARGARET SHEWRING

Lecturer in Theatre Studies, University of Warwick

CAMBRIDGE
UNIVERSITY PRESS

Published by the Press Syndicate of the University of Cambridge
The Pitt Building, Trumpington Street, Cambridge CB2 1RP
40 West 20th Street, New York, NY 10011–4211, USA
10 Stamford Road, Oakleigh, Melbourne 3166, Australia

© Cambridge University Press 1993

First published 1993

Printed in Great Britain at the University Press, Cambridge

A catalogue record for this book is available from the British Library

Library of Congress cataloguing in publication data
Theatre and government under the early Stuarts / edited by
J. R. Mulryne and Margaret Shewring.
p.   cm.
Collected essays originating from a conference held at Stratford on Avon in October 1987,
and a seminar at the University of Warwick in November 1988.
Includes index.
ISBN 0 521 40159 3
1. Theater – England – History – 17th century.
2. Theater and state – England – History – 17th century.
3. Theater – Political aspects – England – History – 17th century.
I. Mulryne, J. R.   II. Shewring, Margaret.
PN2592.T46   1993
792'.0942'09032 – dc20   92–33796   CIP

ISBN 0 521 40159 3 hardback

In memory of
Margot Heinemann

Contents

ix

Contributors

SIMON ADAMS is Senior Lecturer in History at the University of Strathclyde. He has published numerous articles on aspects of Elizabethan and early Stuart politics and foreign policy, and is co-editor of *England, Spain and the Grand Armada, 1585–1604* (1991)

MARTIN BUTLER is Lecturer in English at the University of Leeds, author of *Theatre and Crisis 1632–42* (1984) and of *Ben Jonson: Volpone* (1987), and editor of *The Selected Plays of Ben Jonson* vol. II (1988)

RICHARD DUTTON is Professor of English at the University of Lancaster. He is the author of *Mastering the Revels: The Censorship of English Renaissance Drama* (1991), *Ben Jonson: to the First Folio* (1983) and *William Shakespeare: A Literary Life* (1989) and co-editor of *The New Historicism and Renaissance Drama* (1992).

JULIA GASPER took her D.Phil. at Somerville College, Oxford, in 1989. She now teaches at Mansfield College, Oxford. Her book *The Dragon and the Dove: the Plays of Thomas Dekker* was published by Oxford University Press in 1990.

MARGOT HEINEMANN was until her death in 1992 Fellow of New Hall, University of Cambridge. Her work on seventeenth-century drama and society included *Puritanism and Theatre* (1980), and essays in *Political Shakespeare* (1985), *The English Revolution Revived* (1988) and *The Cambridge Companion to English Renaissance Drama* (1990). She also wrote studies on literature of the 1930s and a novel, *The Adventurers* (1960).

JAMES KNOWLES lectures in Medieval and Renaissance Literature at the University of Dundee. His main research interests lie in John Marston, the relationship between early Jacobean drama and politics and Midlands culture in the seventeenth century.

KATHLEEN MCLUSKIE is Senior Lecturer in English and American Literature and Pro-Vice-Chancellor at the University of Kent. She is author of the 'Plays and Playwrights' section of *The Revels History of Drama in English*, vol. IV (1981), and of *Renaissance Dramatists: Feminist Readings* (1989) and editor of Webster's *The Duchess of Malfi*.

J. R. MULRYNE is Professor of English and former Pro-Vice-Chancellor, University of Warwick. He is General Editor of the Revels Plays and of Shakespeare's Plays in Performance, and author and editor of studies on Shakespeare and Elizabethan and Jacobean drama. With Margaret Shewring he has edited and contributed to collections of essays including *War, Literature and The Arts in Sixteenth Century Europe* (1989), *Theatre of the English and Italian Renaissance* (1991) and *Italian Renaissance Festivals and Their European Influence* (1992).

GRAHAM PARRY is Reader in English at the University of York. He is author of *Hollar's England, The Golden Age Restor'd, Seventeenth Century Poetry: the Social Context* and *The Seventeenth Century: the Intellectual and Cultural Context of English Literature, 1603–1700*

MARGARET SHEWRING is Lecturer in Theatre Studies, University of Warwick and associate General Editor of Shakespeare's Plays in Performance. She has published an edition of Sir Robert Howard's *The Great Favourite*, and studies of Shakespeare, Elizabethan drama and Max Reinhardt. *This Golden Round: The Royal Shakespeare Company at the Swan* (jointly with Ronnie Mulryne) appeared in 1989.

Preface

The essays collected in this volume take their origin from a conference jointly sponsored by the Graduate School of Renaissance
Studies of the University of Warwick and the Shakespeare Institute
of the University of Birmingham, held at Stratford-upon-Avon in
October 1987. Some essays are revised and developed versions of
papers offered at the conference; others have been specially invited
for inclusion here. Almost all the contributors took part in a follow-
up seminar at the University of Warwick in November 1988. At
both conference and seminar, shared discussion of the volume's topic
benefited from the participation of colleagues whose work does not
appear in this collection, but whose knowledge and advice influenced a number of contributions. We are grateful in particular to
Professor Muriel Bradbrook, Mrs Julia Briggs, Mr Leo Salingar,
Professor Jerzy Limon, Professor Andrew Gurr, Dr Blair Worden
and Dr Janet Clare. Since the seminar, versions of the papers have
gone back and forth between the editors and the contributors for
further revision and up-dating. We should like to thank each of our
colleagues for patience, forbearance and tact. We also owe a debt of
gratitude to Sarah Stanton and Cambridge University Press, who
have been unfailingly encouraging, and to Pauline Wilson and
Charmaine Witherall for skilled secretarial help.

R.M. and M.S.

xiii

CHAPTER I

Introduction: theatre and government under the early Stuarts

J. R. Mulryne

Something scarcely less than a revolution has taken place in recent years in political readings of Shakespeare and of his Stuart contemporaries and successors. The revolution, like most revolutions, has not been bloodless. Possibly its most obvious aspect, in particular to those not directly involved, has been the academic hard knocks that have been exchanged between those who have taken up front-line positions. Attacks and counter-attacks signal in academic matters more than the normal growth of scholarly knowledge: questions of value and ideology are involved. Some participants have seen in the debate over Stuart drama nothing less than the reflection of a changing cultural awareness, one that offers the opportunity to bring about practical change, in teaching strategies, in institutional structures, even in society itself. Others have distanced themselves from these aims, and rejected the implied value-judgements, while not being unaffected by the new perspectives. Again like most revolutions, this revolution has conserved a good deal, despite signals in some quarters to the contrary.

Some ten or twelve years after the first studies in what came to be known as 'new historicist' and 'cultural materialist' interpretation seemed an opportune moment to bring together a collection of essays by established scholars that, while not being methodologically committed, would draw on and advance recent interpretation. It also seemed appropriate that the invited essays, though they could not be comprehensive, should nevertheless address a wide range of theatre texts, broadly defined, across the whole period between the accession of James I and the Civil War. Readers of the volume will, we hope, be stimulated by contributions that seek to offer a current interpretation of political theatre, in its various forms, over one of the most debated periods of English history.

Setting a political context for Renaissance plays has been

common practice, especially in the field of Shakespeare studies, since early this century, and before. Yet the terms in which the discussion is conducted have significantly changed, and in two distinct though related ways. The first has been the emergence of genuinely inter-disciplinary work between scholars trained in departments of history and those from departments of literature and theatre, with influen-tial contributions from philosophy and the social sciences. From the perspective of literature departments, it is tempting to see this development as a symptom of that crisis of English which sends teachers of a methodologically restricted discipline in search of new fields to practise in. It is true that some scholars have so regarded it, and departmental boundaries have been patrolled, trespass alleged, and a perhaps even higher level of mutual doubt entertained. Yet at best a genuine re-orientation of scholarly interest has taken place, a change from within, and the results have been impressive.

This institutional realignment derives from a theoretic re-positioning which though logically prior may be seen as the second of the major developments. To write of setting a political 'context' (or 'background') for seventeenth-century plays is to employ a language inappropriate to the newer scholarship. Theatre is now seen crucially as agent, and not or not merely reflection, of the events and issues of its time, a culturally and politically active receiver and transmitter of social energies.[1] To use Jonathan Goldberg's formula: 'language [including theatre] and politics are mutually constitutive ... society shapes and is shaped by the possi-bilities in its language and discursive practice'.[2] Such a stance has been anticipated, if not theoretically formulated, by scholars such as G. K. Hunter and J. W. Lever,[3] but has now become an altogether more conscious assumption. The outcome has been a shift of focus that is also by implication a theoretic revaluation. As Don Wayne phrases it, stressing the politically active role of theatre:

These texts are now being studied in relation to a broader range of representational strategies of legitimation or contestation in Elizabethan and Jacobean culture. In such criticism the figure of *Power* has displaced that of the *Idea* which was the essential constituent of Renaissance scholar-ship in Tillyard's generation.[4]

Readers of the present collection may note that, considered super-ficially in institutional terms, the new directions of scholarly practice are only partially reflected: Simon Adams alone among our contri-butors teaches in a department of history, while the others come from academic training in literature and theatre. Yet, at a more serious level, the essays collected here do respond to the new emphases: in stressing political effect more than literary or theatrical 'quality', in consciously extending the boundaries of the canon, in evaluating the cultural influence of censorship and control, in the leading attention given to previously marginal forms such as masque and civic pageantry, and in the manner in which, and the extent to which, historical evidence is assessed and deployed. The essays are on the surface non-theoretical, but they assume in their methods and their interests many of the conclusions of recent theory. If they largely avoid the allusiveness of some new historicist writing, they share many of its assumptions about the social role of theatre. In both regards, they may be seen as situated within one sector of a British more than an American development of the recent scholarship of Renaissance drama.[5]

The gains and limitations of the newer scholarship have been described and assessed elsewhere,[6] so that no more than a summary is appropriate here. Certain directions of interest have quite clearly emerged. The left-of-centre stance of critics contributing to the movement known as cultural materialism derives from the work of their mentors, Christopher Hill and Raymond Williams. With the shift of emphasis in their writing from idea to power (in Wayne's terms) has gone an increased stress on economic as well as political factors in social experience, and on the power-relations of gender politics. Marxist readings of historical process, with the human subject constructed by economic and ideological forces, have replaced more traditional understandings of human identity. There has been a readiness in much of the newer criticism to extrapolate from Stuart political theatre models and lessons applicable to the modern world, and equally a readiness to read back twentieth-century experience into the political and theatrical life of the seventeenth century. These approaches have been justified both by claims about the incipient modernity of Stuart mentalities, and by deconstructionist theories of reading; they may also be seen to sit easily alongside directorial practices in twentieth-century theatre. Among modern dramatists, Brecht has become the chosen theorist by whose light Stuart political drama has come to be read, both by reason of his own creative interest in the theatre of the period, and by reason of the theory and practice of alienation, differentiating our experience from the past while engaging us with it. All of this has been underpinned by explorations of the analogies to be drawn between political and theatrical display. Here in particular the concerns of cultural materialism and new historicism converge, with critics of both schools interpreting the conflicts inherent in the theory and practice of Stuart absolutism. New historicists have in general identified in political practices strategies of containment which, while admitting subversive tendencies, have also neutralised them; the alternative stress on unresolved conflict has tended to appear in the work of cultural materialists. Yet the separation of the two approaches should not be too rigidly insisted upon: the emphasis of some of Stephen Greenblatt's recent new-historicist writing, for example, while continuing to acknowledge the strategies of containment, nevertheless lays stress on the contingency of texts seen as 'the sites of institutional and ideological contestation'.[7]

The stimulus of this work to new thinking about Stuart drama, even among those who refuse any of the new labels, has been enormous, especially as it follows a period of relative decline in the interpretation of Renaissance theatre, at least outside Shakespeare. There have been losses, perhaps, as Walter Cohen has remarked,[8] in the nuanced interpretation of the detail of theatre texts; the readiness to emphasise explanatory matrices (in life or in theatre) has on occasion caused the interpreter to lose sight of subtlety, uncertainty, change-of-mind and muddle. The displacement of providentialist and essentialist readings of history has sometimes led only to the imposition of equally determinist models. A. D. Nuttall argues that Marxism may be considered the 'most spectacular version of essentialism in modern times', and Marxist explanations have been to the fore in discussion of Stuart theatre and politics.[9] Whether we accept Nuttall's assessment or turn it down – and it applies more straightforwardly, he would agree, to British critics such as Jonathan Dollimore than to Americans like Louis Montrose or Stephen Greenblatt – there can be little doubt that the newer scholarship will need to come to terms even more thoroughly with a nuanced 'close reading' of theatre texts, along the way to realising its full potential. It will have to adapt also (the point is not entirely a separate one) to the specifically performance characteristics of theatre texts, and not only from a theoretical standpoint, where significant gains have been made. Misunderstood Brechtianism in the modern theatre has sometimes undervalued emotion, and there are indications of a similar tendency in the newer criticism.[10] Most significantly, some recovery may be needed of a more thoroughly comprehensive and re-balanced sense of the intellectual and imaginative culture of the period. The wish to displace conservative stereotypes, broadly Christian-humanist and elitist in derivation, has resulted in an unwarranted foregrounding of politically and religiously subversive views. We have been helped to see close up, and with greater clarity, some of the grain of people's lives, in the economic sphere and in gender politics especially; in recent criticism the underprivileged, the marginal and the unusual (even the bizarre) have been acknowledged. Some re-emphasis may now be required on some of the less conflictual elements in social and political experience, from faith and charity to loyalty and altruism. The profit-and-loss account of the newer scholarship shows a healthy credit balance, and one that is drawn on in this volume; but here and elsewhere there are signs that a newer revisionism is needed and under way.

II

Within the newer scholarship, as outside it, the political plays of Shakespeare have continued to receive overwhelming critical and theatrical attention. Partly for this reason, we have not included separate discussion of Shakespeare in the chapters that follow. It may therefore be appropriate to offer at this point some brief commentary and assessment.

Shakespeare criticism over the last five years, according to R. S. White's summary, has undergone, like Stuart theatre generally, what he calls an 'unprecedented re-definition'. What once looked like the impending marginalisation of Shakespeare, understood as a 'canonical' and 'arch-conservative' writer, has been deflected instead into the presentation of 'a much more progressive figure'.[11] This newer account, testimony as much as anything to the resilience of Shakespeare as cultural icon, takes its departure from the displacement (itself by now thoroughly traditional) of E. M. W. Tillyard's account of the dramatist as orthodox political theorist. Yet a progressive Shakespeare seems to run counter to much in the plays, and there is a good deal to be said for the historian Blair Worden's view of Shakespeare conducting his political analyses from *within* rather than in opposition to contemporary prejudices and perceptions. Worden sees providentialism, so central a preoccupation of both supporters and detractors of a conservative Shakespeare, as an occasional rather than a dominant feature of the playwright's thinking. He shows him accepting monarchy as the normal – and sanctioned – form of government, as well as sharing contemporary fears of insurrection and a contemporary distaste for extreme religious attitudes. The plays could only have been written, Worden argues, in an age which was also the age of Machiavelli, and of an incipient Tacitean, non-providentialist, reading of history. Yet Shakespeare's *œuvre*, he says, 'shows none of the self-conscious and risky preoccupation with the new politics and the new history to be found in Jonson or Chapman or Daniel'.[12] This balanced account, persuasive as it is, may nevertheless be limited by a tendency to regard the plays as documents, rather than as agents in a socio-political process. Margot Heinemann takes the more inclusive view when, for example, she reads *Richard II* as inviting its audience to search for answers to the insoluble questions of royal authority: 'it is not the answer', she writes, 'but the question that subverts'. 'The drama', she adds, 'gives people images to think with.'[13] Such images render the plays subversive in effect, if subversion is understood as a conscious awareness of the fictions and suppressions of rule, with the potential, at least, of stimulating political change.

One outcome of the reinterpretation of Shakespeare and politics has been the interest recently taken in such plays as the three parts of *Henry VI*, where earlier dismissal of the plays' failure as formal structures has been converted into admiration for 'realistic' non-coherence and bleakness of word and action. *King John*, too, has been re-evaluated, with its corrosive view of the king in office and its exposure of the venal motives that lead to war, of the ignoble behaviour of church and state, and of the patriotism that if it triumphs does so in circumstances and through language that set question marks over against traditional values; Deborah Warner's celebrated production for the Royal Shakespeare Company exactly caught the instabilities, potentially anarchic, of the play's portrayal of political motivation and action.[14] The second tetralogy of histories, frequently performed in this century, has recently undergone its own re-emphasis. In a moment of crisis in the 1590s, *Richard II* was censored (or so it appears) for raising questions of deposition and succession too directly; but the self-undermining of kingship is now most often played as continuous, not momentary. Henry V in criticism and performance is now seen not as hero-king, but as one agonising over matters of legitimacy, and uncomfortably addressing the issue of national solidarity when vulnerably exposed in war. Most of all, the *Henry IV* plays disquietingly picture the conflicts of value that surround monarchic rule, personal, chivalric and in the initiation and conduct of battle. The second part in particular provides just those images to think with that, while a censor might have difficulty in identifying passages to excise, nevertheless may be interpreted as implicitly subversive. Whether in Whitehall or Gloucestershire, the questioning of established pieties is insistent, and the play's innovative dramaturgy, what Trevor Nunn identified as its subtle and disturbing rhythms, its Chekhovian scenic structures, makes its own case by means of the subversion of expected theatre forms. *2 Henry IV*, to use Stephen Greenblatt's words, 'seems to be testing and confirming a dark and disturbing hypothesis about the nature of monarchical power in England: that its moral authority rests upon a hypocrisy so deep that the hypocrites themselves believe it'.[15] If the Admiral's Men lost out in the inter-theatre rivalry of the years when Shakespeare was writing his histories, it may now be argued it was because the genius of their opponents' principal dramatist was not merely in some undifferentiated sense more creatively ample, but more acutely and disturbingly political.

The histories fall just outside the period dealt with in this volume, but they form the basis of political thought on which Shakespeare's later theatre builds. A play such as *Measure for Measure* has recently been given political readings emphasising the uses and abuses of power, and *Troilus and Cressida*, always interpreted as a disquieting play, morally, philosophically and politically, has received performances, such as those by Manfred Wekwerth and Joachim Tenschert for the Berliner Ensemble (Edinburgh, 1987) or by Howard Davies for the Royal Shakespeare Company (Stratford-upon-Avon, 1985), that lay stress on social and political failure. The tragedies, considered in a political perspective, have received something of a similar re-direction. *Coriolanus* has been much discussed. The play evidently provides a model of a society where the sinews that should hold it together have become overstretched to the point of rupture, and where the alternative modes of authority, hierarchic and representative, that in a late Renaissance state must be reconciled if the society is to be viable, are each disabled by flaws, personal and structural, at the heart. Jonathan Dollimore has shown how the *virtus* Coriolanus so strenuously seeks is ambiguously a matter of personal essence and derivative from the values of *realpolitik*; the implication is 'the radically contingent nature not just of personal identity but, inseparably, of the present historical conjuncture'.[16] Stanley Cavell confirms Dollimore's insight, seeing the play as questioning the most basic understandings out of which the *polis* is constructed.[17] If *Coriolanus* is politically contemporary, it is so, not or not primarily because of references, veiled or open, to corn riots or to individual players on the political scene, nor does its value lie in forecasting the approaching Revolution (though its pre-vision of the unhappily irresolute condition of the Revolution's later stages would have made it then a remarkably current piece). Rather it provides, again, a country of the mind that audiences may explore in the construction of their own, potentially subversive, political awareness.

Other tragedies construct equally disturbing political worlds. *King Lear* invites its audiences to imagine a time when division, not integration, characterises political and family life, where kingly and paternal want of intelligent feeling are intensified to the point of madness, and where reconciliation cannot practically accommodate the destructive forces. If we say that, considered politically, all this serves as tribute, by inversion, to the integrative ideals of James's commonwealth, we ignore the overwhelmingly *disintegrative* force of the play experience, overlook its disruption of state, family, reason, even the discourse of theatre itself (language, costume, stage-perspective) and confine to moral and political platitude what the audience's imagination receives as experiential truth. We overlook also the Jacobean audience's recognition, unconscious or aware, of the current parallels, however partial and qualified, of tyrant king, unfeeling father, corrupt judge.[18] Margot Heinemann has empha-sised the social dimension of the play's exploration of disorder:

The central focus is on the horror of a society divided between extremes of rich and poor, greed and starvation, the powerful and the powerless, robes and rags, and the impossibility of real justice and security in such a world.[19]

Read in this way, the tragedy's effect is the enlargement of consciousness that in a repressive state is politically unwelcome, and in a state selectively and intermittently repressive, such as James's, is resisted by authority only when too acutely specific for comfort (the history of Shakespeare production in the formerly communist European countries offers an instructive parallel).[20] The greater works of theatre, in the seventeenth century as today, both inform popular consciousness and influence as well as ride the stream of history.

It may seem that other Shakespearean tragedies can only with some strain be considered political. Patently, issues of perception, of affection and malice, sit at the heart of *Othello*, though even here a testing of the values of soldiership, the values that in considerable degree underprop the nation state, offers a political perspective. *Julius Caesar* and *Antony and Cleopatra* more directly address questions of government. In the former, too, the place of rhetoric in public life, and the perils of opinion and rumour, invite an audience to see events in the contemporary world in a newly conscious way; Richard Wilson shows how through allusion to 'the radical subversiveness of carnival' the play mimics a crucial juncture in the precarious cultural reconstruction of the absolutist state.[21] In the latter the displacement of attention is not so much historic and geographical as evaluative: which loyalties are ultimate, and which provisional? Jonathan Dollimore shows how only a mistaken reading of *Antony and Cleopatra* can perceive love and *virtus* as simple antagonists: 'the language of desire', he writes, 'far from transcending the power relations which structure this society, is wholly in-formed by them'.[22] The play's extraordinary dramaturgy, as now understood through interpretation and performance, expresses theatrically the unstable mutuality of desire and political power.

Some commentators have thought the Last Plays more royalist and orthodox than their precursors. But if Peter Greenaway's *Prospero's Books*, at one extreme, can construe *The Tempest* as a visual tapestry of Renaissance commonplace, other interpretations (Peter Brook's *La Tempête*, Yukio Ninagawa's Japanese adaptation) recognise the unsettling questions of authority, as well as of reason, creativity and illusion, of which a Jacobean audience would have been aware. Paul Brown has written a challenging interpretation of the play as 'a limit text in which the characteristic operations of colonialist discourse may be discerned – as an instrument of exploitation, a register of beleaguerment and a site of radical ambivalence'.[23] More, *The Winter's Tale* patently sets question marks beside royal behaviour, even if it also offers a visionary future. Glynne Wickham and others have identified specific connections between these plays, as well as *Cymbeline* and *Two Noble Kinsmen*, and events at court.[24] There is more reason still to connect *Henry VIII*

with court auspices.[25] Yet the objection to seeing the plays as no
more than a confirmation of court values is not merely Sir Henry
Wotton's grumpy remark that *Henry VIII*'s mimicry of court practices was 'sufficient in truth within a while to make Greatness very
familiar, if not ridiculous',[26] perceptive as that remark is about the
perils of demystification in a hierarchical society. The subject-
matter of the plays overtly charts royal mismanagement and self-
blame as much as, or more than, achievement, and so potentially
invites subversive construction.

This account differs in its emphasis from some of the best-known
new historicist readings of the political plays. Leonard Tennenhouse sees pre-revolutionary drama as largely 'a vehicle for dissemi-
nating court ideology'.[27] Stephen Greenblatt, brilliantly articulate
in describing the contradictions of absolutist culture, nonetheless
emphasises its powers of containment. Greenblatt's perceptions and
stances are underpinned by a rehearsal of the dilemmas of self-
fashioning that render the individual's attempts at creating a stable
subjectivity at best temporary and at worst self-cancelling. Authority, sacred or secular, is rooted, Greenblatt tells us, in a contradiction of its own most cherished ideals: 'the charismatic authority
of the king, like that of the stage, depends upon falsification'.[28] But
he adds:

It is precisely because of the English form of absolutist theatricality that
Shakespeare's drama, written for a theatre subject to state censorship, can
be so relentlessly subversive: the form itself, as a primary expression of
Renaissance power, helps to contain the radical doubts it continually
provokes.[29]

The calculus is a nice one, between audience credulity and audience
scepticism; and performance, not only in theatre history but originally, could be decisive.[30] The lesson of history is that the centre
could not hold. In the real world, the closure of the theatres was not
just a practical event but a cultural one, and one the proleptic seeds
of which were sown long before. Shakespeare criticism of the last few
years has made us aware of the plays' political function in mirroring
as well as influencing the unstable world of its time; if the stress has
arguably fallen too heavily on the plays' oppositional effects, this has
been a necessary corrective for which the counterbalancing
awareness of the integrative if imperilled ideals to which the plays
pay tribute is now being re-supplied.

III

Stephen Greenblatt has contrasted with the tense balance of Shakespeare's political plays what he describes as 'the unequivocal, unambiguous celebrations of royal power with which the period abounds'. These celebrations – masques, royal entries, progress entertainments and the like – have, he says, 'no theatrical force and have long since fallen into oblivion'.[31] In an obvious sense he is right; with scarcely an exception, the masques and entertainments have not been revived, thus failing to participate in what Greenblatt calls the *energeia* of revival.[32] But their lack of 'theatrical force' may nevertheless consort with political significance of a more complex kind than Greenblatt allows. The social simplifications to which he points – a homogeneous, elite, audience, an apparent common participation in royalist fantasy – conceal strains and contradictions to which masquing texts and masquing occasions testify. The relation of anti-masque to masque (a creative strategy to which Ben Jonson was early led) bears a certain resemblance to the subversions that yet affirm royal authority in Greenblatt's analysis of the histories. To this degree, the masques and entertainments may be construed as reinforcements of court culture. Yet the practical circumstances of performance – mishap and unreadiness, ill-grace on the part of the principal spectator, squabbling ambassadors and ill-behaved courtiers – point to something other than hours and minutes of elite fantasising. Moreover, the texts of masques and entertainments reveal, when set beside current events and current preoccupations, a series of strategic adjustments, suppressions and re-makings that are in themselves both directly and by implication political. The essays by Graham Parry and Martin Butler in this volume show how these adjustments, and the content and temper of the masques, vary as the political life of the Stuart court varies, making them more sensitively political, in both general and particular ways, than has commonly been thought.

It may be useful to pursue this question of the current significance of the court entertainment a little further, in order to open up more fully the complex of senses in which masquing occasions may be read as political.

In obvious ways, the masque is the theatre-form its original presenters would most readily have identified as directly concerned with theatre and government; and it is the form which, although serious work began well before the advent of the newer scholarship, has most directly benefited from it. Masques throughout the Stuart period were, as Martin Butler phrases it, 'at the point of intersection between politics and the arts,'[33] and the political resonances of the masque have become increasingly clear over the past fifteen years or so. Important work has also been done on the role of masques as endeavours of art, not least in establishing the work of Inigo Jones as the most notable and sustained contribution to theatre design in the history of the British stage.[34] Work on the music and dance of the masques has been less fully integrated into the general account of the form, no doubt because of the range of scholarly expertise such an undertaking requires.[35] Concentrating on the politics of the masque, it is easy to forget that dances represented the most extended part of the performance, and were intricately choreographed; that the bands accompanying the performance routinely numbered dozens of lutanists and violinists, woodwind players, trumpets and brass, and included named soloists of distinction; that the music was composed by the leading court composers of the day; that the songs were performed by trained and accomplished singers; that professional actors spoke the text; and that preparing, directing and co-ordinating all of this called for skill of a high order. The lavish financial outlay on masques and entertainments has been sufficiently interpreted politically, but less than due emphasis has perhaps been placed on the role of the masque as developing artistic experiment and competence across a wide range of art-forms, and as edging Britain into the European mainstream of courtly magnificence. It is salutary to be reminded, as Graham Parry reminds us below,[36] that contemporaries viewed the masques primarily in these terms, so far as surviving commentary records, referring to the excellence or failure of the spectacle, the elegance or otherwise of the dancing, and even the generic propriety of the contrivance – thus situating the politics of the masquing occasion in the history of aesthetics rather than the history of government.

Yet the masque *was* directly political, by virtue of its occasion and its audience, as well as its content. The occasion itself is charged with political implication, due to its privileged status as a festival moment. The masque performance *represents* the British court in 'magnificence' and aesthetic sophistication as well as subject-matter – before a European and not merely a British audience. But within the broad politics of international esteem (and aside from the parochial, though important, politics of ambassadorial rivalry), what are the political implications of subject-matter and reception? The difficulty for the interpreter is to know where to draw the boundaries of interpretation, which meanings to hold in focus and which to neglect. While it is true that Festival books and the printing of masque texts (or the preparation of scribal or holograph presentation copies) sought to provide some kind of permanence, the very uniqueness of the masque-occasion requires attention to be given to the specific moment, to the persons involved, to current disputes, factional groupings, styles of behaviour. Martin Butler expresses the challenge from the point of view of the masque writer who 'had tactfully to negotiate the complex statements and counter-statements passing in the event between King, Queen, Prince and Lords';[37] situating the writer in this way illuminates the embarrass-ments, tonal disjunctions, ellipses and suppressions to which the interpreter needs to be alert in commentary on the printed text.[38] It also provides a perspective on the sense in which, as in all occasional writing, but in a marked way in the masque, the author is consciously and not merely inevitably *decentred*. Such decentring invites political interpretation. So too, not infrequently, does the choice of subject-matter. The most evident case, so far as the early Stuart masque is concerned, is the topic of chivalry, with its impli-cation of a backward-looking political stance and a preference for militarist solutions to international politico-religious disputes.[39] Yet a taste for chivalric exercises could consort perfectly well, when the options closed down, with support for James's pacifist policies in a particular instance. The difficulty is to reconcile interpretation of broad cultural developments with the micro-politics, not always fully recoverable, of a particular occasion. The newer scholarship has taught us to pose these questions but not always as yet provided us with the means to answer them.

The entertainments for Henry in 1610 and 1611 provide a clear example of the complexities that confront the commentator on the political significance of masques. Stephen Orgel has remarked on the aesthetic instability that attaches to the conflation, or confusion, of the role of spectator and participant on any such occasion; here in the entertainments for Henry that essentially precarious relationship is put further at risk by the real if disavowed tensions between the political stance of Henry's party, recognisable if nowhere sharply defined, and that of James himself. As Graham Parry explains

below, 'an oppositional note' entered the writing of masques in the
years before Henry's early death (in 1612), and was sustained in the
afterglow of that traumatic event during the celebrations associated
with the Palatine wedding. How emphatic such dissent might have
become can be glimpsed in the distorting mirror of the so-called
Masque of Truth, an entertainment expressing in extreme form the
Protestant-alliance views associated with Henry.[40] The masque was
devised but not performed; so that suppression or self-censorship (or
conceivably accident) kept from public view and public hearing the
factional sentiments its text expresses. Yet in a real sense such sentiments are there as part of the political mind-set of the original audiences of masques and entertainments that *were* performed, from the
Barriers and *Oberon* to *The Lords' Masque* and *Tethys' Festival*, colouring
their reception. Parry also explains how international events – the
diplomatic crisis over the succession to the Duchy of Cleves – con-
ditioned the response of the *Barriers* audience to the attitudes to military aggression there presented. As the international scene changed,
so minds will have interpreted differently (and writers will have
differently presented) the political orientation of the entertainments –
in *Oberon*, for example, where no more than a few months later the
interpretive embarrassments relate not to questions of factional politics but to the fulsomeness of the praise for James, 'a god, o'er kings'
who teaches men 'by the sweetness of his sway, / And not by force'.[41]

Political adjustments to international policies or regal vanity are
by no means the finest mesh through which the original audience's
political response will have passed. A month or so after the presentation of the *Barriers*, Salisbury was called on to address a sceptical
House of Commons (as he had addressed the House of Lords)
arguing for financial supply for James in order to permit, among
much else, the public creation of Henry as Prince of Wales, and using
in his argument as instances of parliamentary approval just those
princes of Wales also cited, and their deeds exemplified, in the *Barriers* entertainment.[42] On 11 June 1610, days after Henry's creation,
Salisbury is once more with the Commons, pleading on James's
behalf for ratification of the Great Contract (seen as essential to
James's financial survival) and recurring in his speech to the magnificence of the creation festivities:

The creation of his son hath been performed with greatness, honor and
magnificence. If the expense of that be thought too much, I answer none of
both Houses, I am sure, will think it, and no man could expect that this

should be the first precedent of frugality in that kind, when not only all men ought to persuade the King to be that with honor which was so much to our comfort, but even private men opened themselves like marigolds against the sun to see such a glorious star as did assure the public and private fortunes of all men.[43]

In the minds of Salisbury's audience, though he rhetorically denies it, and perhaps in his own, there was evident resistance to such conspicuous expenditure at a time of royal bankruptcy; his words' tortuous syntax and unaccustomed (and strained) metaphors signal his embarrassment. How far was any such resistant stance an aspect of the politics of the Barriers, and then of *Tethys' Festival* (performed on 5 June 1610 as part of the creation festivities) and of *Oberon* (danced 1 January 1611, just before James dissolved his parliament)? Within the same span of time (on 25 March 1610) a proclamation was issued on James's behalf suppressing John Cowell's *The Interpreter*, promising stricter control of publishing, and fulminating against those who 'in these our dayes doe not spare to wade in all the deepest mysteries that belong to the persons or State of Kings or Princes, that are gods upon Earth'.[44] How far would the potential ironies, of disclosure and suppression, of benevolence and tyranny, of god-like privilege and mortal anxiety, consort together in the elite audience's mind to modify the political meanings of the current masques? To draw masques into the political arena (where in any case they demand to be) invites a multiplicity of perspectives, not all of which may be capable of reconciliation, and not all of which may be judged in keeping with the masque-writers' 'intention'. Yet each contributes to the politics of the occasion, and thus to the tensioned and complex interrelationships between theatre and government.

IV

The canon of political drama in the Stuart and late Elizabethan periods has been drawn up, as Julia Gasper remarks (pp. 190–1 below), with scant attention to the work of 'popular' playwrights such as Dekker, Heywood and Rowley, or their anonymous or forgotten collaborators. Recent theatrical performance has to an extent mitigated this neglect. Trevor Nunn's *The Fair Maid of the West*, for instance, a conflation of the two parts of Heywood's play, 'quite literally stormed the audience' at the Swan Theatre in Stratford-upon-Avon.[45] Yet response to the performance characteristically emphasised enjoyment while neglecting significance: 'mellow humanism', 'transforming magic', 'a feeling of well-being and happiness and generosity that pervaded the evening'.[46] Only Nunn himself insisted that 'the incident we *must* be serious about is the friendship that grows up between the young white sea-captain and the black Jaffa'.[47] Issues of race and of colonisation were understood by Nunn as implicit in even the most 'mellow' of theatre-pieces; and the uneasy relationship, as it has come to be understood, between adventure, trade and socio-political order could be seen as anticipated if not explored.

In line with this seriousness, some attention is now being given to the 'popular' plays in terms of the success with which they negotiate the controversial issues of the day. They are being read, that is to say, as historical documents that show the impress of social and political tensions and contribute to their development. Thus Alexander Leggatt finds in Dekker's *The Shoemaker's Holiday* not only class tension and embarrassed anger at the mutilations of war but also, in the play's ending, an apparently ideally functioning society compromised by awkwardness and strain.[48] *The London Prodigal*, too, though implying 'something fundamentally secure, familiar and reassuring'[49] may be read, Leggatt urges, as endorsing a set of values that sits not altogether comfortably alongside the formal hier-archical structures of official Stuart doctrine. Margot Heinemann takes this further when she remarks in the plays of Heywood and others the emergence of 'a new heroic model' who is a 'type of civic courage'[50] offering an implicit challenge (especially given the equiv-ocations over honour in King James's court)[51] to officially received and conscious ideologies. Even the raising of the English Bible to iconic status, in *If You Know Not Me* and elsewhere, 'had political and democratic connotations ... there were still those who thought a religion based on reading the Scriptures dangerous to the social order'.[52] One might argue indeed that Heywood's democratisation of learning in his four *Ages* plays, part though it is of a much wider social process, undermines the privileged exclusivity of learning (a stance shared, for example, with the mockery of privileged edu-cation in Middleton's *A Chaste Maid*). Leggatt remarks that two of the most visible of London's institutions, Bedlam and Bridewell, come into question in the two-part *The Honest Whore* for their social inutility; Dekker, he says, can 'use the fringe areas of his plays to suggest that the world is more intractable than conventional theatre allows'.[53] Such veiled subversion, a potential impetus to social change, while it marks the functioning of theatre at most times, is politically significant in a period overtly conscious, as the Stuart period was, of the need to exercise control of theatre performance.

If popular plays are being read for their implicit, perhaps unconscious, social and political criticism, there are plays for the same audience that, with varying degrees of candour, express a conscious political programme. Kathleen McLuskie demonstrates in this volume (pp. 225–31) how the popular audience for Dekker and Heywood shared 'a political culture which was oppositional but also loyal, which claimed popular support but was principally concerned with aristocratic values' (p. 225); in plays addressed to such an audience, specifically *Sir Thomas Wyatt* and *Edward IV*, she uncovers 'a politics of negotiation among contradictory alternatives', a collision of values that is reflected in the generic complexity of the dramatic form. Yet certain popular plays (including *Sir Thomas Wyatt*) may appear to wear their political allegiance to militant Protestantism (a stance not in favour at court) quite plainly on their sleeves. In 1977 Judith Spikes grouped together what she called 'elect nation' plays that derive their political philosophy, and to a considerable degree their narrative, from John Foxe's *Acts and Monuments*.[54] The group included Heywood's *If You Know Not Me* Parts I and II, Samuel Rowley's *When You See Me You Know Me*, Dekker and Webster's *Sir Thomas Wyatt*, and was epitomised in Dekker's *The Whore of Babylon* (in Julia Gasper's words 'the definitive militant Protestant play').[55] These plays were followed rather later by Shakespeare's *Henry VIII* and Thomas Drue's *The Duchess of Suffolk*. While there are now reservations about the emphasis on patriotism as distinct from religion in Spikes's analysis,[56] and while discriminations need to be made between the viewpoints of different plays, the existence of a group of such plays designed to counsel authority in ways authority might be reluctant to go, and to raise issues of sovereignty and obedience that were distinctly controversial, is bound to be of interest to the commentator on theatre and government. The analysis in this case, initially at least, can deal with matters of apparently conscious intent. A brief discussion of one such play may reveal how politically allusive the popular theatre can be, seeking to exercise, it may be argued, direct political influence, as well as exemplifying the culture of current politics.

Samuel Rowley's *When You See Me You Know Me*, one of the least discussed of these plays, shares their common characteristic of an overtly Protestant viewpoint. Played by 'the high and mightie Prince of Wales his servants', Rowley is himself designated on the titlepage 'servant to the Prince'; the subject-matter of the play, a 'Chronicle Historie of King Henry the eight' features 'the birth and virtuous life of Edward Prince of Wales'.[57] The play thus takes its place among the documents of expectant anticipation which militant Protestant writers addressed to Prince Henry (as later to his sister Elizabeth and her husband the Palsgrave) in the hope of influencing policy. The text refers extra-dramatically to the prince:

> KING HENRY: Now *Iane* God bring me but a chopping boy,
> Be but the Mother to a Prince of Wales
> Ad a ninth Henrie to the English Crowne
> And thou mak'st full my hopes ...   (lines 265–8)

The 'chopping boy' born to be Prince of Wales was in the play's history Edward VI, but the 'ninth Henrie' in an audience's mind in 1604 or 1605 was surely the present prince, son to King James. The identification continues throughout, culminating in the scene of pageantry that ends the play, when no less a figure than Charles V delivers an eulogy:

> True honoured off-spring of a famous King,
> Thou dost amaze me ...   (lines 2,899–900)

The Prince's reply is a model of decorum:

> Yes my good lord, in him there's Maiesty,
> In me there's love with tender infancie.   (lines 2,907–8)

Rowley is here negotiating what Roy Strong calls 'the great divide' between Henry and James.[58] A similar allusiveness may distinguish the scenes where the young Prince Edward resists learning in favour of tennis. James's despairing ambition for his son's scholarly progress is well known; the Venetian ambassador in 1607 reported:

He studies, not with much delight, and chiefly under his father's spur, not of his own desire, and for this he is often admonished and set down.[59]

It would be difficult to identify the play's unfortunate Browne, who has his backside whipped to encourage the prince to study, with any particular member of the 'little academy' of aristocratic youths (including Essex and William Cecil) set up around Henry soon after his arrival in London.[60] Yet the general aptness of the parallel is evident;[61] additionally, there may be allusion to James's propensity for bestowing honours, in the lines where Edward decides to knight Browne in recognition of his self-denying services on his behalf:

> WAL: What wilt thou knight him, Ned?
> PR: I will; my father ha's knighted many a one, that
> never shedde drop of blood for him; but hee ha's
> often for mee ...   (lines 1,856–9)

The point is not the incidental satire of James, common enough in contemporary plays, but the broader socio-political implications of Rowley's handling of a relationship that so directly recalls the most important players on the political scene in 1605. Rowley makes his sectarian points by showing Cranmer's tutoring of the prince, and in the virtual hagiography of Catherine Parr, 'a strong Lutheran' (line 2,125), who disposes of the Catholic case by a populist attack on the use of Latin, on pilgrimages and on belief in Purgatory (lines 2,253 ff). Thus the play's overt stance in matters of religion is made plain enough. Yet the *indirect* advice to James may be more significant still. King Henry accepts his son's knighting of Browne; the play thus juxtaposes chivalry with youngsters' games, and the scars of battle with the whip marks on a boy's backside. The effect is not so much parody of official attitudes or court ceremony as the endorsement of a generosity of outlook that can accommodate the exalted and the trivial. The play's King Henry could scarcely be regarded as a model for James; he is unpredictable, frequently irate, and not consistently sound on points of doctrine or the religious settlement. But his ebullient spirit and his contact with the people would surely be understood as implicit instruction for the recessive and iso-lationist James. The most inventive scenes in the play show Henry going disguised into night-time London, and when arrested trans-forming the prison into the court:

> WILL: M. Constable, you have made the Counter
> This night, the royal Court of *England's* King.
> [HENRY]: And by my crowne I sweare, I would not for
> A thousand pound t'ware otherwise.

The play's popular appeal consists in its diminishing the distance, even asserting the identity, between court and City; the connections are insisted upon, in language and incident throughout. They are intimated, too, in the figure of Black Will, the court jester whose humour derives from city jocularity rather than courtly jest. Even more, the rather moving episodes where Henry has to choose the life of his child or that of his queen, as she lies stricken in childbed, form the emotional climate within which matters of state are presented. The effect is to humanise, in a popular sense, the play's politics. Paradoxically perhaps, it may be argued that the popular plays, easy-going and 'mellow' as they are often taken to be, may contribute more fully to the circulation of social energy, and the redefinition of political norms – through their effect on their audience's mental images – than more sophisticated and canonical theatre-pieces.

V

Alexander Leggatt concludes a recent discussion of the popular plays by setting out the central position occupied in so many of them (for reasons clear enough) by lust and adultery. The implications are directly social:

Disloyal adulterous wives lose not so much their immortal souls as their places in a world that could have given them security. And they themselves become, like the prostitutes who haunt the fringes of these plays, damaged goods.[62]

The metaphoric connections Leggatt identifies in the popular plays between sin, social marginalisation and commercial unfitness become the insights that animate many plays by writers accepted as part of the literary canon, such as Middleton, Massinger and Jonson. A summary account of some of these plays and playwrights may help to set the frame within which the more focused studies in this volume are placed.

   The habitual association of women with merchandise, and sexual success with commercial cunning, marks out a central territory of Middleton's writing in particular. Thus Bianca, in *Women Beware Women*, understood by Leantio in virtually the same terms as the goods he factors – the idiom is common, and not only in Middleton – becomes by the play's end the property of a socially more powerful man: acquisitiveness by the exercise of power comes close to being vindicated – or shown at any rate as 'realistic' – as Bianca expresses consent to her rape and Leantio to his seduction (by a socially and financially more privileged woman) as they flaunt their gains in a scene (IV.v) of fine dressing and name-dropping. Only then does a last judgement impose a solution by insisting on the inexorable links between sin and death. The chief interest of the tragedy lies precisely in the disjunction between values that align loving, sex and social and commercial success, and those that close off such links (a disjunction that determines the play's ironic mode). It is set in Florence, but the incidental compliment to James, for 'wisdom' and 'judgement', only reminds us that its true topic is contemporary London.[63] Middleton's intensely practised knowledge of London ways, perfected through a long series of citizen comedies, identifies as crucial the tension between religion and social order on the one hand, and sexual and commercial prowess on the other. Thus his tragedy may be said to epitomise a crisis of values that has distinctly political implications.

Margot Heinemann has convincingly shown the subtle and pervasive links between Middleton's dramaturgy and what she calls 'the growing trends of Parliamentary Puritan criticism and opposition inside and outside the court'.[64] Those links are sometimes directly allusive; much more often they operate through establishing a dramatic equivalent to the tensions that characterise society's values. Middleton's finest comedy, *A Chaste Maid in Cheapside*, refers in its title to social and sexual disequilibrium; its characteristic mode consists of patterns of human behaviour that parody social ideals and human events and practices – birth and christening, family unity and promiscuity, fecundity and infertility, social rituals and regulation – in the service of an utterly disenchanted sense of how men and women behave in a society dominated by commercial values and social competitiveness.[65] The result is a comedy of high-spirited instability. This is appropriately termed 'oppositional theatre' when the connections are drawn that show how such instability undermines the increasingly fragile and theoretic definitions of social structure offered by those occupying positions of authority. That widening gulf makes itself felt in much of the writing of the time, dramatic and non-dramatic.

It would not be difficult to show how the instabilities of Middleton's work are replicated in other major playwrights up to the closing of the theatres. Webster, for instance, has been read increasingly as a writer whose long-acknowledged interest in the fragmentation of personality, of language and of theatrical idiom – a dramaturgy as innovative as it is precarious – can be seen as implicitly political in character. Jonathan Dollimore's association of the

decentring of the tragic subject in *The White Devil* with 'the demystifying of state power and ideology'[66] summarises in the newer idiom
what has long been discerned as the play's deliberate social and
moral incoherence;[67] but it also invites attention to its political *effect*,
in constituting at least for the time the audience's sense of the
power-relations between the privileged and the powerless, whether
socially, financially or in terms of gender. Webster's other great
play, *The Duchess of Malfi*, might be said even more powerfully to
associate power and privilege with violence and insanity, in a text
that takes its starting-point from a discussion of social order; it seems
almost as if the disintegrating structures of the play, in theatrical
idiom as in mental states and language, incorporate the human
non-viability of a society based on social and gendered power.
Chapman too, especially in *Bussy D'Ambois* and the *Byron* plays, may
be read as offering a searching critique of the political ideology that
derives from or depends upon the heroic, in itself the implicit
value-structure both of tragedy, as conventionally understood, and
of at least the overt practices and official language of the late
Renaissance court. If Jonathan Dollimore is correct in reading
Bussy's 'exclusion and poverty' as forcing on him 'a vantage point
from which he experiences the relative worthlessness of the social
order and, simultaneously, his dependence upon it',[68] then the
conflicts of value the play incorporates offer a remarkable commentary on the self-contradictions of Stuart absolutism, and the strains
within the official ideologies of James's court (which the masques, in
another and more deferential way, reflect and influence). Some
recent critics have found in Marston's work what Alexander Leggatt
calls 'the conservatism, the sense of a good world violated, that lies
behind so much Jacobean writing'. But Leggatt's complementary
sense of Marston's 'posturing child actors' expressing through the
overt theatricality of his plays' dramaturgy not only 'a real yearning
for order' but 'a real shock at its violation' seems closer to evoking
the implicitly subversive effect of plays whose subject-matter again
and again concerns itself with court values and court figures – and
their necessary fascination with appearance – but whose dramatic
effectiveness depends not upon shoring up those values but upon a
radical and sustained destabilising of the stage–audience relationship that casts into doubt the values' persuasiveness.[69] Above all,
perhaps, the plays of Jonson demonstrate theatrically the profound
incoherence that derives from and feeds back into the social ideolo-

gies of the period. Only rarely concerned in an overt way with political issues, in *Sejanus* especially, Jonson nevertheless explores in the great plays the contradictions of social energy and social value – competitiveness, greed, desire – which inform and destabilise the value-structure of more obviously political drama. If *Sejanus* was thought seditious when first performed it may have been for reasons more temporary and less comprehensively significant than was justified. The play's inherent ideological stance, holding together as it does a searing exposure of the realities of power and an attempted vindication of the need for hierarchy, is poignantly representative of the political contradictions of its time.[70] Just these contradictions, paralleled in the exuberant but uncomfortable dramaturgy of *Volpone*, *The Alchemist* and *Bartholomew Fair*, characterise the theatrical statement Jonson's playwriting makes; his whole career, indeed, rooted in the actualities of city merchandising and city fashion, but deferring to the values and privileges of the court, might be read as exemplary of the strains, practical and ideological, which were soon to make the effective government of Stuart England an impossibility.

A discussion such as the foregoing of the implicit ideologies of Stuart theatre, so far as canonical amphitheatre plays are concerned, is not only inadequate but patently selective. I have made no mention, for example, of tragicomedy, often read as socially and politically orthodox, though even that genre has been interpreted, by Walter Cohen especially, as showing a variousness of attitude that may include subversive possibilities.[71] Valid comment on dramatists of the later period, such as Ford and Shirley, would require a complex analysis of the social and political circumstances which render their plays no more than oblique commentary on prevailing ideology. Massinger offers in *A New Way to Pay Old Debts* a fascinating case of an unresolved tension between aristocratic and mercantile values, country ideals and city, with the former prevailing, yet unpersuasively: mirroring the conflicts, in a prejudiced way, of his own society. In *The Roman Actor* he develops the insights of Jonson's *Sejanus* into a self-questioning critique of the moral power of the drama itself, thus in some sense writing the obituary of the ideologically engaged play. Each of these, and others, would have to be included in any full and balanced account of theatre and government in these years. The essays that follow, various in their approaches and interests as they are, may be read as a contribution to that continuing, unresolved, discussion.

NOTES

1 See Stephen Greenblatt, *Shakespearean Negotiations* (Berkeley and Los Angeles, 1988; Oxford, 1990), especially chap. 1, 'The Circulation of Social Energy', pp. 1–20.
2 Jonathan Goldberg, *James I and the Politics of Literature* (Baltimore and London, 1983), p. xi. See also, for example, Jonathan Dollimore and Alan Sinfield, eds., *Political Shakespeare: New Essays in Cultural Materialism* (Manchester, 1985), p. 2.
3 G. K. Hunter, *John Lyly: The Humanist as Courtier* (London, 1962). J. W. Lever, *The Tragedy of State* (London, 1971; rev. edn, 1987).
4 Don E. Wayne, 'Power, Politics and the Shakespearian Text', in Jean E. Howard and Marion F. O'Connor, eds., *Shakespeare Reproduced: The Text in History and Ideology* (New York and London, 1987), p. 58.
5 Walter Cohen, 'Political Criticism of Shakespeare' in *ibid.* and Wayne, 'Power, Politics' both identify contrasting tendencies in recent British and American scholarship in the field.
6 See, for example, the essays cited in notes 4 and 5. See also the introduction to Jonathan Dollimore, *Radical Tragedy*, 2nd edn (New York and London, 1989); H. A. Veeser, ed., *The New Historicism* (London and New York, 1989); Jean E. Howard, 'The New Historicism in Renaissance Studies', *English Literary Renaissance*, 16 (1986) 13–43; and Edward Pechter, 'The New Historicism and Its Discontents: Politicising Renaissance Drama', *PMLA* 102 (1987) 292–303; Annabel Patterson, '"The Very Age and Body of the Time, its Form and Pressure": Rehistoricizing Shakespeare's Theater', *New Literary History*, 20 (1980) 83–104. Richard Wilson and Richard Dutton, eds., *New Historicism and Renaissance Drama* in the Longman Critical Readers series (London, 1992), with an excellent introduction and postscript by Wilson and Dutton, appeared too late to be drawn on in this volume.
7 See Greenblatt, *Shakespearean Negotiations*, 'The Circulation of Social Energy'. The quoted phrase comes on p. 3. For studies relevant to the issues summarised in this paragraph see, for example, Catherine Belsey, *The Subject of Tragedy, Identity and Difference in Renaissance Drama* (London and New York, 1985); Jonathan Dollimore and Alan Sinfield, eds., *Political Shakespeare: New Essays in Cultural Materialism* (Manchester and Ithaca, NY, 1985); John Drakakis, ed., *Alternative Shakespeares* (London and New York, 1985); Steven Mullaney, *The Place of the Stage: Licence, Play and Power in Renaissance England* (Chicago and London, 1988); Stephen Greenblatt, ed., *Representing the English Renaissance* (Berkeley, Los Angeles, London, 1988).
8 See Cohen, 'Political Criticism of Shakespeare', especially p. 29.
9 A. D. Nuttall, 'Point of Wonder', review of Stephen Greenblatt, *Marvellous Possessions: The Wonder of the New World* (Oxford, 1991) in *London Review of Books*, 13, no. 23, 5 December 1991, p. 13.

10 Compare Tom McAlindon, 'Tragedy, *King Lear*, and the Politics of the Heart', *Shakespeare Survey*, 44 (1992) 85–90.

11 R. S. White, 'Critical Studies', *Shakespeare Survey* 44 (1992) 223.

12 Blair Worden, 'Shakespeare and Politics', *Shakespeare Survey* 44 (1992) 1–15, p. 4.

13 Margot Heinemann, 'Political Drama', in A. R. Braunmuller and Michael Hattaway, eds., *The Cambridge Companion to English Renaissance Drama* (Cambridge, 1990), p. 177.

14 Deborah Warner's production of *King John* opened at The Other Place, the studio theatre of the Royal Shakespeare Company in Stratford-upon-Avon, in May 1988 and transferred to the Pit (Barbican Theatre, London) in May 1989.

15 Stephen Greenblatt, *Shakespearean Negotiations*, p. 55.

16 Jonathan Dollimore, *Radical Tragedy*, p. 229.

17 Stanley Cavell, '"Who Does the Wolf Love?" Reading *Coriolanus*', in Stephen Greenblatt, ed., *Representing the English Renaissance*, pp. 197–216.

18 For a discussion of the play's 'dangerous matter' of current political references, see Gary Taylor and Michael Warren, eds., *The Division of the Kingdom:Shakespeare's Two Versions of 'King Lear'* (Oxford, 1983).

19 Margot Heinemann, '"Demystifying the Mystery of State": *King Lear* and the World Upside Down', *Shakespeare Survey* 44 (1992) 78. Tom McAlindon, citing Bakhtin, rightly warns against a too-restrictive account of the politics of *Lear* by emphasising the place of 'emotional shock and pity' in the play's 'politics of the heart'. See 'Tragedy, *King Lear*', 85–90.

20 Productions such as the Bulandra Theatre's *Hamlet*, for example, with its caricatures of the Ceaucescu regime (performed at the Royal National Theatre in London, September, 1990) were tolerated in Communist Romania, either as a safety-valve, or because (as Richard Eyre's programme note suggested) 'the code was one that could be read by an audience but not challenged by the censors'.

21 See Richard Wilson, 'Shakespeare's Roman Carnival', *English Literary History*, 54 (1987) 31–44.

22 Dollimore, *Radical Tragedy*, p. 207.

23 Paul Brown, '"This thing of darkness I acknowledge mine": *The Tempest* and the Discourse of Colonialism', in Jonathan Dollimore and Alan Sinfield, eds., *Political Shakespeare*, pp. 47–71, p. 68.

24 See, for example, Glynne Wickham, '*The Two Noble Kinsmen* or *A Midsummer Night's Dream Part II*', in George Hibbard, ed., *The Elizabethan Theatre*, VII (London, 1980), pp. 167–96.

25 See R. A. Foakes, ed., *Henry VIII*, New Arden Shakespeare (London, 1957), but cf. Julia Gasper, pp. 207–8 below. Blair Worden persuasively identifies the early Tudor aspects of the court represented in *Henry VIII*, contrasting them with the late sixteenth-century characteristics of the

other histories, whatever the period in which these plays are ostensibly set (see Worden, 'Shakespeare and Politics', pp. 12ff.).

26 Quoted in Andrew Gurr, *The Shakespearean Stage, 1574–1642* 2nd edn (Cambridge, 1980), p. 226.

27 Leonard Tennenhouse, *Power on Display: The Politics of Shakespeare's Genres* (New York and London, 1986), p. 39.

28 Greenblatt, *Shakespearean Negotiations*, p. 63.

29 *Ibid.*, p. 65.

30 I agree with Walter Cohen, 'Political Criticism of Shakespeare', pp. 18–39, that Greenblatt's ideological stance, shared with others, limits the power of a good deal of new-historicist analysis. I am less persuaded, however, by his claim that reception study of sixteenth-century performance would clarify the matter decisively: the evidence is so scanty (and often difficult to interpret) and the links between theatre experience and behaviour in the real world are far from simple or direct.

31 Greenblatt, *Shakespearean Negotiations*, p. 63.

32 Greenblatt does not take into account the widespread and often lavish publication of Festival books commemorating otherwise ephemeral occasions such as royal entries and dynastic marriages, nor the publication of masque texts and distribution of presentation holograph or scribal copies. Admittedly these texts are arguably much less potent in their social effects than performance itself.

33 See p. 118 below.

34 Pre-eminently in Stephen Orgel and Roy Strong, *Inigo Jones: The Theatre of the Stuart Court*, 2 vols. (New York and London, 1973).

35 But see Andrew J. Sabol's monumental *Four Hundred Songs and Dances from the Stuart Masque* (Providence, Rhode Island, 1978, 1982).

36 See pp. 113–14.

37 Butler, 'Private and Occasional Drama', *The Cambridge Companion*, p. 138.

38 For a discussion of such literary discomforts in a printed masque text see my chapter '"Here's Unfortunate Revels": War and Chivalry in Plays and Shows at the Time of Prince Henry Stuart', in J. R. Mulryne and Margaret Shewring, eds., *War, Literature and the Arts in Sixteenth-Century Europe* (London, 1989), pp. 165–89, and my essay 'Tradition and Experience: Chivalry and the Commonplace in *Prince Henry's Barriers* and Samuel Rowley's *When You See Me You Know Me*', in M.-T. Jones-Davies, ed. *Expérience, coutume, tradition au temps de la Renaissance* (Paris, 1992).

39 See, for example, Mervyn James, *Society, Politics and Culture: Studies in Early Modern England* (Cambridge, 1986), esp. chap. 8, pp. 308–415, and Roy Strong, *Henry Prince of Wales and England's Lost Renaissance* (London, 1986).

40 David Norbrook, '"The Masque of Truth": Court Entertainment and

International Protestant Politics in the Early Stuart Period', *The Seventeenth Century* 1 (1986) 81–110.

41 *Oberon*, ed. Richard Hosley, lines 274–7, in *A Book of Masques in Honour of Allardyce Nicoll*, ed. T. J. B. Spencer and S. W. Wells (Cambridge, 1967), pp. 60–1.

42 See Elizabeth Read Foster, ed., *Proceedings in Parliament 1610* 2 vols. (New Haven and London, 1966), II, pp. 13 and 356.

43 *Ibid.*, p. 136.

44 *Stuart Royal Proclamations* ed. J. F. Larkin and P. L. Hughes (Oxford, 1973), p. 247.

45 See Trevor Nunn, 'The Director in the Swan', in Ronnie Mulryne and Margaret Shewring, *This Golden Round: The Royal Shakespeare Company at the Swan* (Stratford-upon-Avon, 1989), p. 65.

46 Michael Billington and Mulryne and Shewring, in *ibid.*, pp. 56, 29.

47 Trevor Nunn, in *ibid.*, p. 64.

48 Alexander Leggatt, *English Drama: Shakespeare to the Restoration 1590–1660* (London and New York, 1988), p. 169.

49 *Ibid.*, p. 193.

50 Margot Heinemann, 'Political Drama', p. 197.

51 See Mervyn James, *Society Politics and Culture*.

52 Heinemann, 'Political Drama', p. 198.

53 Leggatt, *English Drama*, p. 173. The first part of *The Honest Whore* was written in collaboration with Middleton.

54 Judith Doolin Spikes, 'The Jacobean History Play and the Myth of the Elect Nation', *Renaissance Drama* ns, 8 (1977), 117–49.

55 See Julia Gasper, *The Dragon and the Dove: The Plays of Thomas Dekker* (Oxford, 1990), p. 9.

56 See, for example, Richard Bauckham, *Tudor Apocalypse* (Oxford, 1978), and Gasper, *The Dragon and the Dove* and her chapter in this volume.

57 Samuel Rowley, *When You See Me You Know Me*, ed. F. P. Wilson, Malone Society Reprints (1952). See pp. 198–200 below for Julia Gasper's account, with its somewhat different emphasis.

58 Strong, *Henry Prince of Wales*, p. 14.

59 *Calendar of State Papers, Venetian 1603–7*, quoted in Strong, *ibid.*, p. 14.

60 Strong, *Henry Prince of Wales*, p. 42.

61 There may be another parallel with the experience of the young Prince Henry in the play's references to 'a letter from your royal sister, young *Elizabeth*' (line 2,389) in scene xii when the prince receives letters from both Mary and Elizabeth. Henry's sister Elizabeth wrote to him often, even at this young age (see Miss Benger, *Memoirs of Elizabeth Stuart, Queen of Bohemia* (London, 1825), I, pp. 67, 84–5.) In the play Mary's letter is rejected as 'foolish heresies', while Elizabeth's is sisterly and straightforward, a lesson in Protestant rhetoric.

62 Leggatt, *English Drama*, p. 186.

63 *Women Beware Women*, ed. J. R. Mulryne, The Revels Plays (London, 1975), I.iii.93.

64 Margot Heinemann, *Puritanism and Theatre: Thomas Middleton and Opposition Drama Under the Early Stuarts* (Cambridge, 1980), p. viii.

65 See J. R. Mulryne, *Thomas Middleton*, Writers and Their Work (London, 1979), pp. 17–23.

66 Dollimore, *Radical Tragedy*, p. 231.

67 See my discussion 'Webster and the Uses of Tragicomedy', in Brian Morris, ed., *John Webster*, Mermaid Critical Commentaries (London, 1970), pp. 131–56.

68 Dollimore, *Radical Tragedy*, p. 183.

69 Leggatt, *English Drama*, pp. 118, 119.

70 For a discussion of the censorship of *Sejanus* see the edition by Philip J. Ayres, The Revels Plays (London, 1990); for a wider discussion of censorship and the Stuart stage see Janet Clare, *Art Made Tongue-Tied by Authority* (Manchester, 1988) and Richard Dutton, *Mastering the Revels* (London, 1991).

71 See Walter Cohen, *Drama of a Nation: Public Theater in Renaissance England and Spain* (Ithaca, NY, 1985) and his essay, 'The Politics of Golden Age Spanish Tragicomedy', in Nancy Klein Maguire, ed., *Renaissance Tragicomedy: Explorations in Genre and Politics* (New York, 1987), pp. 154–75.

CHAPTER 2

Early Stuart politics: revisionism and after

Simon Adams

More than a decade has passed since the publication of Conrad
Russell's *Parliaments and English Politics, 1621–1629*,[1] and its place as
the central work of what has been termed the 'Revisionist School' of
early Stuart history is still undisputed. If on the surface a narrative
of parliamentary politics, it is also a work that has posed major
questions about the background to the Civil War and the nature of
the early Stuart polity. These questions have in turn transformed
decisively the intellectual framework of the period. The debate has
spread to encompass other institutions of Stuart politics – the court,
the counties, the church – and the history of the sixteenth century as
well. Such sweeping revisionism has not been entirely welcome;
much has been thrown into flux, few adequate surveys exist and the
non-specialist faces a forbidding task in trying to grapple with the
subject.[2] The best recent appraisals of revisionism have been concerned primarily with the causes of the Civil War.[3] An historiographical study focused on the debate over the nature and structure of
the early Stuart polity, on the other hand, has not yet been
attempted. The absence of such a study supplies a justification for
the present essay. The approach to be adopted must be a post-
revisionist one, in the sense that if all the revisionist arguments are
not found convincing, the questions posed still need answering. The
historiographical context is a broad one, but it is in the nature of the
subject that it cannot be adequately treated in a briefer compass.
The issues raised affect not simply seventeenth-century studies, but
the whole of the early modern period.[4]

I

Revisionism, it has been claimed, is a critical rejection of the 'Whig
tradition', a term derived ultimately from Herbert Butterfield's

celebrated essay *The Whig Interpretation of History*. The term is under-
standably a convenient one, but it is also a misnomer. Butterfield
was less concerned with the historiography of the Stuart period than
with what he identified as a general nineteenth-century positivist
assumption that those opposed to 'change and innovation' were
unworthy of 'historical understanding'.[5] Few serious historians
would now dispute his general propositions. Nevertheless the concerns that have shaped Stuart revisionism were less a general Whig
tradition than the intellectual framework of Tudor and Stuart
history first erected by the Liberal historians of the mid- to late-
nineteenth century. The central figures of this school were the trio of
Froude, Gardiner, and Motley, rather than the more obvious
Macaulay.[6] Their significance is derived from the straightforward
fact that they were the first to create an archivally based narrative
for the period from 1529 to the Civil War. The gap left between
Froude's conclusion in 1588 and 1603 was to some degree filled by
Motley, whose *History of the United Netherlands* was heavily based on
English archives and provided a detailed account of the Anglo-
Dutch relationship after 1585. There has been considerable debate
over their use of sources, both at the time and since, but nevertheless
their employment of the Public Records distinguished their work
from that of their predecessors. As a consequence their intellectual
influence has been far more extensive and subtle than often allowed
for. The shared outlook (together with the shared contemporary
popularity) is a further reason for including Motley – together with
the fact that he also initiated the American connection that has had
such an influence on the subsequent development of the field.

What justifies characterising this school as Liberal rather than
Whig are three concerns shaped directly by the intellectual climate
of the period from 1840 to 1880: their hostility to the aristocracy, the
specific nature of their anti-Catholicism and their nationalism.[7] At
the risk of glib superficiality, the Liberal hostility to the aristocracy
may be attributed to the resistance of the House of Lords to reform
and in particular to the circumstances of the passage of the Great
Reform Bill of 1832. With the exception of an enlightened minority,
the Lords appeared to be a purely reactionary interest. By extension,
aristocratic politics in general were essentially selfish and anarchic.
For proof, one needed to look no further than Shakespeare's portrait
of the Wars of the Roses. The very phrase 'baronial anarchy' was
almost a tautology. Such an interpretation of aristocratic politics

had two major (and long-lived) consequences. The first was the justification for a strong monarchy. The historical role of the house of Tudor was thus the final curbing of a nobility that had nearly destroyed the country in the Wars of the Roses. As late as 1966, we can find no less an authority than A. G. Dickins commenting on the reign of Henry VIII: 'Despite Henry's moral blemishes, the common Englishman might have fared much worse than he did under Henry's rule, since the mad forces of disorder inherited from the previous century had been less fully exorcised than is commonly supposed.'[8]

In order to control the nobility the Tudors employed the gentry to govern the country. The connection between the 'rise of the gentry' and the history of parliament was the second major consequence. There were sound constitutional reasons for seeing the House of Commons as the active – if not necessarily progressive – force in the growth of parliamentary government. But since the House of Commons was above all else the representative of the gentry, this in turn made the gentry not only the dominant force in the post-medieval history of parliament, but also the active and progressive force in the body politic. In illustration, one need turn no further than to Gardiner's paeans on the gentlemen of England.[9]

Liberal anti-Catholicism also needs to be set in its precise context: that of the post-1848 papacy of Pius IX and the publication of the Syllabus of Errors. If there was one concern that essentially defined nineteenth-century Liberalism, it was the belief that the great achievement of modern civilisation had been the obtaining of religious and intellectual liberty. The Renaissance and the Reformation were the first stages of the process. To Froude, the defeat of the Spanish Armada marked the decisive point in the transformation of 'the England of a dominant church and monasteries and pilgrimages into the England of progressive intelligence'.[10] Motley's preface to the *History of the United Netherlands* contained similar reflections:

The deep-laid conspiracy of Spain and Rome against human rights deserves to be patiently examined ... History has few so fruitful examples of the dangers that come from superstition and despotism and the blessings which flow from the maintenance of religious and political freedom as those afforded by the struggle between England and Holland on the one side, and Spain and Rome on the other.[11]

Gardiner saw the Thirty Years' War in the same terms: 'the unity of the subject ... must be sought in the growth of the principle of religious toleration as it is adopted or repelled by the institutions under which Germany and France ... are living'. The lesson could be seen in contemporary Germany:

Whatever else had been lost, Protestantism had been saved. Wherever Protestantism had firmly rooted itself there sprang up in the course of time a mighty race of intellectual giants ... When Bavaria, scarcely more than two generations ago, awoke to the consciousness that she had not more than the merest rudiments of education to give to her children, she had to apply to the Protestant north for teachers.[12]

This argument should not, however, be caricatured. It was not so much one that Protestantism itself led to prosperity: the real spur to progress was religious toleration. The historic connection between Liberalism and nonconformity was forged in the struggle against the established church. Nor was it a coincidence that none of the trio was a member of the Church of England. Froude, despite his clerical childhood and his early flirtation with the Oxford Movement, had become an agnostic by the 1850s; Gardiner was by upbringing an Irvingite; Motley, of course, was a New England Congregationalist. Thus as an established Church, the Church of England was preferable to Rome only in its more moderate aspects. For Froude, the Anglican hierarchy of Elizabeth's reign had no moral credibility at all, and was only sustained by the queen's refusal to accept Presbyterianism. There was no half-way house: 'Puritanism was a living force in England; Catholicism was a dying superstition.'[13] The true advances of toleration were also made by the 'Puritans' – under the Dutch Republic and then the Cromwellian Protectorate.

But what also attracted them to Puritanism was its moral fibre. The heroic military austerities of the Sea Beggars, Gustavus Adolphus and the New Model Army were evidence of the moral superiority of Protestantism. 'As is always the case [Gardiner opined] the physical decline of the population was accompanied by moral decadence.'[14] The growth of Arminianism under the Stuarts sapped the moral fibre of the country. Gardiner described the conflict between Arminianism and Puritanism in very revealing terms:

Such a doctrine [Arminianism] would offer a refuge to many who but for it would have fled from the uncongenial teaching of Puritanism into the arms of the Church of Rome. It would gather round it all the growing love of aesthetic decoration, of colour, and of music. Beyond that, it appealed to one side of human nature, its weakness, its dependence upon outward surroundings, its need of a curb upon irreverence and thoughtlessness. But to men of a strong and highsouled temperament it was nothing but Popery in disguise bringing the spirit under outward and material bondage.[15]

If the moral force of Puritanism inspired the Commons to resist the despotism of the Stuart monarchy, moral force was also essential to mid-nineteenth-century nationalism. This conception of nationalism was one of national (even racial) genius (e.g. the Anglo-American genius for representative government), destiny, greatness and decline.[16] Thus Froude felt it necessary to apologise for halting in 1588, when the years that followed 'were rich in events of profound national importance ... The national intellect, strung by the excitement of sixty years, took shape in a literature which is an eternal possession of mankind.' The literary flowering at the end of Elizabeth's reign marked it as an era of national greatness, which stemmed from the 'greatest achievement in English history, the "breaking of the bonds of Rome"', that had established true national independence.[17] Gardiner and Motley, no less than Froude, were influenced by contemporary theories of the influence of Great Men. Although neither Froude nor Motley considered Elizabeth I of the same stature as their heroes Henry VIII and William the Silent, she was clearly superior to her immediate successors. For Gardiner the first two Stuarts presided over an era of national decline; revival was only to come under Cromwell.

Posing the question in this way, however, created a further dilemma that was difficult to resolve. If the 'Tudor Century' was one of national greatness, it was essentially an English one. If the nation was redeemed by the Puritans both in parliament and during the Interregnum, this too was an English phenomenon. But 1603 had ushered in a British monarchy: was this the first stage in the progression towards a British nation? Froude saw English rule in Ireland as doomed on national and racial grounds, but between England and Scotland a British national identity could at least be forged from a common Protestantism. Gardiner also sensed the difficulties. Although he saw the Scottish nobility as 'self-seeking and unruly', and commented on Ireland's 'joyous disregard of the decencies of civilised existence', nevertheless he accepted Scottish and Irish reactions to the policies of English governments as legitimate expressions of national sentiment.[18]

II

Much succeeding scholarship can be seen as a refining of these themes. The first half of the present century has been dominated by two broad approaches. The first can also be termed Liberal, for its chief concern lay with the history of parliament. In it the Anglo-American connection was most strongly represented. Two allied schools – at London (A. F. Pollard and J. E. Neale) and at Yale (Wallace Notestein and his successors) – divided the field between them, a division most obvious in the years between the wars when London undertook the preparation of the biographical *History of Parliament*, and Yale the publication of the parliamentary diaries. Neale was initially concerned with two basic questions, whether the Elizabethan parliaments were packed, and, following from that, the significance of the 'gentry invasion' of the borough seats. The first he found easy to disprove; the second he discovered to be one of the most important trends of the period. By 1604 the number of true burgesses sitting for borough seats had dwindled to a distinct minority. The membership of the House was composed overwhelmingly of country gentlemen, who, he considered, gave the institution its vitality.[19]

Neale also discovered that opposition to the crown in the Commons under Elizabeth was far more extensive than had been allowed for. His explanation for it was the influence of Puritanism – essentially tracing Gardiner back into the sixteenth century. For this argument his much-praised reconstruction of the events of the 1559 parliament was crucial.[20] In discovering a radical Calvinist party in the Commons that only obtained part of what it wanted in the Elizabethan religious settlement, he was able to posit a basic political tension that lasted from 1559 to 1640. Two further consequences followed. Puritanism inspired a continuity of political activity that enabled him to speak of 'the opposition' or the 'Puritan opposition'. Moreover, Puritanism itself was 'politicised', for it was now seen as an organised political movement with potentially revolutionary ends. It was only held in check by loyalty to Elizabeth and her native political skill, features conspicuously absent from the succeeding reigns.[21]

Two further features of Neale's Elizabethan parliaments deserve attention. The first was his notoriously cavalier attitude to the House of Lords, which he simply regarded as unimportant. This is now seen as one of the main weaknesses of his interpretation of the events of 1559.[22] Why were the nobility so tame? The answer he discovered in the patronage of the crown, which enabled the queen to lure them into the court nexus and to control them.[23] This argument was further elaborated by Wallace MacCaffrey, who saw the Tudor employment of patronage as part of a process of civilising the nobility. The bastard feudalism of the Wars of the Roses was thus transformed into the court politics of the seventeenth century. However, the process was not entirely a smooth one, for MacCaffrey also discovered the signs of a 'crisis of patronage' at the beginning of the seventeenth century, when demand began to outrun the crown's limited supply.[24] Yet the importance assigned to patronage raised a further question that was not fully resolved. If the 'patronage system' was so extensive, how were so many of the country gentlemen in the Commons able to remain independent? The closest Neale came to providing an answer was the suggestion that there was a substantial decline in the morality of the court at the end of the reign and a major increase in corruption. This alienated the independent gentry, created factions of 'ins' and 'outs' from those who did and those who did not obtain patronage, and thus shaped the moral climate of the Stuart court.[25]

Neale's other major contribution was his emphasis on the increasing procedural and tactical sophistication of the Elizabethan Commons, which, he claimed, reflected the growing importance its members assigned to their business and their role in government.[26] This point had been advanced explicitly by Wallace Notestein in his famous British Academy Raleigh Lecture of 1924, 'The Winning of the Initiative by the House of Commons'. Notestein posited a decisive tactical advance in the 1620s, including the use of money bills to obtain redress of grievance, that enabled the Commons to gain control of legislation by 1640.[27] Notestein's student D. H. Willson developed one of the subsidiary arguments of this thesis in his study of the parliamentary activities of the Stuart privy councillors.[28] Willson drew attention to the decline in the numbers and quality of privy councillors in the Commons in Stuart as compared to Elizabethan parliaments, which weakened decisively the crown's control of the House. A further contribution to the development of tactics argument was J. H. Hexter's *The Reign of King Pym*, which attributed much of John Pym's influence in the Long Parliament to his tactical ability.[29] Hexter also strengthened the case for continuity of opposition by tracing the existence of a 'Middle Group' back into the 1630s, through their involvement in such organisations as the Providence Island Company. Christopher Thompson in his 1971 Alexander Prize essay 'The Origins of the Politics of the Parliamentary Middle Group, 1625–1629' pushed its origins even further back into the mid-1620s.[30] No less important was the fact that this Middle Group included several quite important peers (the 3rd Earl of Warwick and 4th Earl of Bedford), and therefore spanned both Commons and Lords.

Possibly the last pre-revisionist example of this school was Derek Hirst's *The Representative of the People?*, which argued for an increasingly active and more numerous electorate (particularly in the economically important boroughs) in the years leading to 1640.[31] The American branch also produced four monographic studies of Jacobean parliaments: Notestein's own attempt to write a Nealean narrative for 1604 to 1610, Moir on 1614, Zaller on 1621, and Ruigh on 1624.[32] Of these Ruigh is clearly the most interesting and best researched. He initiated some of the main lines of the reconsideration of Jacobean parliamentary history by showing that not only had James not become the cipher Gardiner had claimed he was in 1624, but that he also successfully prevented parliament from dictating his foreign policy.

The second twentieth-century line of approach was influenced equally by sociology and by Marxism, for their proponents shared several major concerns. The first was the refining of the association between Protestantism and progress into the relationship between Calvinism and capitalism attributed to Max Weber. The second was the introduction of the Marxist interpretation of history as the conflict of economically determined social classes and the identification of the events of the English seventeenth century as the English bourgeois revolution. Less clear, however, was who constituted the revolutionary class. For R. H. Tawney the revolution was the result of a major redistribution of landed property between 1540 and 1640 in favour of the gentry and at the expense of the crown, the church and, most significantly, the nobility.[33] The success of the gentry, he argued, lay in their more capitalist approach to the economic potential of their estates, the smaller size and greater compactness of which enabled them to exploit them more effectively than their noble rivals. Their progressive economic outlook made them the equivalent of a bourgeoisie.

Tawney thus refined the relationship between the nobility and the gentry into one of economically competitive social classes. The decline of the nobility was less the result of the policies of the crown than of its own obsolete social and economic attitudes. The gentry were both more imbued with Puritanism and more austere in personal expenditure, while the nobility were forced by rank and their obsolete social code into conspicuous consumption. Less clearly answered was the question of whether Puritanism inspired the austerity (as Weber had argued) or whether men of this economic outlook found Puritanism attractive. The tension between the nobility and the gentry was addressed at great length in the most distinguished post-Tawneyian work of this school, Lawrence Stone's *The Crisis of the Aristocracy 1558–1641*.[34] Stone was, in fact, unable to find the clear evidence of the economic decline of the nobility that he had expected and was forced to fall back on a 'crisis of confidence' among the peerage in the early seventeenth century. This was caused by a weakening of its social status following a political and military decline from fifteenth-century bastard feudalism, the consequence of new forces unleashed by the sixteenth century, of which the growing self-confidence of the gentry in the House of Commons was part.

The celebrated 'gentry controversy' need not be re-fought here, but it raised several issues that later influenced revisionism. The most important was H. R. Trevor-Roper's counter to Tawney's 'rise of the gentry'.[35] This was also an economically determinist argument, but one that suggested that what might be termed 'serious money' was not to be made in agriculture, but at court and in the City. The gentry dependent solely upon their estates were a declining class, and it was their revolt against an economically parasitical court that constituted the Civil War. The tension between court and country was thus a very real one, and the politics of patronage a major issue. The provincial gentry were clearly not the beneficiaries of patronage, for this was confined to the court. The 'country' was to some degree defined by those discontented at being cut off from the patronage of the crown. But if patronage had served as the cement of the political system in the sixteenth century, why did it fail to do so in the seventeenth? Stone found two answers to this question. One was the tension between supply and demand; the other was the decision of James I in particular, and Charles while the Duke of Buckingham was alive, to concentrate their largess on their favourites and immediate court circles.[36] These two arguments were not entirely compatible, for the tension between supply and demand suggested a basic structural weakness in the political system, while the concentration on favourites was the consequence of personal political misjudgement.

The alternative Marxist approach has been most fully advanced by Christopher Hill. This developed two main themes: Puritanism as an ideology in the Marxist sense, and the re-direction of attention towards the sub-parliamentary class, 'the middling sort', as the key revolutionary social group of the period. The growth of Puritanism as an ideology can again be traced back to the association between Calvinism and capitalism. What Hill sought to show was that both the Puritan clergy and the Puritan laity shared ideas on economic, social and political issues that helped intellectually to subvert the established order and usher in the new commercial society.[37] 'The middling sort' addressed what even contemporaries appreciated to be the most awkward aspect of the English social system, the distinction between the gentry and other commoners.[38] It encompassed a broad group of men – lesser gentry, prosperous freeholders (and even leaseholders), smaller merchants and traders, as well as the less established members of the professions – whose general economic position was roughly similar. They possessed some landed property, or enjoyed some form of economic security and employed servants; they were also consumers on a moderate scale, and probably literate. Politically their position was not easy to define: they were clearly below the level of the magistracy, let alone that of MPs, yet many possessed the franchise, and would serve in village and lesser municipal office, and on juries. It was on them that the bulk of taxation (particularly parliamentary subsidies) fell. To Hill they were the real revolutionary class in the sense that it was they who provided the broad base of parliamentary support and it was to them in particular that Civil War radicalism appealed. The history of the early seventeenth century was therefore essentially that of their progressive alienation from the political status quo and their growing self-confidence. Puritanism provided the ideology that united them with those MPs and peers who broke with the king in 1641–2.[39]

Before leaving this survey of the field as it stood in the early 1970s, it is worth noting the subjects that had not been covered. The concern was overwhelmingly with the causes of the Civil War, with increased attention being paid to the broader social aspects as against the apparently old-fashioned emphasis on parliamentary politics. The Stuart 'political system' itself and its institutions and personalities had hardly been examined at all. The nearest thing to a study of the central government was Gerald Aylmer's work on the Caroline 'Civil Service'.[40] Few of its personalities – in contrast to the leading Elizabethans – had been the subject of serious biographies. D. H. Willson produced one on James himself, but apart from raising the important question of why so apparently successful a king of Scotland was such a disaster in England, and presenting the king's 'pacificism' in a sympathetic light, it marked no new advances.[41] Of James's councillors, Lionel Cranfield was the subject of two major biographies, but he could hardly be considered typical.[42] The court itself was, to all intents and purposes, unknown territory.

III

For several important respects John Morrill's *The Revolt of the Provinces* deserves to be considered the first revisionist work.[43] There were, however, some precursors. Although no coherent rival school to those described above had emerged, there had been a few outsiders. Possibly the earliest was R. G. Usher, who in 1910 published a study of Archbishop Bancroft that portrayed him in a positive light, less the persecutor of Puritans than the creator of a coherent Anglican church.[44] Several years later he published a highly critical study of Gardiner's 'historical method', in which he argued that Gardiner, who worked in great haste, had simply selected his evidence to suit his case.[45] In 1965 G. R. Elton published his essay on the Commons 'Apology' of 1604, which has given him a certain claim to have initiated the argument that too much early Stuart history had been written looking backwards from 1642.[46]

The significance of *Revolt of the Provinces* lay in its conversion of the arguments that emerged from the debate over the gentry into a new explanation for the political tensions of the pre-1640 period. One general conclusion of the gentry debate (possibly the only one) was the need for closer examination of individual counties. It thus inspired a substantial number of county studies in the 1960s and 1970s. Of these, one of the earliest was also possibly the most radical: Alan Everitt's *The Community of Kent and the Great Rebellion 1640–60*.[47] Everitt was the first Stuart historian to advance uncompromisingly the 'county federalist' thesis – though Neale had nodded towards it.[48] In broad terms this is an argument that throughout the early modern period England was essentially a federation of counties. Political loyalty was focused on county rather than country; there was a real sense of 'county community'; and in times of crisis the first response was to rally to county solidarity. In his study of Elizabethan Norfolk A. H. Smith redefined the general tension between court and country into a specific one between court and county.[49] After the death of the 4th Duke of Norfolk in 1572, the county became to all intents and purposes a gentry republic, factionalised between those who sought to implement the demands of the crown and those who saw their primary political duty as that of protecting their community from external exactions.

Morrill's book combined his own work on Civil War Cheshire with a sophisticated re-working of the county-community argument. The country opposition of 1640–2 he divided into an 'Official Country' and a 'Pure Country'. The 'Official Country' were the distinct group of MPs and peers disenchanted with the king for ideological reasons, who (he suggested) saw themselves as an alternative administration. Although Morrill devoted very little attention to them, they look very much like Hexter and Thompson's Middle Group. The 'Pure Country' – MPs who saw themselves as representing their communities – were his real interest. If they were allied to the 'Official Country' in temporary opposition to the personal rule in 1640–1, the grounds of their opposition were quite different. They were essentially opposed to centralising government, rather than the immediate political complexion of the court. What had alienated them were certain specific measures of the personal rule – the Book of Orders and the way in which ship money had been levied – which were seen as a revolutionary break with established practice. Their politics were localist and defensive, as was to be seen in their hostility to similar governmental pressure during the Civil War and Interregnum.

From this thesis three further broad arguments emerged. The first was that 'county federalism' and localism represented a major structural problem for an English government. The second was that the function of MPs in such a system was specifically that of local representation. The local community thus formed a definite constituency, and it was with their grievances that these MPs were primarily concerned. Those MPs interested in 'national issues', on the other hand, were a distinct minority. The third (arising from this latter point) was the question of whether there was indeed a national political culture. A study of Cambridge University by Victor Morgan reinforced this argument: the two universities were not 'centralising' institutions, for the strong local links embodied in the collegiate system reinforced provincial identities.[50] Anthony Fletcher in his study of Stuart Sussex drew a similar conclusion. While the greater gentry may have operated in a national social nexus (as revealed by their marriage patterns) the lesser gentry (the leaders of Hill's middling sort) were markedly more local in outlook and contacts.[51]

This reinterpretation of the politics of the county communities has formed one of the two main themes of the revisionist debate. The other was specifically parliamentary. It has been developed above all in the work of Conrad Russell, though some of the issues were addressed in Kevin Sharpe's collection *Faction and Parliament*.[52] This book was planned a year before the publication of Russell's now famous essay 'Parliamentary History in Perspective, 1604–1629',[53] but it was not published until 1978. It was followed a year later by Russell's *Parliaments and English Politics*, and by then there had been considerable cross-fertilisation. Russell's essay, 'Parliamentary History in Perspective', was essentially a refutation of Notestein's 'Winning of the Initiative'. Russell discovered no real tactical innovations, no attempt to use supply to obtain redress of grievances, and no continuity of opposition. To use the phrase made famous by *Parliaments and English Politics*, parliament was an event rather than an institution. What then were parliamentary politics about? This was explained in *Parliaments and English Politics*. From the point of view of the crown parliaments were primarily occasions for the raising of revenue, and in this respect they were failures.[54] The crisis of the monarchy lay in its inability to raise sufficient revenue to conduct modern warfare; therefore it had no alternative but to make peace or to turn to other methods. In advancing this case Russell developed a second important argument: that the crown's foreign policy and military strategy in the 1620s were perfectly straightforward. Any rejection of them in parliament arose not from ideological or political principle, but from the localist provincialism of the majority in the Commons. The impact of localism on parliamentary politics, as advanced by both Morrill and Russell, became the main argument of the first stage of revisionism.

But if localism was one ground of 'opposition', there were also others. The first was court factionalism; the second a specific religious tension arising in the later 1620s from the increased prominence of Arminianism. For Russell, the latter was the essential cause for the alienation of John Pym (and by extension his associates in the 'Official Country' or Middle Group).[55] The Russell thesis thus led directly to two other major revisionist debates: the nature of court and aristocratic politics and the relationship between Puritanism and Arminianism. Before turning to them, however, a further refinement of this view of parliament should be taken into account. It was made by Mark Kishlansky in his article 'The Emergence of Adversary Politics in the Long Parliament' and his book *Parliamentary Selection*.[56] He argues that the decisive change in parliamentary behaviour was the acceptance of majority voting, whether in the House of Commons or in elections, and that this was a result of the pressures of the Civil War. Thus before the 1640s the Commons had sought to achieve consensus, which made a sustained opposition impossible. In elections the aim throughout was to avoid contests. *Parliamentary Selection* was intended to rebut Hirst's thesis of the growth of a politically aware electorate in the years to 1640, but it should be noted that Hirst and Kishlansky are not always dealing with the same elections: Hirst's emphasis is on the larger boroughs, Kishlansky's on the county seats.

IV

The debates over the politics of the court and the nobility and over the relationship between Puritanism and Arminianism raised issues that extend beyond the immediate confines of the early seventeenth century, and reveal the more sweeping aspects of revisionism. Given the ignorance of the Jacobean court in the mid-1970s, Russell's emphasis on the role of court factions in parliamentary politics raised questions to which there were no immediate answers. Since then the subject has undergone some major advances.

Three main lines of approach can be distinguished. The older view of the tension between crown and nobility in the sixteenth century received its most sophisticated treatment in a series of articles by M. E. James during the course of the 1970s.[57] However, the publication of the papers of K. B. Macfarlane in 1973 on the nobility in the fourteenth and fifteenth centuries re-opened the subject.[58] Instead of an anarchic nobility needing the control of a strong crown, an essentially co-operative relationship menaced if anything by a tyrannical crown was posited. Bastard feudalism was no longer purely the raising of private armies; the Wars of the Roses were caused by weakness in the crown rather than ambition in the nobility. This theme has been developed in the work of J. R. Lander, but some of the most influential Macfarlanites have been Scottish and Irish historians.[59] If this view of relations between crown and nobility was accurate, then the apparent weakness of the institutions of central government in Scotland and Ireland did not mean that their polities were essentially more primitive than England's.

Recent work on the Tudor nobility has stressed co-operation with the crown and the importance of the nobility in the governing of the realm.[60] A similar emphasis can be found in G. R. Elton's re-phrasing of the court and country relationship in his three 'Tudor Government: the Points of Contact' lectures, where he sought to show that the three key institutions of Tudor government (court, privy council and parliament) were not hostile to the country, but the means by which the political nation as a whole came together.[61] If this was indeed the case under the Tudors, then it raised the question of whether the system continued to function under the Stuarts. Kevin Sharpe, in his essays on the Personal Rule, has made the most explicit use of the Eltonian framework. Far from being a novel rejection of parliamentary government, the 1630s saw a return to an established pattern of administration by the privy council and the county communities.[62]

In the course of arguing against the court and country tension, Elton has adopted a position on the significance of court factiona-lism similar to Russell's. In several essays he has sought to show that what might appear to be instances of 'opposition' to the crown, whether in parliament or in the localities, were in fact the activities of court factions taking their struggles into the country.[63] The new interest in court factionalism has also been influenced by David Starkey's major transformation of the study of the court as an institution.[64] This began as a revision of Elton's *Tudor Revolution in Government*, which had posited the destruction of the medieval pattern of household government in the reign of Henry VIII and the separation of the 'working' government from the court. Starkey's study of the Henrician privy chamber suggested that this was too

radical: the privy chamber remained at the centre of politics, and
the key issue of court politics was that of access to the monarch. On
access the distribution of patronage, and consequentially court
factionalism, would revolve. This approach to court politics in the
period to 1640 was outlined in the three essays that Starkey, Sharpe
and I contributed to *History Today* in 1982–3 (albeit with somewhat
different conclusions), and in the collection of essays on the court
that Starkey edited in 1987.[65] The contributions to the latter by
Sharpe and Neil Cuddy were the first attempts to explore the
Jacobean and Caroline courts in Starkey's terms.[66] The new interest
in the structure of the court has also led to more serious consideration of the queen's household. To date this has focused on the
household of Henrietta Maria; Anne of Denmark's has yet to be
explored.[67] In the meantime an ambitious reappraisal of the politics
of the Stuart nobility has been advanced by J. S. A. Adamson.[68]

The sophistication of the new approach to court politics is also
reflected in the quality of the recent biographies of Stuart court
figures. Of these the most important is Roger Lockyer's life of the
Duke of Buckingham.[69] Lockyer provides the most detailed account
of the later Jacobean court to date, although he argues that Buckingham's consolidation of his position at court was influenced less by
English precedent than by his observation in 1623 of Olivares'
relationship to Philip IV of Spain. Lockyer's account of Buckingham's politics reinforces Russell's interpretation of the 1620s. He
considers Buckingham's foreign policy and military strategy defensi-
ble; the failure of the English war effort is attributed to the localist
outlook of MPs and personal enmities at court. What Lockyer did
not tackle, however, was the nature of Buckingham's clientele.[70]
Who constituted it, whether they shared a coherent outlook, and
whether they spread into the country as a whole remains to be
explored. Linda Peck's study of Henry Howard, Earl of Northampton, is essentially a pre-Starkey work, and one very much
influenced by Neale's concern with patronage and corruption.[71] She
does show, however, that Northampton made a greater intellectual
contribution to Jacobean government than he has been given credit
for and points to the need for a much more serious exploration of the
'Spanish faction'.[72]

The 3rd Earl of Pembroke, perhaps the most debated of Stuart
court figures next to Buckingham, has been the subject of two recent
studies.[73] They have not, however, completely revised the older

view that while Pembroke participated actively in court and parliamentary politics, he was not prepared to do so decisively. Part of the enigma surrounding Pembroke is undoubtedly archival in origin: a considerable quantity of Northampton's papers survive and much of Buckingham's correspondence can be reconstructed, but only fragments of Pembroke's can now be traced. It is revealing that of the two recent studies, Brennan emphasises the pressures on Pembroke to act as inheritor of an Elizabethan Protestant aristocratic tradition, while Gebauer, noting that Pembroke was in some senses James I's first English favourite, argues that the real inspiration for his politics was his intense jealousy of the Duke of Buckingham.

Like the debate over the court and the nobility, that over religion spans both the sixteenth and seventeenth centuries. At its heart perhaps is the vexed question (about which contemporaries were no clearer) of the identification of a Puritan. The taking of sides in 1642 does not help with those who did not survive till then. Acts of nonconformity, which would include emigration to the Netherlands and New England, may place too great an emphasis on the separatist wing. Support for different conceptions of ecclesiastical polity is difficult to trace in those persons who were not otherwise nonconformists. A predilection for a certain type of divinity may help to define allegiances among the clergy, but for the laity evidence is much more limited.[74] Patronage can provide a valuable indicator, but it cannot be taken for granted, nor does it help for those social groups below the level of potential patrons.

Any discussion of Puritanism must also take into account the protean influence of Patrick Collinson, not least because his views have shifted over the years. In his earliest work the influence of Neale's 'Puritanism as a Political Movement' can be detected.[75] Yet the great *Elizabethan Puritan Movement* reveals something else.[76] Collinson is not particularly sympathetic to the openly Presbyterian wing of Elizabethan Puritanism, rather he points to the widespread influence of Calvinist divinity among both the court and the Elizabethan episcopate – raising the question whether there could be Puritan bishops, and thus subverting the older definition of Puritanism as anti-episcopalianism. In *The Religion of Protestants* this is further expanded into an argument that between 1559 and 1625 a low-church Calvinism formed the natural centre of gravity of English Protestantism. The stature of the Elizabethan and Jacobean episcopate (as exemplified by Archbishops Grindal and Abbot) is thus redeemed. By pursuing a low-church policy, tolerant towards Protestant nonconformity, and uncompromising towards Catholicism, they essentially defused much Puritan criticism.[77]

Such a view of the church has also been advanced by Peter Lake and Nicholas Tyacke. Lake's *Moderate Puritans and the Elizabethan Church* made clear the willingness of a very influential body of Cambridge theologians to remain within the church so long as its theology remained Calvinist.[78] Tyacke's essay 'Puritanism, Arminianism and Counter-Revolution' is now famous for advancing the 'Calvinist consensus' thesis – although the phrase does not appear in it.[79] Until the later 1620s the dominant theological allegiance of the Church of England was Calvinist. The advancing of Arminian clergy by the king and Archbishop Laud thus marked a revolutionary break with the past with major political implications. As has been seen, this argument strongly influenced Russell's interpretation of the alienation of John Pym and the Middle Group. They were less motivated by constitutional matters *per se* than by religion. The wider impact of Arminianism was similarly revolutionary, in that it was seen to challenge what were regarded as the established practices and outlook of the church. James I's ecclesiastical policy thus obtained a retrospective justification: for all his hostility to Presbyterianism, he had successfully maintained a moderate (in Protestant terms) consensus.[80]

This view of the church has come under attack on two fronts, distinct on one level, but sharing a common emphasis on the minority status of Puritanism. The earlier is Christopher Haigh's dismissal of the popularity of the Protestant Reformation.[81] In essence he argues that there was in fact no popular upswell against the pre-Reformation church. The Henrician Reformation was primarily an act of state, and Protestantism remained a minority faith largely confined to the literate. The destruction of popular Catholicism was the result of the actions of the state and the strategic errors of the émigré Catholic clergy, who sought to win back the gentry instead of the population as a whole, rather than any positive evangelical achievement by the Protestant clergy. Puritanism, for all its apparent hostility to the ecclesiastical establishment, was no more popular. True popular loyalty in religion lay in a sacramental faith, which by the beginning of the seventeenth century had become 'parish Anglicanism'. To this body of opinion Laudianism or Arminianism possessed a distinct appeal.[82]

The other attack has been mounted by P. G. White.[83] This rephrased an older argument that the Calvinist consensus in the church before 1625 was more apparent than real. Not only were the Thirty-Nine Articles not explicitly predestinarian, but both the Elizabethan and the Jacobean church had contained an established anti-predestinarian wing. The Caroline Arminians had a perfectly respectable pedigree and were in no sense revolutionary. The revival of sacramental religion during the personal rule was less innovatory than the activities of Pym and his allies, who sought to have the decrees of the Synod of Dort embodied in statute.

One final major revisionist issue remains to be discussed: 'The British Problem', which in a sense is a rephrasing of the older national question.[84] The year 1603 saw not just the accession of James I to the English throne, but also the first king of England, Scotland and Ireland. This created a totally new context for English politics, for England's monarchs were now operating in a British context. James's claim to statesmanship becomes the more credible.[85] The contemporary debates over the Union of Scotland and England have consequentially been re-examined.[86] Where previously James's advancing of the Union was seen as idealistic in conception but impractical in execution, it is now argued that the failure of the Union in 1606–7 was caused by the conservative localism of the English parliamentary classes. English prejudice against the Scots was the real villain of the piece, not an overly ambitious grand design of the Stuart monarchy.

V

The wide range of areas under debate permits little immediate resolution. What can be outlined, however, are the subjects, both general and specific, upon which attention is focusing. Possibly the weakest link in the revisionist chain is the localist argument. This has come under attack from a number of quarters, and it is clear that the 'localist mentality' may have been overstated.[87] A certain distortion may have crept in through the choice of counties initially studied (Kent, Cheshire and Norfolk), for these possessed particularly strong local identities, arising in part from unique institutions. Also worth noting is the small role the City of London has played in this heavily provincial debate. Only Robert Ashton has emphasised the importance of the City to the political system.[88]

A further controversial element in this conception of politics is the importance of factionalism. The all-pervading influence of factionalism has been accepted in some quarters as near-axiomatic, and it has been seen as the explanation of much that might have previously appeared as 'principled' opposition.[89] This may be taken too far: the existence of factions should be proved rather than assumed.[90] Part of the problem lies in the implicit connection drawn between factionalism and patronage, which also needs to be explored more than it has been. Indeed, the unquestioned assumption that there was such a connection obscures major transformations in the nature of the patronage of the crown, and shifts of policy in its employment.[91] There may also be major differences in the ways individuals exploited their own private patronage. Thus the argument for a distinct pattern of politics between c. 1500 and 1640 defined by faction and patronage may itself have to be revised.

The reservations about the importance of localism also pose major questions about the theses advanced by Morrill and Russell. If localism was not the overwhelming motive for opposition in the 1620s and 1630s, what was? Here the difficulties of dealing with either decade in isolation emerge. Given that the opposition involved was primarily focused on financial issues (ship money in the 1630s and parliamentary taxation in the 1620s), can the influence of the earlier Stuart financial debates be dismissed? In this context it is revealing that the two specific areas most subject to debate are ship money and the war policy of the 1620s.[92]

The parliamentary session of 1624 has attracted more attention recently than any of the others.[93] It is easy to see why. This session apparently launched England into the Thirty Years' War, thereby reversing James's policy of strengthening Anglo-Spanish diplomatic relations. The expressed willingness of parliament to support a war would be used in retrospect to provide the crown with a justification for its later financial demands. None of the more recent contributors have queried Ruigh's demonstration of James's deliberate delaying tactics. Yet much debate has been inspired by the question of 'success' and the significance of the apparent honeymoon between the Duke of Buckingham, Prince Charles and the House of Commons. Are the murmurs of disquiet at the possible levels of taxation involved to be dismissed as the views of a minority, or of an intimidated majority? Nor can an interpretation of this session be divorced from consideration of its successor in 1625. By then the 'honeymoon' was definitely over. Was it the result of events between the two (the French marriage and the Count of Mansfeld's expedition being the most obvious candidates), or did it reflect the fact that the popularity of the war had been limited all along? Answers to these questions demand careful examination of both 'public opinion' and the course of diplomacy.

The role to be assigned to public opinion in the 1620s and 1630s is the area where the debate over politics and that over religion overlap most clearly. But as difficult as it may be to establish the views of members of the court or of parliament on matters of politics or religion, it is another question when the broad mass of the population is concerned. The revisionist concentration on parliament and the court has meant that this level of politics has been neglected to some extent in recent work.[94] Such questions as the 'popularity' of various forms of religion, the response to demands for taxation and the nature of broader political loyalties and attitudes must now be reopened in a post-revisionist context. Given the present appreciation of the complex relationship between politics and culture, these subjects should provide a fruitful ground for the future collaboration of historical and literary scholarship.[95]

NOTES

Place of publication is London, unless otherwise stated.

1 (Oxford, 1979).

2 D. Hirst, *Authority and Conflict: England 1603–1658* (1986) and R. Lockyer, *The Early Stuarts: A Political History of England 1603–1642* (1989), are the only surveys that deal with the issues raised by revisionism.

3 R. Cust and A. Hughes, 'Introduction: After Revisionism', in Cust and Hughes, eds., *Conflict in Early Stuart England: Studies in Religion and Politics* (1989), pp. 1–46. A. Hughes, *The Causes of the English Civil War* (1991).

4 As argued by J. C. D. Clark, *English Society 1688–1832: Ideology, Social Structure and Political Practice during the Ancien Regime* (Cambridge, 1985), and *Revolution and Rebellion: State and Society in England in the Seventeenth and Eighteenth Centuries* (Cambridge, 1986).

5 H. Butterfield, *The Whig Interpretation of History* (1931), p. 4. Cf. Clark's observations in *Revolution and Rebellion*, p. 15.

6 J. A. Froude, *History of England from the Fall of Cardinal Wolsey to the Defeat of the Spanish Armada*, 12 vols. (1856–70). S. R. Gardiner, *History of England from the Accession of James I to the Outbreak of the Civil War 1603–1642*, 10 vols. (1905). J. L. Motley, *The Rise of the Dutch Republic*, 3 vols. (1855); *History of the United Netherlands from the Death of William the*

Silent to the Twelve Years' Truce 1609, 4 vols. (1860–7); *The Life and Death of John of Barneveld, Advocate of Holland*, 2 vols. (1874).

7 In the interval between the first and final versions of this essay, J. S. A. Adamson has published a perceptive study of Gardiner, which rehearses several of the points made here both more substantially and with greater elegance, 'Eminent Victorians: S. R. Gardiner and the Liberal as Hero', *Historical Journal*, 33 (1990) 641–57.

8 Introduction to A. F. Pollard, *Henry VIII* (New York, 1966), p. xix.

9 E.g. *History of England 1603–42*, IV, pp. 35–6, 263–4.

10 *History of England 1529–88*, XII, p. 476.

11 *History of the United Netherlands*, I, preface, p. iii.

12 *The Thirty Years' War 1618–1648* (1881), pp. v, 216.

13 *History of England 1529–88*, XII, pp. 498ff.

14 *Thirty Years' War*, p. 214.

15 *History of England 1603–42*, VII, p. 11. See Adamson's discussion of Gardiner's 'use of "character" as a recurrent term of explanatory art', 'Eminent Victorians', 643ff.

16 See the reflections of A. F. Pollard on the failure of parliamentary institutions in 'semitic or negroid communities', quoted in G. R. Elton, *F. W. Maitland* (1985), p. 63. See also Gardiner on the moral stature of Sir John Eliot, *History of England 1603–42*, V, p. 186.

17 *History of England 1529–88*, XII, pp. 475, 510.

18 *History of England 1603–42*, VII, p. 286; VIII, p. 3.

19 *The Elizabethan House of Commons* (1949), esp. chaps. 1 and 7 (pp. 138–41).

20 'The Elizabethan Acts of Supremacy and Uniformity', *English Historical Review*, 65 (1950) 304–42. *Elizabeth I and Her Parliaments*, 2 vols. (1953–7), I, chaps. 2–3.

21 *Elizabeth I and Her Parliaments, passim.*, esp. conclusion.

22 A point made explicitly in N. L. Jones, *Faith by Statute: Parliament and the Settlement of Religion 1559*, Royal Historical Society, Studies in History, 32 (1982); see my review, *History*, 69, (1984) 317.

23 'The Elizabethan Political Scene', British Academy Raleigh Lecture, 1948, repr. in *Essays in Elizabethan History* (1958), pp. 59–84.

24 In S. T. Bindoff *et al.*, eds., *Elizabethan Government and Society* (1961), pp. 95–126.

25 'Elizabethan Political Scene', pp. 78–84.

26 'The Commons' Privilege of Free Speech in Parliament' in R. W. Seton-Watson, ed., *Tudor Studies* (1924), pp. 257–86, and *Elizabeth I and Her Parliaments*.

27 *Proceedings of the British Academy* XI (1926), 125–76, repr. in L. S. Sutherland, ed., *Studies in History: British Academy Lectures* (Oxford, 1966), pp. 145–203.

28 *The Privy Councillors in the House of Commons, 1604–1629* (Minneapolis, 1940).

29 J. H. Hexter, *The Reign of King Pym* (Cambridge, Mass., 1941).
30 *Transactions of the Royal Historical Society*, 5th ser., XXII (1972) 71–86.
31 *The Representative of the People? Voters and Voting in England under the Early Stuarts* (Cambridge, 1975).
32 W. Notestein, *The House of Commons, 1604–1610* (New Haven, 1971). T. C. Moir, *The Addled Parliament of 1614* (Oxford, 1968). R. E. Zaller, *The Parliament of 1621. A Study in Constitutional Conflict* (Berkeley, Calif., 1971). R. E. Ruigh, *The Parliament of 1624: Politics and Foreign Policy* (Cambridge, Mass., 1971).
33 'Harrington's Interpretation of His Age', *Proceedings of the British Academy*, XXVII (1941), repr. in Sutherland, *Studies*, pp. 238–61. 'The Rise of the Gentry, 1558–1640', *Economic History Review*, 11 (1941) 1–38.
34 (Oxford, 1965, repr. 1979). For more recent observations by Stone on the broader question, see 'The Bourgeois Revolution of Seventeenth-Century England', *Past and Present*, 109 (1985) 44–54.
35 *The Gentry 1540–1640, Economic History Review Supplement*, 1 (Cambridge, 1953), developed in a wider context in 'The General Crisis of the Seventeenth Century', in Trevor Aston, ed., *Crisis in Europe 1560–1660* (1965), pp. 59–95.
36 *Crisis of the Aristocracy*, chap. 8.
37 Esp. in *Society and Puritanism in Pre-Revolutionary England* (1964) and *The Intellectual Origins of the English Revolution* (Oxford, 1965).
38 Sir Thomas Smith provides the best-known example, see *De Republica Anglorum*, M. Dewar, ed. (Cambridge, 1982), pp. 71–6.
39 An argument developed in B. Manning, *The English People and the English Revolution* (1976). See also C. Hill, 'Parliament and the People in Seventeenth-Century England', *Past and Present*, 92 (1981) 100–24, and Hughes, *The Causes of the English Civil War*.
40 *The King's Servants: The Civil Service of Charles I, 1625–1642* (1961).
41 *King James VI & I* (1956).
42 M. Prestwich, *Cranfield: Politics and Profit under the Early Stuarts* (Oxford, 1966). R. H. Tawney, *Business and Politics under James I: Lionel Cranfield as Merchant and Minister* (Cambridge, 1958). See also M. J. Havran, *Caroline Courtier: The Life of Lord Cottington* (1973) and M. V. Alexander, *Charles I's Lord Treasurer: Sir Richard Weston, Earl of Portland (1577–1635)* (1975).
43 *The Revolt of the Provinces: Conservatives and Radicals in the English Civil War, 1630–1650* (1976).
44 *The Reconstruction of the English Church*, 2 vols. (New York, 1910).
45 *A Critical Study of the Historical Method of Samuel Rawson Gardiner* (St Louis, 1915). I am grateful to John Morrill for bringing this to my attention some years ago.
46 'A High Road to Civil War?' in Elton, *Studies in Tudor and Stuart Politics and Government*, 3 vols. (Cambridge, 1974–83), II, pp. 164–82.

47 (Leicester, 1966).

48 *Elizabethan House of Commons*, p. 19.

49 *Country and Court: Government and Politics in Norfolk, 1558–1603* (Oxford, 1974).

50 'Cambridge University and the "Country" 1560–1640', in L. Stone, ed., *The University and Society*, 2 vols. (Princeton, 1974–5), I, pp. 183–245.

51 A. Fletcher, *A County Community in Peace and War: Sussex 1600–1660* (1975), chap. 2.

52 *Faction and Parliament: Essays on Early Stuart History* (Oxford, 1978, repr. 1985).

53 *History*, 61 (1976) 1–27.

54 See also 'Parliament and the King's Finances', in C. Russell, ed., *The Origins of the English Civil War* (1973), pp. 91–116; and 'The Nature of a Parliament in Early Stuart England', in H. Tomlinson, ed., *Before the English Civil War: Essays on Early Stuart Politics and Government* (1983), pp. 123–50. Russell has continued to emphasise this issue in his more recent work, *The Causes of the English Civil War* (Oxford, 1990), and *The Fall of the British Monarchies 1637–1642* (Oxford, 1991).

55 'The Parliamentary Career of John Pym', in P. Clark *et al.*, eds., *The English Commonwealth 1547–1660* (1979), pp. 147–65. See also Russell, *Fall of the British Monarchies*, pp. 100–1.

56 'The Emergence of Adversary Politics in the Long Parliament', *Journal of Modern History*, 69 (1977) 617–40. *Parliamentary Selection: Social and Political Choice in Early Modern England* (Cambridge, 1986).

57 See 'English Politics and the Concept of Honour 1485–1642', and 'At a Crossroads of the Political Culture: the Essex Revolt, 1601', in M. E. James, *Society, Politics and Culture: Studies in Early Modern England* (Cambridge, 1986), pp. 308–415, 416–65.

58 *The Nobility of Late Medieval England* (Oxford, 1973). Macfarlane is now undergoing revision; see P. R. Coss, 'Bastard Feudalism Revised', *Past and Present*, 125 (1989) 27–64.

59 J. R. Lander, *Politics and Power in England, 1450–1509* (1976). J. M. Brown, ed., *Scottish Society in the Fifteenth Century* (1977), introduction and chap. 3; J. Wormald, 'Bloodfeud, Kindred and Government in Early Modern Scotland', *Past and Present*, 87 (1980) 54–97; *Lords and Men in Scotland: Bonds of Manrent: 1442–1603* (Edinburgh, 1985), chap. 1. S. G. Ellis, *Tudor Ireland: Crown, Community and the Conflict of Cultures* (1985). For a revision of Wormald, see K. M. Brown, *Bloodfeud in Scotland 1573–1625: Violence, Justice and Politics in an Early Modern Society* (Edinburgh, 1986).

60 G. W. Bernard, *The Power of the Early Tudor Nobility: A Study of the Fourth and Fifth Earls of Shrewsbury* (Brighton, 1985). H. Miller, *Henry VIII and the English Nobility* (Oxford, 1986).

61 G. R. Elton, 'Tudor Government: The Points of Contact: 1. Parlia-

ment, 2. The Council, 3. The Court', in *Studies in Tudor and Stuart Politics and Government*, III, pp. 3–57.

62 'The Personal Rule of Charles I', in Tomlinson, ed., *Before the English Civil War*, pp. 53–78; 'Crown, Parliament and Locality: Government and Communication in Early Stuart England', *English Historical Review* 101 (1986) 321–50; both reprinted in *Politics and Ideas in Early Stuart England* (1989), pp. 101–22, 75–100.

63 'Politics and the Pilgrimage of Grace' and 'Arthur Hall, Lord Burghley and the Antiquity of Parliament', in *Studies in Tudor and Stuart Politics and Government*, III, pp. 183–215, 254–73. *The Parliament of England, 1559–1581* (Cambridge, 1986), chap. 14.

64 'The King's Privy Chamber, 1485–1547', unpublished Ph.D. diss. (Cambridge University, 1974). See also the essays in C. Coleman and D. Starkey, eds., *Revolution Reassessed: Revisions in the History of Tudor Government and Administration* (Oxford, 1986).

65 D. Starkey, 'From Feud to Faction: English Politics c. 1450–1550'; S. Adams, 'Faction, Clientage and Party: English Politics 1550–1603'; K. Sharpe, 'Faction at the Early Stuart Court', *History Today* 32 (Nov. 1982) 16–22 (Dec. 1982) 33–9; 39 (Oct. 1983) 39–46. D. Starkey, ed., *The English Court from the Wars of the Roses to the Civil War* (1987).

66 'The Revival of the Entourage: the Bedchamber of James I, 1603–1625'; 'The Image of Virtue: the Court and Household of Charles I, 1625–1642' 173–25, 226–60. See also Cuddy, 'Anglo-Scottish Union and the Court of James I, 1603–1625', *Transactions of the Royal Historical Society*, 5th ser. XXXIX (1989) 106–24. The Caroline court of the early 1630s is discussed in L. J. Reeve, *Charles I and the Road to Personal Rule* (Cambridge, 1989).

67 For Henrietta Maria, see R. M. Smuts, 'The Puritan Followers of Henrietta Maria in the 1630s', *English Historical Review*, 93 (1978) 26–45; C. Hibbert, *Charles I and the Popish Plot* (Chapel Hill, 1983), and 'The Role of a Queen Consort: the Household and Court of Henrietta Maria, 1626–1642' in R. G. Asch and A. Birke, eds., *Princes, Patronage and the Nobility: The Court at the Beginning of the Modern Age* (Oxford, 1991), pp. 393–414. A brief introduction to the problems raised by Anne of Denmark can be found in A. J. Loomie, 'King James I's Catholic Consort', *Huntington Library Quarterly*, 34 (1971) 303–16.

68 'The Baronial Context of the English Civil War', *Transactions of the Royal Historical Society*, 5th ser., XL (1990) 93–120. See also R. G. Asch, 'Krone, Hof und Adel in den Ländern der Stuart Dynastie im frühen 17 Jahrhundert', *Zeitschrift für Historische Forschung*, 16 (1989) 185–220.

69 *Buckingham: The Life and Political Career of George Villiers, First Duke of Buckingham 1592–1628* (1981). Also published during the 1980s were Roy Strong, *Prince Henry and England's Lost Renaissance* (1986); M. D. Young, *Servility and Service: The Life and Work of Sir John Coke*, Royal Historical Society, Studies in History, 45 (1986); R. E. Schreiber, *The Political*

Career of Sir Robert Naunton 1589–1635, Royal Historical Society, Studies in History, 24 (1981) and *The First Carlisle: Sir James Hay, First Earl of Carlisle as Courtier, Diplomat and Entrepreneur, 1580–1636*, Transactions of the American Philosophical Society, 74, pt. 7 (1984); M. V. Hay, *The Life of Robert Sidney, Earl of Leicester (1563–1626)* (Washington DC, 1984).

70 See my review, *English Historical Review*, 98 (1983) 625–8.

71 *Northampton: Patronage and Politics at the Court of James I* (1982): see also 'Corruption and the Court of James I: the Undermining of Legitimacy', in B. C. Malament, ed., *After the Reformation: Essays in Honor of J. H. Hexter* (Manchester, 1980), pp. 75–94.

72 The 'Spanish Faction' of the court of James I still needs an adequate study; some preliminary observations on that of Charles I can be found in A. J. Loomie, 'The Spanish Faction at the Court of Charles I, 1630–8', *Bulletin of the Institute of Historical Research*, 59 (1986) 37–49.

73 M. G. Brennan, *Literary Patronage in the English Renaissance: The Pembroke Family* (1988). A. Gebauer, *Von Macht und Mäzenatentum: Leben und Werk William Herberts, des dritten Earls von Pembroke* (Heidelberger Forschungen 28, 1987).

74 See, however, J. T. Cliffe, *The Puritan Gentry: The Great Puritan Families of Early Stuart England* (1984), and N. Tyacke, *The Fortunes of English Puritanism, 1603–1640*, Friends of Dr Williams Library, 44th lecture, 1989.

75 Esp. 'John Field and Elizabethan Puritanism', in Collinson, *Godly People: Essays on English Protestantism and Puritanism* (1983), pp. 335–70.

76 (1967).

77 *The Religion of Protestants: The Church in English Society 1559–1625* (Oxford, 1982). On Grindal, see Collinson, *Archbishop Grindal 1519–1583: The Struggle for a Reformed Church* (1979); on Abbot, K. Fincham, 'Prelacy and Politics: Archbishop Abbot's Defence of Protestant Orthodoxy', *Historical Research*, 61 (1988) 36–64. See also P. Lake, 'Matthew Hutton – A Puritan Bishop?', *History*, 64 (1979) 182–204, and the forthcoming collection edited by K. Fincham, *The Early Stuart Church*.

78 (Cambridge, 1982).

79 In Russell, *Origins of the English Civil War*, pp. 119–43. See also his *Anti-Calvinists: The Rise of English Arminianism, c. 1590–1640* (Oxford, 1987).

80 K. C. Fincham and P. G. Lake, 'The Ecclesiastical Policy of James I', *Journal of British Studies*, 24 (1985) 169–207. Tyacke, however, still considers Puritanism a revolutionary force, see *Fortunes of English Puritanism*, and 'The Ambiguities of Early-Modern English Protestantism', *Historical Journal* 34 (1991) 743–54.

81 'Puritan Evangelism in the Reign of Elizabeth I', *English Historical Review*, 92 (1977) 30–58; 'From Monopoly to Minority: Catholicism in Early Modern England', *Transactions of the Royal Historical Society*, 5th

ser., XXXI (1981) 129–47; 'The Continuity of Catholicism in the English Reformation', *Past and Present*, 93 (1981) 37–69; 'The Church of England, the Catholics and the People', in C. Haigh, ed., *The Reign of Elizabeth I* (1984), pp. 195–220.

82 This theme is also developed by John Morrill, see 'The Church in England, 1642–49' in J. Morrill, ed., *Reactions to the English Civil War* (1982), pp. 89–114.

83 'The Rise of Arminianism Reconsidered', *Past and Present*, 101 (1983) 34–54, and, more recently, *Predestination, Policy and Polemic: Conflict and Consensus in the English Church from the Reformation to the Civil War* (Cambridge, 1992). See also S. Lambert, 'Richard Montagu, Arminianism and Censorship', *Past and Present*, 124 (1989) 36–68. For a critique of this argument, see P. Lake, 'Calvinism and the English Church', *Past and Present*, 114 (1987) 32–76.

84 Outlined in C. Russell, 'The British Problem and the English Civil War', *History*, 72 (1987) 395–415. For Russell, the 'British Problem' is central to the outbreak of the Civil War, and explored at length in his *Causes of the English Civil War* and *Fall of the British Monarchies*.

85 J. Wormald, 'James VI and I: Two Kings or One?', *History*, 68 (1983) 189–209. See also Cuddy, 'Anglo-Scots Union and the Court of James I'.

86 B. Galloway, *The Union of England and Scotland 1603–1608* (Edinburgh, 1986). For an Irish approach to the question of English 'nationality', see S. Ellis, 'Crown, Community and Government in the English Territories 1450–1575', *History*, 71 (1986) 187–204, also taken up in J. Guy, *Tudor England* (Oxford, 1988), chap. 13.

87 A. Hughes, 'Militancy and Localism: Warwickshire Politics and Westminster Politics, 1643–1647', *Transactions of the Royal Historical Society*, 5th ser. XXXI (1981) 51–68; and 'Local History and the Origins of the Civil War', in Cust and Hughes, *Conflict in Early Stuart England*, pp. 224–53. A. Fletcher, 'National and Local Awareness in the County Communities', in Tomlinson, *Before the English Civil War*, pp. 151–74. C. Holmes, '"The County Community" in Stuart Historiography', *Journal of British Studies*, 19 (1980) 54–73. For specific instances, see P. Lake, 'The Collection of Ship-Money in Cheshire during the Sixteen-Thirties: a Case-Study of Relations Between Central and Local Government', *Northern History*, 17 (1981) 44–71, and R. Cust, *The Forced Loan and English Politics 1626–1628* (Oxford, 1987).

88 *Reformation and Revolution, 1558–1660*, Paladin History of England (1984); *The City and the Court 1603–1643* (Cambridge, 1979).

89 See, for example, A. Wall, 'Patterns of Politics in England, 1558–1625', *Historical Journal*, 31 (1988) 947–63.

90 See S. Adams, 'Eliza Enthroned? The Court and its Politics', in Haigh, *Reign of Elizabeth I*, pp. 55–77; 'The Dudley Clientele and the House of Commons, 1559–1586', *Parliamentary History*, 8 (1989) 216–39;

'Favourites and Factions in the Elizabethan Court', in Asch and Birke, *Princes, Patronage and the Nobility*, pp. 265–88. For a recent example of the older view, see S. Doran, 'Religion and Politics at the Court of Elizabeth I: the Habsburg Marriage Negotiations of 1559–1567', *English Historical Review*, 104 (1989) 908–26.

91 Discussed in more detail in Adams, 'The Patronage of the Crown in Tudor Politics: The 1590s in Perspective' in J. A. Guy, ed., *The Reign of Elizabeth I: Court and Culture in the Last Decade* (Cambridge, forthcoming). See also R. G. Asch, 'The Revival of Monopolies: Court and Patronage during the Personal Rule of Charles I, 1629–1640', in Asch and Birke, *Princes, Patronage and the Nobility*, pp. 357–92.

92 On ship money, see Lake, 'Collection of Ship Money in Cheshire'; K. Fincham, 'The Judges' Decision on Ship Money in February 1637: the Reaction of Kent', *Bulletin of the Institute of Historical Research*, LVII (1984) 230–7; N. Bard, 'The Ship Money Case of William Fiennes, Viscount Saye and Sele', in *ibid.*, L (1977) 177–84.

93 Apart from Ruigh's monograph, and the relevant chapters of Russell, *Parliaments* and Lockyer, *Buckingham*, see also Adams, 'Foreign Policy and the Parliaments of 1621 and 1624' in Sharpe, *Faction and Parliament*, pp. 139–71, T. Cogswell, *The Blessed Revolution: English Politics and the Coming of War, 1621–1624* (Cambridge, 1989), and M. D. White, 'Buckingham, War and Parliament: Revisionism Gone Too Far', *Parliamentary History*, 4 (1985) 45–69.

94 But see T. Cogswell, 'England and the Spanish Match', in Cust and Hughes, *Conflict in Early Stuart England*, pp. 107–33.

95 As in the collections edited by L. L. Peck, *The Mental World of the Jacobean Court* (Cambridge, 1991), and K. Sharpe and P. Lake, *Politics and Culture in Early Seventeenth Century England* (forthcoming).

CHAPTER 3

Ben Jonson and the Master of the Revels

Richard Dutton

Thomas Dekker's *Satiromastix: Or the Untrussing of the Humorous Poet* (1601) palpably lampoons two Jonsons. One is a 'staring Leviathan' with a face 'puncht full of oylet-holes, like the cover of a warming-pan' who 'hast such a terrible mouth, that thy beard's afraid to peep out' (v.ii.258–9) and who is portrayed on stage 'in his true attire', which is verminous. The other is a high-minded but self-conceited satirist, who 'must be call'd Asper, and Criticus, and Horace' (i.ii.376), characters from Jonson's own plays *Every Man Out of His Humour, Cynthia's Revels* and *Poetaster.*[1] Among the 'hits' that Dekker scores in this comprehensive 'untrussing' is the accusation that, behind the unprepossessing Jonson's repeated pose as the railing poet, lies an ambitious toady, anxious to 'beget ... the reversion of the Master of the King's Revels' (iv.i.189–90).[2] The Master of the Revels, responsible for the censoring and licensing of most plays for public performance in the London area, was the very embodiment of authority as far as the theatrical world was concerned.[3] Given Jonson's antagonistic relationship with various forms of authority at this time, it is odd that Dekker should accuse Jonson of this particular ambition.

Jonson's first recorded association with the theatre was as an actor in, and co-author of, *The Isle of Dogs*, performed by Pembroke's Men at the new Swan Theatre in 1597, which was denounced to the privy council as a 'seditious play'. Jonson and others were imprisoned for two to three months, while the privy council placed a general restraint on playing, and even issued directives for the dismantling of all theatres, though they were not enforced.[4] Subsequently Jonson was obliged to change the ending of *Every Man Out of His Humour* (1599), as he grudgingly acknowledges in the quarto text: 'It had another *Catastrophe* or conclusion at the first playing: which (διὰ το τὴν βᾰσίλισσαν προσωποποϊεῖσθαι [because of the impersonation of the Queen]) many seem'd not to relish it: and therefore 'twas since alter'd'.[5] Given that Jonson did not restore the original version when he printed the play, we may suspect that it was official intervention rather than popular opinion that forced the change on him. Certainly it was official intervention which ensured that the 'Apologetical Dialogue' he appended to *Poetaster* (1601) was 'only once spoken upon the stage' and furthermore not allowed to be printed with the quarto in 1602: 'Here (Reader) in place of the Epilogue, was meant to thee an Apology from the Author, with his reasons for the publishing of this book: but (since he is no less restrain'd, than thou depriv'd of it by Authority) he prays thee to think charitably of what thou hast read, till thou mayst hear him speak what he hath written' (H. & S, IV, p. 317, note). Some facet of the play clearly got Jonson into trouble with the law, since in dedicating the folio text to the lawyer, Richard Martin, he describes it as one 'for whose innocence, as for the Author's, you were once a noble and timely undertaker to the greatest Justice of this kingdom' (p. 201) – presumably referring to a prosecution by an aggrieved party before the Lord Chief Justice, Sir John Popham. None of this suggests that Jonson was meekly trying to curry favour with those powerful enough to procure for him a responsible court post, least of all that of Master of the Revels.

Moreover, away from the stage, his life was hardly conducted with an eye to the main chance. In September 1598 he had killed his fellow actor Gabriel Spencer in a duel and escaped hanging only by pleading benefit of clergy – the increasingly anachronistic exemption from the death penalty for those able to read 'neck verse' from the Bible. Nevertheless, he did not escape entirely unscathed; all his goods were confiscated, and he was branded with the Tyburn T at the base of his thumb, marking that his life was forfeit to the state for any subsequent offence. Moreover 'then took he his religion by trust of a priest who visited him in [Newgate] prison. thereafter he was 12 years a Papist' ('Drummond', lines 249–51). Conversion to Roman Catholicism at the instigation of an underground missionary priest was hardly the calculated act of a man bent on self-advancement. Nevertheless, Dekker's satiric gibe would have been pointless if at least some of the audience had not recognised in it an approximation to the truth. And it proved extremely prescient. Twenty years later, on 5 October 1621, Jonson was indeed granted the reversion to the post of Master of the Revels: that is, he acquired the right of possession on the death or removal from office of the present incumbent, Sir George Buc, and that of Sir John Astley, who held a prior reversion. Buc retired insane in 1622 and so, for the last fifteen years of his life, Jonson was only a heart-beat away from taking on the authority of the Master of the Revels: a remarkable – almost ironic – reversal, it would seem.

Of course, Jonson at the end of James's reign was a very different figure from Jonson at the end of Elizabeth's. Both of Dekker's caricatures had been transformed: the 'lean . . . hollow-cheekt scrag' (v.ii.261–2) had given way to the 'mountain belly' of 'On My Picture Left in Scotland', and the railing poet had quit the 'loathed stage' to become the smooth-tongued panegyrist of dozens of court masques and aristocratic entertainments. The reversion to the Mastership, rumour had it, was the king's reward for the most recent of these, *The Gypsies Metamorphosed*, a vehicle for the royal favourite, Buckingham, performed an unparalleled three times in August–September 1621. It is easy to read into the transformation a hypocritical abandonment of principles on Jonson's part, or a simple capitulation to the 'authority' he scorns when explaining to readers why he cannot print his 'Apologetical Dialogue'. But Jonson's career is fraught with problems of self-definition, coming as it does at the very beginning of a transformation in the status and function of literature succinctly outlined by Alvin Kernan: 'An older system of polite or courtly letters – primarily oral, aristocratic, amateur, authoritarian, court-centered – was . . . gradually replaced by a new print-based, market-centered, democratic literary system.'[6] Renaissance play-texts were in the vanguard of this change, products of a marriage between 'court-centered' patronage and 'market-centered' capitalist enterprise, within which the role of the author – his standing in society, the nature of his responsibility to both patrons (including the acting companies who employed him) and audiences, the copyright of his writing, the limits on his self-expression – was both ill-defined and in transition.

Jonson's insistence on the title of 'poet' against that of 'playwright', the self-conscious re-drafting of theatrical scripts for the different audience of print (and the retention somehow of the right to reproduce those scripts in the different medium, against the usual practice of the acting companies that commissioned them), the constant spelling out of contractual relationships between himself and his paymasters (whether they be his aristocratic patrons or the

'grounded judgements' in the public theatres) – these are all symptomatic not so much of personal vanity as of a genuine insecurity in a
role that Jonson was having to create for himself. The publication of
his *Works* in 1616 is rightly seen as a key moment in the history of
English letters, incorporating a claim to classic status for himself and
to canonical status for those of his writings, including a select nine
plays, given permanence by 'the book'.[7] But, as David Riggs points
out: 'The success that came his way upon the publication of the folio
and the grant of the [royal] pension ... raised Jonson to such an
eminence that he ceased, ironically enough, to write for publication,
and reverted to the ways of the gentlemanly amateur.'[8] Jonson was
never able to relax into a single, stable self-definition, and his
attitude to the role of Master of the Revels must be seen in relation
to this constant state of flux and its attendant anxieties. The case for
this is the more compelling if we appreciate that the Master of the
Revels was not, as is often assumed, simply the repressive agent of an
authoritarian regime, but an ambivalent intermediary in the cultural politics of early modern England, where the theatre itself hung
indeterminately between the feudal past and the commercial future.
He was the bridge between court patronage and the market
economy. It seems likely that Jonson himself came to appreciate this
in the highly charged years just before and after the accession of
James I, between *Poetaster* (1601) and *Volpone* (1606).

The so-called 'War of the Theatres', of which *Poetaster* and *Satiromastix* were the last shots, was itself symptomatic of the anxieties
surrounding dramatic authorship at this time. While it might be
true, as Reavley Gair maintains, that 'there is a high probability
that the Poetomachia was a purely contrived situation, a seventeenth-century version of a modern publicity campaign to control
taste', David Bevington is also correct in observing that 'the purely
commercial aspects of a theatrical rivalry [do not] explain away the
basic dividing issue of the proper role of satire in a commonwealth
shaken by religious and dynastic uncertainties'.[9] 'The proper role of
satire' points to the parallel question of the role, function and status
of the satirist, the author, which becomes a key issue in these plays.
Jonson in particular was extremely sensitive to these matters in all
his 'comicall satyres' (whether or not they were strictly contributions to the 'War of the Theatres'), not least because he was
obliged to attend to the ways in which the state was alert to them
and attempting to contain the problems they posed for it. It is hardly

coincidental that the Poetomachia overlaps with the bishops' ban in the summer of 1599 on the printing of satires and epigrams, and their order for the burning of several controversial works, notably those of Gabriel Harvey and Thomas Nashe; or that these restrictions in turn came within a month of the privy council's ban on the printing of English histories without the written permission of its own members, a ban inspired by Dr John Hayward's *The First Part of the Reign of Henry IV*, which was construed as drawing subversive parallels between Richard II and Elizabeth.[10] In such measures we may detect not only an awareness of the subversive potential of printed literature (licensing of the press dated back to 1538, and Lord Burghley himself had been a press licenser under Edward VI), but also a glimmering recognition of the commercially autonomous author as a new species and problem, which would need to be contained.

In the case of writing for the theatre, the restraints were neither sudden nor dramatic, but in some ways (perhaps because public order was more immediately at issue) more thorough. Throughout Elizabeth's reign the privy council had sought to control the acting profession by limiting their numbers, resisting their tendency to float free of the social framework, and placing restraints on their freedom of movement. The 1572 Act for the Punishment of Vagabonds, for example, removed the right to patronise actors (which had previously extended to knights and even gentlemen) from all persons below the status of baron. In 1574 a directive required that the actors' wearing a patron's livery must represent a genuine attachment to his service (and so authority), not just a convenient fiction. The 1598 Act which replaced that of 1572 removed the right of justices of the peace to grant licences to actors without aristocratic patronage. Within the London area (towards which most of these measures were primarily directed) the *Isle of Dogs* affair precipitated a move for even tighter controls. Although the order for the dismantling of all the theatres came to nothing, it was followed by a directive the following February restricting playing to only two companies specifically licensed and under the patronage of members of the privy council, who were moreover both cousins of the queen: 'none [may] be suffered hereafter to play but those two formerly named belonging to us, the Lord Admiral and Lord Chamberlain, unless you shall receive other direction from us'.[11] In June 1600 those two companies were further restricted to the use of one nominated theatre each (the Fortune and Globe respectively) and to only two performances each per week (Chambers, *ES* IV, pp. 329–31). But already pressures were at work to undermine what seems to have been the privy council's very clear purpose. By late 1599 or early 1600 two boys companies, the Children of Paul's and the Children of the Chapel, were revived after lying dormant for a decade or more. Protected by their licences as adjuncts of choir schools, they were not affected by the privy council's restrictions, and their revival seems to have been an attempt to exploit an under-supply in the market created by the restrictions on the adult companies. That cartel was also directly challenged, first by Derby's Men and latterly by a joint company of Worcester's and Oxford's Men, both using the Boar's Head Theatre. And the latter, at least, had royal approval (Chambers, *ES* IV, pp. 334–5).

Nevertheless, the aim of the privy council to contain the theatrical profession within a closed circle of its own licensing and patronage remained clear, and the translation of this to exclusively royal patronage after 1603 was merely an adaptation to fit the circumstances of the new monarchy, not a radical change of policy. In *Poetaster* (written for the Children of the Chapel, outside the adult cartel) Jonson casts a critical eye on the dangers of such arrangements. Asinius Lupus is an asinine wolf of a magistrate, determined to further his own interests by denouncing true poets as a threat to public order and to the emperor. Significantly, his agents and abettors include the (adult) actors, Histrio and Aesop ('your politician'), specifically associated with 'your Globes, and your Triumphs' (III.iv.201), which inevitably suggests the Chamberlain's Men. They lay information with the authorities against both Ovid and Horace (that is, in the sense that Dekker construed it, against Jonson himself) for which Aesop is promised 'a monopoly of playing, confirm'd to thee and thy covey, under the Emperor's broad seal, for this service' (v.iii.123–5). E. K. Chambers asks: 'Can the Aesop episode be a reminiscence of the part played by Augustine Phillips in the Essex innovation?' He is referring to the special performance of the Richard II play by the Chamberlain's Men on the eve of the rebellion and the fact that the authorities' only response was to ask Phillips, one of their principal members, some not very searching questions. They performed at court as usual only days later, on the eve of Essex's execution.[12] Whether Jonson is making a specific allusion or not, the broad accusation of collusion between unscrupulous politicians and compliant actors is clearly made. Horace denounces those who

> vomit forth
> Their own prodigious malice; and pretending
> To be the props, and columns of [Caesar's] safety,
> The guards unto his person, and his peace,
> Disturb it most, with their false lapwing-cries. (iv.vii.49–53)

Lupus is fitted with ass's ears, while Horace demonstrates that the true poet is a more trustworthy servant of the emperor and the state than whose who ostensibly protect them.

It is consistently part of Jonson's strategy to associate his own integrity (like that of his surrogates, Asper, Criticus and Horace) with the authority of the monarchs he serves, while misreadings of his works are put down to blatant folly or malicious misconstruction. But protestations of integrity did nothing to deflect Dekker's ridicule: *Satiromastix* was an unusual joint venture by the Chamberlain's Men and Paul's Boys and so not merely the sour grapes of those in the cartel whose privileges had been circumvented by the resuscitated boys. (The 'War' was never simply a matter of 'public' versus 'private' theatres.) Nor did they deflect the prosecution, to which Jonson alludes in the dedication of his play, or the suppression of his 'Apologetical Dialogue'. In the 'Dialogue' (with a backward glance at Lupus) he had intended to announce that his next project would be a tragedy in the classical manner:

> There's something come into my thought
> That must and shall be sung high and aloof,
> Safe from the wolf's black jaw and the dull ass's hoof.
>
> (lines 237–9)

Ironically that work, *Sejanus*, encountered its own Asinius Lupus in the powerful form of a privy councillor, Henry Howard, Earl of Northampton: 'Northampton was his mortal enemy for brawling on a St George's Day one of his attenders, he was called before the Council for his *Sejanus* & accused both of popery and treason by him' ('Drummond', lines 325–7). The privy council register for this period is missing, so we do not know the date of this; on balance, the evidence suggests that publication in 1605 rather than performance in 1603 was the likelier cause of Northampton's antagonism. But it would seem that either *Sejanus* or Daniel's *Philotas* (1604) was the first *play* to provoke the privy council itself to question the *author* about his intentions, a notable development. Previously, offending plays were deemed to be the responsibility of the acting company that commissioned and performed them, with authorship only one consideration among others. Jonson, for example, does not seem to have been subjected to greater attention or punishment for his part as co-author of *The Isle of Dogs* than were his fellow actors.

Jonson's next play, *Eastward Ho*, encountered yet another Asinius Lupus in the form of the Scottish courtier, Sir James Murray: 'he was delated by Sir James Murray to the King for writing something against the Scots in a play *Eastward Ho* & voluntarily imprisoned himself with Chapman and Marston, who had written it amongst them; the report was that they should then had their ears cut and noses' ('Drummond', lines 273–7). The threat of a second judicial mutilation galvanised Jonson to write to a range of the most powerful people he knew at court. Seven such letters survive, three to the Earls of Salisbury, Pembroke and Montgomery, three to unnamed lords (probably including Lord Chamberlain Suffolk and the king's cousin, Lord D'Aubigny), and one to an unnamed lady, possibly Lucy, Countess of Bedford.[13] It may be a mark of desperation that Jonson turned not to a single patron but, in effect, to virtually all the major constituencies at court. Of these letters, the most interesting is that to the Earl of Salisbury. Jonson composed it with the utmost care – it exists both in an early draft and in the holograph Salisbury actually received. Significant passages from it were to be reproduced in public, virtually verbatim, in the dedicatory Epistle to *Volpone*, dated 'From my house in the Blakfriars this 11. of February 1607' in the quarto. Given the suppression of the 'Apologetical Dialogue' to *Poetaster*, this was the first general *apologia* by Jonson to see print. It is also the key text in which Jonson acknowledges, and accedes to, the authority of the Master of the Revels.

It should be observed that, between the *Eastward Ho* affair and the writing of the epistle, two non-theatrical events must have shaken Jonson severely. One was the Gunpowder Plot, in which he may well have played a shadowy role (he was certainly seen in the company of Catesby and other plotters barely a month before the plot's 'discovery', and was called in by Salisbury to help track down a missionary priest with information immediately after it). The other was his own 'presentation' before the Consistory Court in January – April 1606 for persistent failure to take the Anglican communion.[14] It is difficult to believe that this concatenation of events did not contribute to the almost defiant, ultramontane conformism of the epistle in its attitude to all forms of law and authority, literary and critical as well as political. As James D. Redwine Jr observes: 'The importance of the *Volpone* criticism ... can scarcely be stressed too often – it marks a turning point in the development of Jonson's critical theory. Up to the time he wrote *Volpone*, his attitude toward the so-called laws would seem to be one of respectful independence.' He cites the dialogue between Cordatus and Mitis in the Induction to *Every Man Out of His Humour* as evidence of Jonson's earlier view of the 'licence' or 'liberty' that may properly be exercised by modern poets. But

'licence, or free power, to illustrate and heighten our invention' is more likely to be attacked as a dangerous tendency of an illiterate age than to be defended on the grounds of classical precedent ... Throughout [the *Volpone* epistle] it is the 'liberty' or 'licence' of contemporary poetry that he attacks most bitterly. And in the *Volpone* prologue, three of Mitis' 'too nice observations' are brought forth as necessary elements ('needful rules') of 'quick comedy'.[15]

The Jonson of the Epistle, possibly chastened by his experiences of *Sejanus* and *Eastward Ho*, besides other matters, is altogether more convinced of the need for 'authority' than any of his earlier manifestations. We should bear this in mind in considering those parts of the Epistle that bear directly on the authority of the Master of the Revels.

In differentiating the integrity of his own 'poems' from 'the too-much licence of Poetasters, in this time' (Epistle, line 14), Jonson acknowledges 'that now, especially in dramatic, or (as they term it) stage-poetry, nothing but ribaldry, profanation, blasphemy, all licence of offence to god, and man, is practis'd ... [but] For my own particular, I can (and from a most clear conscience) affirm, that I have ever trembled to think toward the least prophaneness' (lines 35–8, 43–5). In this he absolves himself of those offences which had precipitated the Act to Restrain Abuses of Players only the year before, and which had placed on the Master of the Revels the most *explicit* responsibilities with which, to the best of our knowledge, he was ever charged ('For the preventing and avoiding of the great abuse of the Holy Name of God in stageplays, interludes, Maygames, shows, and such-like': Chambers, *ES*, IV, p. 338). Jonson then addresses charges to which he knows he is more vulnerable:

And, howsoever I cannot escape, from some, the imputation of sharpness, but that they will say, I have taken a pride, or lust, to be bitter ... I would ask of these supercilious politics, what nation, society, or general order, or state I have provok'd, what public person, whether I have not (in all these) preserv'd their dignity, as mine own person, safe. My works are read, allow'd, (I speak of those that are entirely mine) look into them: What broad reproofs have I us'd? Where have I been particular? Where personal? except to a mimic, cheater, bawd, or buffoon, creatures (for their insolencies) worthy to be tax'd? Yet, to which of these so pointingly, as he might not, either ingenuously have confess'd, or wisely dissembled his disease. (lines 47–60)

He comes then, critically, to the recognition that the purity of his own motives cannot guarantee the innocence of what he writes, which depends in the last resort on its reception:

I know, that nothing can be so innocently writ, or carried, but may be made obnoxious to construction; marry, whilst I bear mine innocence about me, I fear it not. Application is now grown a trade with many; and there are, that profess to have a key for the decyphering of everything: but let wise and noble persons take heed how they be too credulous, or give leave to these invading interpreters, to be over-familiar with their fames, who cunningly, and often, utter their own virulent malice, under other men's simplest meanings. (lines 62–70)

This last section, derived ultimately from Martial's preface to his *Epigrams*, had been used in a different form in the 'Apologetical Dialogue' and in the letter to Salisbury: 'My noble Lord, they deal not charitably, who are too witty in another man's works, and utter, some times, their own malicious meanings, under o[u]r words' (p. 221). The challenge that his works be 'look[ed] into' also figures in the letter to Salisbury:

let me be examin'd, both by all my works past, and this present ... whether, I have ever (in any thing I have written private, or public) given offence to a nation, to any public order or state, or any person of honor, or authority, but have aequally labour'd to keep their dignity, as mine own person safe. (p. 221)

In both contexts, this passage leads to a very particular pay-off. In the letter to Salisbury, Jonson immediately protests: 'If others have transgress'd, let not me be entitled to their follies.' This was not in the early draft of the letter, and is clearly a careful afterthought. Jonson is hinting at something made much more explicit in a letter to the king by Jonson's fellow prisoner, Chapman: '[our] chief

offences are but two clauses, and both of them not our own' (p. 218).
Two particular 'clauses' in *Eastward Ho* had apparently caused most
offence.[16] The usual construction of the passages in the two letters is
that Jonson and Chapman were both tacitly blaming the third
author, Marston (who had apparently absented himself), for these
'clauses', though it is equally possible that they were interpolations
by the actors.

This, in more general terms, is the issue Jonson takes up at the
parallel point in the epistle to *Volpone*: 'My works are read, allow'd,
(I speak of those that are entirely mine) look into them.' He
dissociates himself in this from *Eastward Ho*, which was neither
'entirely mine' nor apparently 'allow'd' – that is, officially licensed.
Chapman begins another letter, to Lord Chamberlain Suffolk, with
a real admission of guilt:

Of all the oversights for which I suffer, none repents me so much, as that
our unhappy book was presented without your Lordship's allowance, for
which we can plead nothing by way of pardon: but your person so far
remov'd from our requir'd attendance; our play so much importun'd, and
our clear opinions, that nothing it contain'd could worthily be held
offensive. (pp. 218–19)

Whoever wrote the two offending 'clauses', it seems that all the
authors were being held responsible for its presentation without
'allowance' – an offence in itself as serious as the satiric libel to which
Murray presumably objected in the first place, since it defied the
whole structure of authority by which the theatres were suffered to
exist. In all probability it was this omission, rather than the libel *per
se*, that rendered this case as serious as it turned out to be. Jonson's
insistence in the epistle that his own 'works are read, allow'd' is his
first public obeisance to that structure of authority, and a significant
change of tack from the defiance he had manifested earlier.

In the context of *Volpone* this obeisance is a formal submission to
the authority of Edmund Tilney, Master of the Revels who, since
1581, had borne a special royal commission: 'we ordain, appoint
and authorise [him] by these presents of all such shows, plays,
players and playmakers, together with their playing places, to order
and reform, authorise and put down, as shall be thought meet or
unmeet unto himself or his said deputy in that behalf'.[17] These
plenipotentiary powers were a development from one of the
Master's existing functions, that of 'perusing and reforming' plays
for performance at court: 'perusing' usually meant seeing a rehearsal

of the play in his quarters in the old palace of St John's, while 'reforming' implied bringing it up to a standard fit for performance before the monarch. Philostrate has this role at court in *A Midsummer Night's Dream*: he has 'perused' Quince's *Pyramus and Thisbe* but (rightly) judged it quite beyond 'reforming', though Theseus chose to ignore his advice.[18] To ensure an adequate supply of royal entertainment Elizabeth's Master of the Revels already had powers to require acting companies to present themselves before him in this way. The 1581 commission should perhaps be seen less as a radical initiative to control the entire theatrical profession (though its wording will bear that construction, and all the powers ultimately exercised by successive Masters derived from it) than a reinforcement of the existing authority the Master had to facilitate his court duties. When Tilney had first been appointed in 1579 he was specifically charged with reducing the cost of court theatricals, which had got out of hand under his predecessor. His success in this (as W. R. Streitberger observes, 'the Revels bills for the 1580s were the lowest in Elizabeth's reign'[19]) was largely due to a policy of relying less on costly masques and more on plays provided by professional actors. To ensure the standard of performance available, Tilney in 1583 created an elite company of players, the Queen's Men, bringing together twelve of the finest actors from the existing companies, under direct royal patronage and his personal supervision. His 1581 powers made all this possible, and were probably granted primarily with that end in view.

But they also made it possible for Tilney to profit legitimately from his position by perusing and licensing plays for public performance, whether or not there was any question of their being put on at court; in these cases, a reading of the 'book' and the appendage of his 'allowance', if he thought it suitable, was sufficient. He could similarly charge for licensing theatres. In short, the situation grew up which we find reflected in Henslowe's papers. Contrary to what many assume, however, this was not a universal arrangement: it applied only to the principal established companies in the London area, those who might realistically be called upon to perform at court. It was, in effect, the beginning of the cartel whose exclusive rights the privy council was to try to enforce in the late 1590s. And we may suppose the arrangement suited the companies concerned well enough. Although it cost them money (a licence for a play cost 7 shillings in the early years of Henslowe's records and rose to £1 by the time Herbert was installed) the Master's 'allowance' effectively established that a play was fit for performance at court, and local justices or city authorities could not presume to enforce a higher standard than that. As early as 1592, the City of London authorities came to regard Tilney as the players' protector rather than their regulator. The Lord Mayor pleaded with the Archbishop of Canterbury to find some way of dealing with abuses associated with the actors, which the Master's authority prevented them from tackling. Whitgift apparently intimated that Tilney might be bought off for a 'consideration', but whether because the Livery Companies were not prepared to pay what he asked or for some other reason, this line of action was not pursued (Chambers, *ES*, IV, pp. 307–9).

Almost from the beginning, therefore, the Master's position was publicly perceived as ambiguous, his licensing motivated as much by personal gain (which depended on keeping the actors under his authority in business) as by zeal for the public good. This may well colour Dekker's gibe in *Satiromastix* about Jonson's ambitions in this direction. And the whole arrangement was doubtless envied and resented by actors excluded from the privileged circle. A case in point would appear to be those, including Jonson himself, involved in the *Isle of Dogs* affair. This company of Pembroke's Men was of recent formation, while the Swan was a new playhouse, and neither came under Tilney's jurisdiction. The privy council's correspondence on the matter is addressed not to him, but to the Surrey magistrates responsible for the Bankside.[20] The limiting of London-based companies to the cartel of two, which immediately followed, did however explicitly involve Tilney. The privy council directive which records it is addressed to him, mentioning 'a third company who of late (as we are informed) have by way of intrusion used likewise to play, having prepared neither any play for her Majesty nor are bound to you, the Masters [*sic*] of the Revels, for performing such orders as have been prescribed and enjoined to be observed by the other two companies before mentioned' (Chambers, *ES*, IV, p. 325). Tilney is enjoined to suppress this third company, and any other not specifically licensed by the council.

In his letter to Salisbury concerning *Eastward Ho* Jonson had ruefully to admit that he had been at fault over *The Isle of Dogs*. Salisbury, who had been on the privy council at the time, doubtless recalled the affair: 'I protest to your Honour, and call God to testimony (since my first error, which (yet) is punish'd in me more with my shame, than it was then with my bondage) I have so attemper'd my style, that I have given no cause to any good man of grief' (p. 221). There is no way of knowing if Jonson's working for Pembroke's Men, or his 'error', was partly inspired by the relative freedom of its not being one of the companies licensed by Tilney, but it is not unlikely. The play *should* have been 'perused' by the Surrey magistrates, but they were perhaps not as adept at spotting 'very seditious and slanderous matter' as we may suppose Tilney had by then become. Moreover, it is clear from reprimands issued in 1601 that the magistrates in both Middlesex and Surrey were less zealous in respect of theatrical matters than the privy council would have liked them to be (Chambers, *ES*, IV, pp. 332–3). Subsequent to *The Isle of Dogs* Jonson had no choice but to work for Henslowe and for the Chamberlain's Men, both adjuncts of the cartel, where his writing must have been subject to the perusal of the Master of the Revels. This may have helped to keep any potential offence in them within bounds. However, one of the critical handicaps we face in trying to understand the censorship of this period is that nothing has survived of the office-books of either Tilney or his successor, Buc. From what we know of Herbert's practice (and even that is far from perfect) they probably kept a record of the plays they licensed, with comments on any major interventions they had felt it necessary to make. But none of this is available to us. So we do not know, for example, if Tilney was involved in making Jonson change the ending of *Every Man Out of His Humour*. It would appear that the original version was staged, and so presumably had Tilney's 'allowance'. But the 'book' Tilney saw may not have been totally frank about the impersonation of the queen by an actor, and he may have intervened subsequently. It is equally possible, however, that someone else in authority did so. Members of the privy council did not necessarily consult the Master if a theatrical matter troubled them. They suspended *all* playing as a result of the *Isle of Dogs* scandal, and Salisbury did the same over Chapman's *Byron* plays, while the Bishop of London for a time prevented performance of Fletcher and Massinger's *Sir John Van Olden Barnevelt* in 1619.[21] In these and other instances there is evidence that even his own superiors did not, at least with any consistency, see the Master of the Revels as their plenipotentiary agent for dealing with the theatres.

Jonson seems to have taken the earliest opportunity to write for the Blackfriars Boys. *Cynthia's Revels* was put on by them in the autumn of 1600, and at court in January 1601. Dekker's gibe that 'your plays are misliked at court' (*Satiromastix*, v.ii.324) suggests that this early bid for royal favour was not successful, though Tilney must have liked it well enough to sanction its performance there. Writing for the boys, Jonson may have avoided the adult cartel, but he nevertheless remained subject to the authority of the Master of the Revels. This, at least, is what we must infer, though the evidence is tenuous. No documentation at all survives about the authority to license plays for 'private' theatres during Elizabeth's reign. Presumably this is because their very existence depended upon royal warrants (the Children of the Chapel, moreover, were members of the queen's own household), and it was taken for granted that their theatrical activities were subject to the authority of the relevant royal official, the Master of the Revels. This (again presumably) remained the case when their theatres re-opened at the end of the reign, although their activities were now unambiguously professional and almost totally distinct from the choir-schools under whose commissions they operated. There is specific evidence in respect of one play staged by Paul's Boys early in 1603. Chapman's lost *The Old Joiner of Aldgate* became the subject of litigation, in the course of which the company's manager testified that he bought the 'book' from the author, 'being licensed by the Mr of . . . the Queen's Majesty's Revels, he not knowing that it touched any person living'.[22] If Paul's Boys were required to license their plays with Tilney, it is most unlikely that the Blackfriars Boys were not. So Tilney, again, may have been responsible for the suppression of the 'Apologetical Dialogue' to *Poetaster*. The 'Dialogue' was not part of the original 'book', and if the boys staged it without further 'allowance', that would have been cause enough for its suppression, irrespective of what it said. Tilney would *not*, however, have been responsible for preventing the 'Dialogue' coming out in print (which may have been a corollary of the litigation about the play). The licensing of plays for the press, as of all other printed matter, was still at this time in the hands of an ecclesiastical commission headed by the Archbishop of Canterbury and the Bishop of London. In 1606 Sir George Buc, who by then held the reversion to the Mastership of the Revels, acquired the authority to license *plays* for the press; this was distinct from his authority to license them for the stage, which did not commence until he succeeded Tilney in August 1610, though thereafter the responsibilities were conjoined under successive Masters.[23]

Sejanus, being a Chamberlain's/King's Men's play, would certainly have come to Tilney before it was staged in 1603, though we
cannot be certain whether it was something that he let through that
incensed Northampton, or whether it was something introduced in
the printed version of 1605 which, as Jonson advertised, 'in all
numbers, is not the same with that which was acted on the public
stage' (Epistle, To the Readers). It is clear, however, that *Eastward
Ho* did *not* come before the Master of the Revels, because it was
outside his jurisdiction. In February 1604 the Children of the
Chapel were re-incorporated as the Children of the Queen's (i.e.
Queen Anne's) Revels; their royal patent gave them the right to
perform: 'Provided always that no such plays or shows shall be
presented ... or by them any where publicly acted but by the
approbation and allowance of Samuel Daniel, whom her pleasure is
to appoint for that purpose' (Chambers, *ES*, II, p. 49). This was a
logical corollary of the fact that James's succession not only installed
a new monarch but also created a second royal household, that of
the Queen Anne (and, indeed, separate establishments for Prince
Henry and Princess Elizabeth, though these were of no immediate
consequence).[24] The queen, with her own council, Lord Chamberlain and other officers, exercised her rights of patronage in respect of
the acting company within her own household – while the authority
of the Master of the Revels now specifically related to that of the
king. This arrangement seems to have led to immediate confusion, in
as much as Daniel chose to stage his own play *Philotas*, which
someone on the privy council (very possibly Salisbury himself) felt
might 'be applied to the late Earl of Essex'.[25] Daniel protested that it
was a case of 'wrong application and misconceiving' but compoun-
ded his error by calling upon one of the lords, the Earl of Devonshire, to testify to his innocence. Devonshire, formerly Lord Mount-
joy and an associate of Essex, did not take kindly to being involved
in this way before his fellow privy councillors. The precise outcome
of all this is unclear, but it does seem that Daniel ceased to act as
licenser for the Queen's Revels company. On the other hand, it is far
from clear who *did* regularly act as licenser for the company in its
bewilderingly various guises thereafter – Children of the Revels,
Children of the Blackfriars, Children of the Whitefriars and, once
more (1610), Children of the Queen's Revels. Its continued anomalous status must partly explain its involvement in so many theatrical
controversies of the day.[26]

In the case of *Eastward Ho*, as Chapman's letter establishes, it was the *king*'s Lord Chamberlain, the Earl of Suffolk (and he in person, not a subordinate like the Master of the Revels), who should have been approached for a licence. The authors and the actors, however, decided to go ahead without worrying about what Chapman tries to pass off as a technicality: 'but your person so far remov'd from our requir'd attendance; our play so much importun'd, and our clear opinions, that nothing it contain'd could worthily be held offensive' (pp. 218–19). Suffolk was with the court at Oxford, and the suspicion must be that (as with the *Byron* plays and *A Game at Chess*, though the latter *was* properly licensed) the actors deliberately waited until the court was away from London before staging a play which they expected to generate something of a scandal. But in this case it was the authors, rather than the actors, who were held accountable for the offence, and the company seems not to have been affected. The explanation would appear to be that, in the case of plays for the 'private' theatres, it was the responsibility of the author(s) to acquire the necessary 'allowance'. That, at any rate, might be inferred from evidence relating to *The Old Joiner of Aldgate*. In the case of *Eastward Ho*, the fact that one of the authors, Marston, was involved in the management of the Blackfriars company may explain why the actors did not query this omission. It would also explain why Marston apparently left London expediently, possibly abandoning the stage altogether, while Jonson (if we can credit his claim that he imprisoned himself 'voluntarily') may not at first have been aware that anything was seriously amiss. For the most part, the fact of licensing itself, and the panoply of court authority and patronage that lay behind it, seems to have protected the actors and their authors from the savage penalties which the law theoretically made available for speaking too freely about great persons or affairs of state. As Philip Finkelpearl observes, 'during King James's reign as in Elizabeth's not one prominent poet or playwright was punished for libel'.[27] The multiply-confused licensing situation of the Blackfriars company best explains why Jonson and Chapman came closest of anyone to spoiling that statistic. This reading of the matter might help to explain how it was that Lady Elizabeth's Men were able to revive *Eastward Ho* in 1613 and indeed present it at court on 25 January 1614. The items that offended Sir James Murray in the first place were perhaps expunged, but the play as a whole was far from anathema, despite the stigma that must have attached to it. Presented within the proper structure of licensed authority, the court was prepared to countenance a surprising range of satirical comment, even aimed at itself.

The epistle to *Volpone* suggests that this is a lesson Jonson learned very thoroughly. The fact of his works being 'read, allow'd' became not merely a defensive concession but something to be prominently asserted. In the 1616 folio of his *Works* all his plays, bar one, bore the inscription: 'With the allowance of the Master of the Revels'. (The exception is *Catiline*, the last play in the volume. That was dedicated to the Earl of Pembroke, by then Lord Chamberlain and the Master's superior; if Pembroke had acknowledged the dedication, mention of the 'allowance' might be superfluous, even insulting.) In that sense, the 1621 reversion is already foreshadowed in the protest-ations of integrity in the 1607 epistle. But to what extent was Jonson compromising himself as an author by this public deference? Reviewing the powers granted to Tilney in his 1581 commission, G. E. Bentley argues: 'The hypotheses so often and so solemnly advanced by many critics and readers of Tudor and Stuart plays about the dramatist's "advice to the Queen" or "protests against the law" or "assertions of his religious dissent" must be made either in ignorance of the powers of the Master of the Revels or in assumption of his incompetence or his venality' (*The Profession of Dramatist*, p. 149). This implies not only that much modern criticism of Renaissance drama is fundamentally misconceived, but also that any writer subject to these powers (much less one publicly vaunting the fact) was severely, even demeaningly, curtailed in the range of his thoughts and their expression. The issue, however, is not in the end the powers that were theoretically vested in the Master of the Revels by his patent, but how he actually functioned and how his role was perceived in the articulate community of early Stuart London.

In the absence of more precise information from his predecessors, this is something we can only gauge with any detail in relation to Sir Henry Herbert, whose approach to his role as censor is most tellingly exemplified in his response to two plays by Massinger, the one originally called *The King and the Subject* (though that was one item that Herbert insisted on changing) and the other eventually called *Believe As You List*. In an unusually full entry in his office-book on the former, Herbert records:

The name of *The King and the Subject* is altered, and I allowed the play to be acted, the reformations most strictly observed, and not otherwise, the 5th of June, 1638.

At Greenwich on 4 June, Mr. W. Murray, gave me power from the king to allow of the play, and told me he would warrant it.

> Monies? We'll raise supplies what ways we please,
> And force you to subscribe to blanks, in which
> We'll mulct you as we shall think fit. The Caesars
> In Rome were wise, acknowledging no law
> But what their swords did ratify, the wives
> And daughters of the senators bowing to
> Their wills, as deities, etc.

This is a piece taken out of Philip Massinger's play, called *The King and the Subject*, and entered here forever to be remembered by my son and those that cast their eyes on it, in honour of King Charles, my master, who reading over the play at Newmarket, set his mark upon the place with his own hand, and in these words:

> This is too insolent, and to be changed.

Note, that the poet makes it the speech of a king, Don Pedro, king of Spain, and spoken to his subjects. (Adams, *Herbert*, pp. 22–3)

Bentley observes of this entry:

In the light of the fact that these lines were written in the time of the protests about ship money and corporate monopolies and other forms of alleged royal tyranny, Massinger must have been naive to think that they would be approved by the Master of the Revels. Such lines, which could easily be thought to express criticism of current actions or policies of the government, are just what the Master of the Revels was appointed to eliminate from plays performed in the London theatres. (*The Profession of Dramatist*, p. 173)

This is typical of the Whiggish attitude to early Stuart government, and so to its dramatic censorship, that has prevailed for much of this century, following the tone set by Virginia Crocheron Gildersleeve's pioneering *Government Regulation of the Elizabethan Drama* (New York, 1908). But there is clearly more to this case than that. Massinger had been a professional dramatist for the best part of twenty years when this occurred (1638), had been dealing with the same Master of the Revels for the last fifteen of them, and was assuredly not naive. Moreover, how did the king come to be involved, if the matter was so straightforward? On another occasion William Davenant complained about Herbert's over-strict 'reformation' of oaths in his play,

The Wits, and prevailed upon Endymion Porter to take the matter up with the king; Charles over-ruled Herbert on certain items (which the latter meticulously recorded, registering his loyal dissent) but was careful in his whole management of the matter not to call the Master's authority into question (Adams, *Herbert*, p. 22). Possibly Massinger, too, found a courtier to take up his case for him. But it is equally possible in this instance that Herbert was nervous enough about the play (he clearly was about the title) that it was he who asked for the king's judgement. Whatever the case, the striking feature of the way Herbert records the matter is his specificity: it is not that the general tenor of the play was at fault, but one particular speech. And even that is not so self-evidently exceptionable that Herbert does not need to spell out that it was spoken by a king of Spain and to his subjects. That is, Herbert is not recording something so patently outrageous that we might think Massinger naive to have tried to get it past him: but something so close to being acceptable that he needs to keep a precise record of how exactly it transgressed and of the king's express opinion in the matter.

It is also striking that there is no suggestion here of taking Massinger to task for being 'too insolent'. While it would have been unacceptable for these lines to be spoken in public, no one is apparently concerned to punish Massinger for thinking the thoughts. The licensing system over which the Master of the Revels presided was one of containment, not of antagonistic repression. Clearly, some dissenting voices must have been excluded altogether by the system, but if what we have of Herbert's records is anything like complete he rarely rejected a play out of hand. On the brink of the Civil War he did lose patience with 'a new play which I burnt for the ribaldry and offence that was in it' (Adams, *Herbert*, p. 23), but that was apparently a unique reaction. Also unusual, but deeply revealing, was a rare decision to refuse a licence to another play by Massinger (rather than use his absolute power to reform its 'dangerous matter', as he did with Thomas Drue's *The Duchess of Suffolk* in 1624): 'I did refuse to allow of a play of Massinger's because it did contain dangerous matter, as the deposing of Sebastian king of Portugal, by Philip the [Second] and there being a peace sworn twixt the kings of England and Spain' (Adams, *Herbert*, pp. 18–19). Sebastian of Portugal died at the battle of Alcacer-el-Kebir in Morocco in 1578, and Philip II of Spain annexed Portugal two years later. Various people claiming to be Sebastian subsequently surfaced, and were an embarrassment to Spain. One surfaced in Vienna in 1598, was hounded out by Spanish diplomatic pressure, and eventually executed by Philip III. In 1601 Henslowe paid Chettle and Dekker for a play, *King Sebastian of Portugal*, which Tilney presumably licensed at that time, when relations with Spain were still antagonistic. Herbert is quite explicit in 1631 that his refusal of the licence is because of the offence it might cause to a now-friendly power. It is more than likely, however, that he was sensitive not only to an issue some forty years old but also to more immediate matters – the struggle by the exiled Elector Palatine to establish his claim to the throne of Bohemia, annexed by Habsburg forces in a manner that Sebastian's history might clearly parallel. Since the Elector was Charles's brother-in-law, his Protestant cause and England's failure to support it were delicate issues.

Five months later, however, Herbert licensed *Believe as You List* without comment (6 May). This survives in manuscript, with the allowance attached. It is set in Roman times and concerns Antiochus the Great but, as C. J. Sisson suggests, 'the most cursory examination' is sufficient to identify it as a re-working of the play earlier refused a licence.[28] While there is no way of knowing what specific items Massinger might have dropped, the 'new' play still shadows Sebastian's case so closely in all but the names and the geography that we might have expected Herbert to continue to draw the line. He clearly knew what Massinger had in mind, and must have suspected that audiences would at least know that the earlier play had been refused a licence; moreover, in 'excusing' the author, the prologue to the new version virtually invites the audience to draw contemporary parallels:

> if you find what's Roman here,
> Grecian, or Asiatic, draw too near
> a late, & sad example, 'tis confess'd
> he's but an English scholar at his best,
> a stranger to cosmography, and may err
> in the countries' names, the shape, & character
> of the person he presents.   (lines 4–10)

As ever, there is room for speculation about collusion, or special pressures being brought to bear to secure a licence for this play. But it is entirely unnecessary. Herbert in fact was only pursuing the line taken by his predecessors. His role was not to repress *all* comment on contemporary affairs, which (given the malleability of allegory) was impossible, but to contain any comment within acceptable limits.

Those limits usually required a modicum of fictional or historical veiling; the speech from *The King and the Subject* clearly breached this principle, while the re-cast *Believe as You List* was deemed adequately opaque. It was not for Herbert to speculate on what Massinger might have been hinting at, even though he knew full well what he had in mind. His responsibility ended with ensuring that none of the powerful constituencies which he was installed to protect could legitimately complain of personal affronts, specific libels or *explicit* comment on matters of state. Such constituencies would include virtually anyone of consequence, particularly at court, and especially (as the original *Believe as You List* demonstrates) foreign ambassadors alert to slightings of their countries. Tangible affronts to any of these would not be tolerated. For example, Herbert was particularly incensed when, after licensing Shirley's *The Ball* as unexceptionable, he discovered in performance that 'there were divers personated so naturally, both of lords and others of the court, that I took it ill' (Adams, *Herbert*, p. 19). The capacity of costume and make-up to break through what might seem adequately veiled on the page was also certainly one contributory factor to the scandalous success of *A Game at Chess*. For the most part, the Master of the Revels must have relied on their ultimate dependence on his continued goodwill to ensure that the actors did not often break the letter *or the spirit* of his 'allowance' in this way; T. H. Howard-Hill has aptly characterised his relationship with them as 'although ultimately authoritarian ... more collegial than adversarial'.[29] At the point of licensing a play, however, he could be concerned only to set decent fictional boundaries. What construction the audience thereafter placed on the plays he 'allowed' was none of his business.

The virtue of being 'read, allow'd' was thus that it pre-empted unauthorised 'construction', Jonson's over-riding concern in the epistle to *Volpone*: while it placed limits on an author's freedom to write exactly as he chose, it absolved him of the risk of being ignorantly or maliciously misconstrued. The Master's allowance (being that of authority itself) precluded anything untoward. Far from impugning the author's integrity, it underwrote it: to challenge (in this instance) Jonson's virtue was to challenge the virtue of the state itself. Such a system of mutual reciprocities might well result in the smug collusion of vested interests which Jonson scorns in *Poetaster*. But in the right hands (and Jonson was always one to insist that the man, not the office, was what counted) it could create a relationship dedicated to higher standards of art and probity in the theatre, while averting potentially tragic confrontations between dramatists and the state, such as occurred with *Eastward Ho*. Jonson's conversion to the cause can, of course, be construed as expedient self-preservation; more charitably, it might be seen as pragmatic idealism. Nowhere in this does Jonson deny his own responsibilities as a writer. As in the Induction to *Bartholomew Fair* (though here with the state itself, rather than the paying customers) Jonson acknowledges a contract in which the two-edged nature of 'licence' mirrors the functional indeterminacy of language itself, allotting both parties mutually agreed rights – and freedoms. In the epistle 'To the Readers' of *Sejanus* he had cited 'truth of argument' as the first office of a tragic writer; in the Epistle to *Volpone* itself he claims that the first 'office of a comic-poet' is 'to imitate justice, and instruct to life' (lines 121–2). 'Truth' and 'life' insist that he confront the present as well as the past, the real as well as the fictional, and, as we have seen, nothing in subjecting himself to the 'allowance' of the Master of the Revels denies him that right, as long as he conducts himself within agreed parameters. It may constrict the method, but not the substance, of what he writes.

If as I have suggested, the man may have weighed more heavily with Jonson than the office itself, a further factor in shaping Jonson's attitude to the post of Master of the Revels must have been the character of those who held it. Tilney was already about 61 at the time of the *Isle of Dogs* affair, virtually two generations older than the 24-year-old Jonson, and it is unlikely that they had much in common. That same year George Buc's interest in the Mastership of the Revels became a matter of public comment for the first time, since John Lyly believed that it had been 'countenanced upon Buc', dashing the 'hopeful item' in it that he had cherished himself for ten years (Chambers, *ES*, 1, pp. 96–7). Buc was then about 34; he did not actually secure the reversion to the Mastership until 1603. We cannot establish for certain that he and Jonson knew each other, although they are likely to have met over the licensing of plays and masques for the press from 1606, and for the stage from 1610. Buc certainly licensed *Epicoene* (though no quarto survives, and it is possible none was actually printed) and *The Alchemist* for the press. (Unaccountably, the other two Jonson quartos from the relevant period, *Volpone* and *Catiline*, are not entered in the Stationers' Register, though given their prestigious dedications, respectively to the

Universities of Oxford and Cambridge, and to the Earl of Pembroke, it seems inconceivable that they were not passed in due form.) But it is quite probable that Buc and Jonson knew each other better than that. Both were friends of Sir Robert Cotton and used his famous library.[30] Both were friends of William Camden, Jonson's old schoolmaster, to the 1607 edition of whose *Britannia* Buc appended Latin verses. Both followed Camden as historians, Jonson in his tragedies, in contributions to Ralegh's *History of the World* and in writing a history of Henry V, which perished when his lodging burned down in 1623, Buc in the historical eclogue, Δαφνίς Πολυστέφᾶνος (1605), in his *Third University of England* (written 1612) and in his *History of Richard III* (published posthumously in 1646; Jonson had written a play, *Richard Crookback* for Henslowe). Jonson is actually mentioned in a marginal note to Δαφνίς and when, around 1620, Edmund Bolton drew up a proposal for an English Academy, Jonson and Buc were both among the eighty or so names he suggested for its first members. Their interests and associations overlapped so much that it is difficult to believe they were not quite well acquainted and, however they got on personally, Jonson must have measured his own credentials for the post against Buc's respected standing as an antiquarian. That a man of such scholarship embodied theatrical 'authority' must have presented Jonson with a tantalising role model.

Moreover in 1621, when Jonson received the reversion to the Mastership, the Lord Chamberlain – and so his potential superior in the office – was William Herbert, Earl of Pembroke; indeed, it is not unlikely that he had a hand in securing it for him, whatever the truth of the rumours of the king's enjoyment of *The Gypsies Metamorphosed*. Certainly there was a usual understanding that the post was in the Lord Chamberlain's gift: Suffolk in that role secured the reversion for his man, Astley, in 1612 and Pembroke was to protest in 1622 when someone tried to secure a further reversion for William Painter, 'a man whom he never saw', putting forward his own agent, John Thoroughgood, instead. Jonson's respect for Pembroke is well attested in the dedication not only of *Catiline* but also of his *Epigrams* to him, while Pembroke not only gave Jonson £20 a year to buy books ('Drummond', lines 312–13) but also, as Chancellor of the University, put him forward for the honorary MA conferred by Oxford in 1619. There seems to have been a degree of genuine mutual respect between poet and patron in this instance.[31]

The obeisance to authority signalled in the epistle to *Volpone* did not end Jonson's problems over his writing, though their severity was much mitigated thereafter. *Epicoene*, for example, appears to be the play referred to in a report by the Venetian ambassador on 8 February 1610: 'Lady Arabella [*sic*] is seldom seen outside her rooms and lives in greater dejection than ever. She complains that in a certain comedy the play-wright introduced an allusion to her person and the part played by the Prince of Moldavia. The play was suppressed' (H & S, v, p. 146). Arbella Stuart's position was a delicate one: as a cousin of the king and a potential claimant to the English throne herself, she had become engaged only days before to Sir William Seymour, who also had a claim, and the pressure on her was intense. Scandalous references to her supposed relationship with Stephano Janiculo, self-styled Prince of Moldavia (see *Epicoene*, v.i.24–5), would have been particularly unwelcome at that time. The identification of the unnamed comedy with *Epicoene* is reinforced by Jonson's protestations in the 1616 text, including a second prologue 'occasion'd by some persons' impertinent exception' and consideration in the dedication of 'how much a man's innocency may be endanger'd by an uncertain accusation'. Conceivably the Master of the Revels's 'allowance' was an inadequate barrier, given the extreme delicacy of Lady Arbella's position. But the play was written for the Children of the Whitefriars – the latest incarnation of the old Blackfriars Boys. As I have already observed, the licensing status of this company in its various guises is indeterminable, so Tilney *may* not have been involved.

In 1633, however, when Jonson already held the reversion but had been forced back to the public stage by the loss of his regular court commissions, Herbert recorded two items specifically relating to him, the only dealings we can tangibly trace between Jonson and a Master of the Revels. On 7 May:

R[eceived] for allowing of *The Tale of the Tub*, Vitru Hoop's part wholly struck out, and the motion of the tub, by command from my Lord Chamberlain; exceptions being taken against it by Inigo Jones, Surveyor of the King's Works, as a personal injury unto him ... £2

and on 24 October:

Upon a second petition of the players to the High Commission court, wherein they did me right in my care to purge their plays of all offence, my Lord's Grace of Canterbury bestowed many words upon me, and discharged me of any blame, and laid the whole fault of their play, called *The Magnetic Lady*, upon the players ... In their first petition they would have excused themselves on me and the poet. (Adams, *Herbert*, pp. 19, 21–2)

Both of these are intriguing. Jones appears to have heard of Jonson's supposed intentions in *The Tale of the Tub* before it was licensed, but approached the Lord Chamberlain to stop his former colleague's satire, rather than Herbert. Does this imply a lack of confidence in the Master of the Revels? Does the wording of Herbert's entry dissociate him either from Jones's view of the matter or the Lord Chamberlain's action? Given the attitudes he expresses elsewhere, he may well have felt that Jones was being unduly sensitive in taking the fictionalised portrait personally. Jonson got his own back the following year, however, by using the satire on 'Captain Vitruvius' in *Love's Welcome at Bolsover*, a royal entertainment commissioned by the Earl of Newcastle. In the context of a private performance before the king and queen, neither the Lord Chamberlain nor the Master of the Revels seems to have raised any objections; Jones's reaction is not recorded. In the case of *The Magnetic Lady*, someone objected to the play in performance, complaining of excessive oaths and blasphemies – which is why it was referred to the High Commission, with Archbishop Laud himself presiding. The King's Men appear to have defended themselves on the grounds that the words were Jonson's and that they had been 'allow'd' by Herbert. Assuming that Laud's ruling was a just one, the actors must have tampered with the 'book' after Herbert's licensing on 12 October 1632 – something which both Jonson ('I have ever trembled to think toward the least prophaneness') and Herbert (remember his severity with *The Wits*) would have been anxious to demonstrate. For both it was a question of maintaining their public integrity: one as Master of the Revels in possession, the other in reversion, though the death of Astley might have reversed those roles at any moment. The arrangement whereby Herbert bought the office from Astley for an annual fee of £150 did not affect Jonson's rights. His reversion would have taken effect as soon as Astley died, but in fact Astley outlived him, Jonson dying in 1637 and Astley in 1640.[32]

It was the closest that Jonson came to being identified with the post that Dekker had taunted him with coveting more than thirty years before and which, despite early reservations, he had come to regard as consonant with his own integrity and aspirations as a writer. Any censorship implicitly demeans the status of authorship.

But the anomalous position of the Master of the Revels, as much the protector of the privileges of the court as the repressor of dissident voices, made him as much the ally of the theatrical profession as its regulator. The stability that his office gave to the exchange of meaning in the early modern theatrical market-place contributed in no small part to the remarkable vitality of the drama of the period; had his office not existed, or if it had been constituted in different terms, the nature of the plays allowed to be written would have been very different. His 'allowance' made for a heterogeneity of expression that was to be silenced in 1642 (ironically, the Commonwealth period permitted other repressed voices to be heard, but not in this medium) and that was not to be heard again on the English stage until the twentieth century. For Jonson, a pioneering modern author in search of his own authority, the Master of the Revels was an acceptable mirror-image of his own aspirations, a fact ironically acknowledged in this interchange between the puppet-master, Lantern Leatherhead, and the would-be censor, Zeal-of-the-Land Busy in *Bartholomew Fair*:

> LEATHERHEAD: Sir, I present nothing but what is licensed by authority.
> BUSY: Thou art all license, even licentiousness itself, Shimei!
> LEATHERHEAD: I have the Master of the Revels' hand for't, sir.
> BUSY: The Master of the Rebels' hand, thou hast; Satan's!
>
> (v.v.12–15)

NOTES

1 References are to the edition of *Satiromastix* in *The Dramatic Works of Thomas Dekker*, Fredson Bowers, ed., 4 vols. (Cambridge, 1953–61), I. 'Criticus' became 'Crites' in the folio *Cynthia's Revels*.

2 I borrow 'ambitious toady' from Cyrus Hoy's admirable introduction to the play in his *Introductions, Notes and Commentaries to Texts in 'The Dramatic Works of Thomas Dekker'* (Cambridge, 1980), p. 194, where he gives a very balanced view of Dekker's tone. It is 'King's' rather than 'Queen's Revels' since the play is notionally set in the reign of William Rufus.

3 I explain below the limits to the Master of the Revels's authority.

4 See E. K. Chambers, *The Elizabethan Stage*, 4 vols. (Oxford, 1924), III, pp. 454–6; IV, Appendix D, cx, cxi, cxii, pp. 322–3. Hereafter 'Chambers, *ES*', cited within text and notes.

5 References to the works of Jonson are to the edition by C. H. Herford and P. and E. Simpson, 11 vols. (Oxford, 1925–52). (Hereafter

'H & S', cited within the text.) This quotation is from vol. III, Appendix x, p. 602. References to Jonson's 'Conversations with William Drummond of Hawthornden' ('Drummond') are to the text in vol. I, pp. 128–78, cited by line numbers. Here, and in all other citations from old-spelling texts, I have silently modernised the spelling.

6 Alvin Kernan, *Printing Technology, Letters and Samuel Johnson* (Princeton, 1987), p. 4.

7 See W. David Kay, 'The Shaping of Ben Jonson's Career', *Modern Philology* 67 (1970) 224–37; Richard C. Newton, 'Jonson and the (Re-)Invention of the Book', in C. J. Summers and T.-L. Pebworth, eds., *Classic and Cavalier: Essays on Jonson and the Sons of Ben*, (Pittsburgh, 1982), pp. 31–58.

8 David Riggs, *Ben Jonson: A Life* (Cambridge, Mass. and London, 1989), p. 258.

9 Reavley Gair, *The Children of Paul's* (Cambridge, 1982), p. 134; David Bevington, *Tudor Drama and Politics* (Cambridge, Mass., 1968), p. 279.

10 I do not think the timing sustains O. J. Campbell's argument that the bishop's ban *led to* the vogue for dramatic satires, which were not subject to the same constraints, but his *Comicall Satyre and Shakespeare's 'Troilus and Cressida'* (San Marino, Calif., 1938) remains an important study of the subject.

11 Chambers, *ES*, IV, p. 325. The relevant passages from the 1572 and 1598 Acts are given by Chambers, *ES*, IV, pp. 270 and 324. The most detailed exploration of the failure of the authorities to pull down the theatres, though not to my mind entirely convincing, is Glynne Wickham's 'The Privy Council Order of 1597 for the Destruction of all London's Theatres' in David Galloway, ed., *The Elizabethan Theatre*, (1969), pp. 21–44.

12 Chambers, *ES*, I, p. 385 note. He uses the term 'innovation' in the antiquarian sense of rebellion or insurrection (as indeed Shakespeare uses it in *Hamlet* — 'the late innovation' associated with the 'inhibition' of the actors – and the subtlest of allusions is probably intended). The record of Phillips's interrogation is printed in E. K. Chambers, *William Shakespeare: A Study of Facts and Problems*, 2 vols. (Oxford, 1930), II, p. 325. On modern 'readings' of this whole affair, see Leeds Barroll, 'A New History for Shakespeare and His Time', *Shakespeare Quarterly* 39 (1988) 442–54.

13 They are printed, together with three from his fellow prisoner, George Chapman, in an appendix to R. W. Van Fossen's Revels edition of *Eastward Ho* (Manchester and Baltimore, 1979), pp. 218–25. References to both Jonson's and Chapman's letters are to that text, whose probable ascription of addressees I follow.

14 See Rosalind Miles, *Ben Jonson: His Life and Works* (London, 1986), pp. 100–2, 106–7.

15 James D. Redwine Jr, ed., *Ben Jonson's Literary Criticism* (Lincoln, Nebraska, 1970), p. xv.

16 Almost certainly the notorious gibe at 'a few industrious Scots ... dispersed over the face of the whole earth' (iii.iii.44–6, ff) and possibly the allusion to James's traffic in knighthoods, rendered in unmistakeable brogue: 'I ken the man weel; he's one of my thirty-pound knights' (iv.i.197–8).

17 The full text of the commission is printed in Chambers, *ES*, iv, pp. 285–7.

18 So the quarto. In the folio the role is given to Egeus.

19 W. R. Streitberger, *Jacobean and Caroline Revels Accounts, 1603–1642*, Malone Society Collections. vol. xiii (1986), p. xxi. (Sections 1 and 2 of the introduction to that volume are the best concise account available of the Revels Office and its workings.)

20 Chambers, *ES*, iv, p. 323. Similarly, in May 1601, they addressed their concern about 'certain players that use to recite their plays at the Curtain in Morefields' to the Justices in Middlesex. The Admiral's Men had by then renounced the Curtain for the Fortune, so this must have been one of the companies of 'strangers' who were occasionally allowed to infringe the cartel for brief periods (Chambers, *ES*, iv, p. 332). Herbert sometimes licensed plays for such troupes, though even then there were doubts about his authority to do so, but there is no record of Tilney being involved with such companies. See J. Q. Adams, *The Dramatic Records of Sir Henry Herbert* (New Haven, 1917), p. 25 and notes 5 and 6. Hereafter Adams, *Herbert*, cited within the text.

21 See G. E. Bentley, *The Profession of Dramatist in Shakespeare's Time, 1590–1642* (Princeton, 1971), p. 178. Hereafter Bentley, *The Profession of Dramatist*, cited within the text.

22 Cited in C. J. Sisson, *Lost Plays of Shakespeare's Age* (Cambridge, 1936), pp. 69–70.

23 There has been much confusion over the transition from Tilney to Buc, who were not uncle and nephew, as Edmond Malone supposed and many authorities still insist. See Mark Eccles, 'Sir George Buc, Master of the Revels', in C. J. Sisson, ed., *Thomas Lodge and Other Elizabethans* (Cambridge, Mass., 1933), pp. 409–506, and my *Mastering the Revels: The Regulation and Censorship of English Renaissance Drama* (London and Basingstoke, 1991), chap. 6.

24 See G. P. V. Akrigg, *Jacobean Pageant* (London, 1962), p. 28.

25 From Daniel's 'Apology', printed with the play in 1605.

26 See my *Mastering the Revels*, chap. 6.

27 Philip J. Finkelpearl, '"The Comedians' Liberty": Censorship of the Jacobean Stage Reconsidered', *English Literary Renaissance* 16 (1986) 123–38, p. 124.

28 *Believe as You List*, ed. C. J. Sisson, Malone Society Reprints (1927), p. v. In the interests of brevity I must leave it to readers to consult this excellent edition to verify the editor's (it seems to me irrefutable) claim.

29 T. H. Howard-Hill, 'Buc and the Censorship of *Sir John Van Olden Barnavelt* in 1619', *Review of English Studies* ns 39 (1988) 39–63, p. 43.

30 See Kevin Sharpe, *Sir Robert Cotton* (Oxford, 1979). Jonson was returning from Cotton's house, with Camden, when he had the visionary premonition of his son's death ('Drummond', 261–72).

31 On Pembroke's determination to retain his authority as Lord Chamberlain over the office of Master of the Revels, see my 'Patronage, Politics, and the Master of the Revels, 1622–40: the Case of Sir John Astley', *English Literary Renaissance* 20 (1990) 287–319. On Jonson's relations with Pembroke, see Robert C. Evans, *Ben Jonson and the Poetics of Patronage* (Lewisburg, 1989), especially pp. 107–18, and David Riggs, *Ben Jonson: A Life*, especially, pp. 179–80, 226, 231–2.

32 The nature of these transactions and their implications is also the subject of my 'Patronage, Politics and the Master of the Revels'.

CHAPTER 4

The politics of the Jacobean masque

Graham Parry

Of all the Stuart theatrical forms, the masque had the greatest potential for political comment, for it was the supreme kind of court entertainment, performed on festival occasions before the monarch, with leading members of the court circle taking on symbolic roles in mythological fantasies whose principal themes were royal creativity and power. Given the exceptional advantages enjoyed by the writers of masques to address an audience composed of the most influential members of the kingdom, it becomes a matter of some interest to know what use these writers made of their privileged condition. Did they contrive the most magnificent occasions of royal panegyric yet devised and compose fictions that were uncritically supportive of the monarch, or did they temper their praise with hints that Whitehall was not a court of unblemished perfections, that King James's wisdom was not entirely Solomonic? In pursuing these questions, we shall find that the early masques were indeed adulatory in their celebration of the new king and the benefits that his reign appeared to have brought, and yet, when the young Prince of Wales began to establish himself as an independent factor in state affairs, the masque writers associated with him were encouraged to strike an oppositional note when the emergence of an alternative centre of authority seemed to be a possibility. The experience of Prince Henry's incipient divergence from King James's policies produced a new tension and complexity in the masque as writers like Jonson and Daniel, whose primary loyalty was to the king and queen, devised entertainments which tried to satisfy both the rising prince and the ruling parents. These tensions continued through the enter-tainments for the Palatine marriage, and thereafter the critical strain remained a feature of the genre, though often relegated to the anti-masque. In the last decade of King James's reign, Ben Jonson, who enjoyed a monopoly on the court masque during this time, was

circumspect in the construction of his devices for his royal patron,
desiring to consolidate the authority of a king whose conduct of
affairs became less assured and less admirable as the reign wore on,
rather than to undermine it by covert criticism. The court might
suffer from disordered humours that could be reviewed in an anti-
masque, but the king and his policies were exalted by all the powers
of art.

To sense the character of the early masques, we might look first at
a song composed by Thomas Campion as part of a celebration of an
Anglo-Scottish marriage at court in 1607:

> Shows and nightly revels, signs of joy and peace,
> Fill royal Britain's court while cruel war far off doth rage, for
>   ever hence exiled.
> Fair and princely branches with strong arms increase
> From that deep-rooted tree whose sacred strength and glory
>   foreign malice hath beguiled.
> Our divided kingdoms now in friendly kindred meet
> And old debate to love and kindness turns, our power with
>   double force uniting.[1]

We find here an anthology of themes that informed the first Jacobean festivals, occasioned by an event that was in itself symbolic of
the new political strength that James's accession had brought to
Britain. Lord Hay, the Scottish favourite of King James at the time,
was marrying Honora Denny, the daughter of an English country
gentleman. James was present at the wedding ceremonies, and the
masque was addressed as much to the king and his concerns as it was
to the couple. The happiness of the united realms, the blessings of
peace, the security from foreign designs and the assurance of a
plentiful succession of Stuarts are all alluded to in this song. Campion's dominant intention in *Lord Hay's Masque* was to praise the
king as the architect of the union between Scotland and England, a
union imitated by the partners of the marriage, who may in consequence expect to know both 'joy and peace'. James certainly
believed that the union of the crowns in his person assured peace to
his kingdoms, which he now insisted be known as Great Britain, for
he took much pride in having restored the ancient unity of the
islands. He regarded his double kingship as a metaphysical triumph
brought about by divine providence, as he explained to parliament
with some insistence in the important early speeches of his reign.[2]
During these first years, one of his cherished designs was to bring

about the political union of England and Scotland to complement the union of crowns, but he was unable to persuade MPs at Westminster that the parliaments, laws and religion of the two countries should be made uniform, an alteration that was essential if true political union was to be achieved. Throughout the sessions of 1605 and 1606, James exhorted parliament to approve of political union, and his arguments were imaginatively supplemented by the Twelfth Night masques of 1606 and 1607, both of which took the opportunity provided by weddings at court to proclaim the virtues of union as a social, political and metaphysical condition. Ben Jonson's masque for 1606, *Hymenaei*, for the marriage of Robert Devereux, Earl of Essex, to Lady Frances Howard, had revealed by a combination of music, dance, ritual and symbolic tableaux the sublime mystery of union as the sustaining power of the universe, and it was in the introduction to this masque that he made his well-known statement, concerning the construction of masques, that 'though their voice be taught to sound to present occasions, their sense, or doth, or should, lay hold on more removed mysteries'. Campion too pulled out all the stops in the interests of royal policy, for, after all, many members of the court audience watching his masque sat in parliament, but he did not pursue the theme of union quite as relentlessly as Jonson had done. Nevertheless, it was an entertainment with a strong political drift.

Campion's fable or 'invention' as he called it was fairly typical of the early masques, involving a highly contrived mythological scenario that was symbolically apt to the occasion and complimentary to the king. Flora and Zephyrus, figures suggestive of spring and fertility, are preparing a bower for the young couple, when Night enters to announce that Diana is enraged that one of her nymphs has defected in favour of marriage. In revenge, she has transformed the beautiful young men of the place, the Knights of Phoebus, into trees. We know we are in the world of marriage comedy, where arbitrary powers enforce impediments to the natural aspirations of the young. However, we rapidly hear that Phoebus Apollo has interceded with Diana, and all is well: the nymph can be married, the knights made men again. Apollo and Diana are the opposed principles of nature, male and female, sun and moon, heat and coldness, that must be reconciled by love if nature is to be genial and creative. But Phoebus is also the sun god of 'this happie western Isle,' King James, 'Brittaines glorious eye,' who, like Apollo, is an oracle of truth, a source of wisdom. His presence ensures that peace and happiness prevail, and that the union of opposed principles takes place. The chief spectacle of the masque is the discovery of the masquers as gilded trees, followed by their transformation into green men, their ritual homage to Diana's Tree of Chastity, and then their glorious appearance in extravagant masquing costume as the Knights of Phoebus as they process to the Bower of Flora. At each stage they dance, and finally they participate in the court wedding festivities as they join with the ladies of the audience for the long-continuing revels.

Clearly, pleasure and festivity predominated in this entertainment, but in its published form Campion took pains to draw attention to the political dimension of the masque. The dedication to 'James King of Great Britain' praises his peaceful union of Scotland and England: 'who can wonder then / If he that marries kingdoms, marries men?' An epigram exploits a familiar motif of early Jacobean iconography by hailing James as the fulfilment of the old prophecy that Arthur would return to 'wield great Britain's state / More powerful tenfold and more fortunate'; then a Latin poem meditates on the mystical marriage of King James to his kingdom. Next follows a poem addressed to Lord Howard de Walden, one of the masquers, which solicits patronage from the Howards, who were politically ascendant at the time. To conclude, Campion turns to the couple in whose honour the 'golden dreame' of the masque was evoked, reminding them that the offspring of their marriage will be authentically British, among the first of a revived race.[3]

The British motif ran through most of the early court entertainments presented before James, and in many ways *Lord Hay's Masque* is characteristic of the state spectacles of the first decade of the century. A recognisable complex of themes recurs: the glory of the union, the imperial condition of James in his new empire of the north, the incomparable peace of Britain with its attendant blessings of prosperity and the flourishing of the arts that make these the Fortunate Isles, hitherto known only in legend. The god-like attributes of the king who professed to rule by divine right are extolled: his wisdom, justice and mercy. Although several of the early masques were commissioned by Queen Anne – Daniel's *Vision of the Twelve Goddesses* (1604), Jonson's *Masque of Blackness* (1605), *Masque of Beauty* (1608), *Masque of Queens* (1609) – as occasions for dancing, disguise and display, they were presented to the king as gifts of state.

Right from the beginning the masque writers recognised the potential that these festivals possessed for affirmative political statement. Before the assembled court and with the foreign ambassadors present, the felicity of Britain under Stuart rule could be proclaimed, and the mysterious powers that constituted the virtue of Stuart kingship could be revealed in scenes of wonder as they exerted an operative influence over the action of the masque.

It was particularly in these early masques, when the genre was new and audiences were somewhat bewildered by the complexity of sensation and idea that a masque transmitted, that the writers took pains to explain their intentions in prefaces and instructive commentary in the printed accounts. Samuel Daniel, who wrote the first masque for the new reign, immediately saw the possibilities for an art form that could be politically coloured. 'These ornaments and delights of peace are in their season as fit to entertain the world and deserve to be made memorable as well as graver actions, both of them concurring to the decking and furnishing of glory and majesty as the necessary complements requisite for state and greatness.'[4] He explained that he had designed the queen's entertainment with the intention to present 'the figure of those blessings, with the wish of their increase and continuance, which this mighty kingdom now enjoys by the benefit of his most gracious majesty, by whom we have this glory of peace, with the accession of so great state and power'. So, the twelve goddesses with their emblems formed a composite of the qualities of good government; Daniel described his tableau of divinities as 'the hieroglyphic of empire and dominion, as the ground and matter whereon this glory of state is built'.[5]

Daniel's *Vision* was predominantly pageant-like in character, with processions of masquers up and down the hall, ritual offerings at a temple, dispersed settings for the action, and little scenery. He viewed his invention as a kind of Platonic figuring, in that he had 'given mortal shapes to the gifts and effects of an eternal power, for that those beautiful characters of sense were easier to read than their mystical *Ideas* dispersed in that wide and incomprehensible volume of Nature'.[6] In the music of the masque he intended to symbolise the harmony of James's rule in Britain, which has now become 'the land of civil music and of rest'. The dances involved numerical patterns, and were 'framed into motions circular, square, triangular, with other proportions exceeding rare', suggestive of order with moral firmness. Overall, Daniel desired his masque to work as a form of sympathetic magic on the court, 'as ever more to grace this glorious monarchy with the real effects of these blessings represented'. Daniel's preface to the masque, framed as a letter to Lucy, Countess of Bedford, uncovers his somewhat cautious and prosaic approach to art: he certainly does not want to take the imagination of his audience by storm, and declares himself reluctant to communicate mysteries or act as a medium for the ineffable. Extravagant beauty and inexplicable effects of wonder he disdains, and though his entertainment was entitled a Vision, there was little of the supernatural about it.

Whereas Daniel declared that he had designed the incidents of his masque 'without observing ... their mystical interpretations', and professed himself sceptical of masques as vehicles for profound learning, Ben Jonson had emphatically different views. Working with Inigo Jones's new perspective stage and with the rapidly evolving technology of lights and motions, he saw the chance to make these state spectacles occasions of wonder and magnificence, secular acts of monarchic worship in an aura of learned mystery. Whatever the spectators thought of these early masques (and many were critical or uncomprehending)[7] and however jerkily the gods went about their celestial business in their chariots or clouds, Jonson was determined that the printed record should render the most glorious account of the event. Through the use of a noble and chromatic prose style, he succeeded in describing the ideal performance to the consummate understanding spectator, evoking the atmosphere of enchantment in which the rituals of action took place, and preserving every detail of the scenery, costume and architecture so that its symbolic significance could be finely appreciated.[8] The effects of light and music were delicately recreated, and the patterns of dance made perfect in retrospect. The erudition that Jonson believed should give firmness to these fictions was emphasised in the prose commentaries that he supplied, for it was an article of faith with Jonson that the masques should have a philosophical and intellectual structure – the 'soul' of the masque as he termed it – which would outlive the transitory vehicle of its display. For both Jonson and Jones the learning should be from Greece and Rome, for that is where poetry and architecture had their origin, where the universe of the mind had been most fully mapped. So the complexity of the masque increased on every level, but its objective remained the magnification of the king, and praise of his virtues and of the wisdom of his rule.

In Jonson and Jones's masques of the first decade, the king possesses the attributes of divinity, and exerts a defining influence over the action. He is the primal source of beauty in the masques of *Blackness* and *Beauty*, the cause of concord in *Beauty*, of union in *Hymenaei*, where he is also praised for his divine judgement, wisdom and 'designing power'. In *The Masque of Queens* he is the field of honour and the pinnacle of fame. As the masques became more elaborate, they discovered still more miraculous powers in the king, but the ground of their acclaim remained the familiar nexus of motifs that made up the political heraldry of James's reign: peace, wisdom, union and empire, and divine favour for the Fortunate Isles of Britain.

The celebration of the known attributes of kingship that characterised the masques of the first decade was, however, no longer vital in the masques honouring Prince Henry, the heir to the throne, who moved to centre stage in 1610 when he was created Prince of Wales. The festivities for that year were mostly under the control of the prince himself, who used them to project his own political identity as it was then forming. The character of Henry's small court was markedly different from his father's: it was chivalric, disciplined and high-principled. Henry revered the memory of Sir Philip Sidney as a Christian knight, and inclined towards a policy of militant Protestantism modelled on Sidney's example. Observers of the prince spoke of his desire to join Henri IV in a campaign against the Habsburg forces and the papacy, of his dream to crusade against the Turks. He supported the efforts of the Virginia Company to make plantations in America that would establish the Protestant faith there and counteract the growth of Spanish Catholicism in the new world. He was known to favour the marriage of his sister Elizabeth to a German prince in order to forge a northern Protestant alliance. In so many ways he was the antithesis of his father, who followed cautious policies of peace, feared entanglement in European military campaigns, and hoped to resolve the religious differences of Europe by theological debate and by marriage alliances which would bind nations in amity. Although the approving could see in James's policies a prudent, statesmanlike concern for slow international reconciliation, the critical might describe them as a cover for inertia. Against Henry's promise of vigorous activism, James looked like a hapless temporiser. It is easy to imagine how Henry carried with him the hopes of young and zealous Englishmen, and equally easy to recognise that King James was wary of his son's enthusiastic stance, and greatly jealous of his popularity.

When Prince Henry planned the festivities for the climax of the Christmas season in 1609–10, to mark his first formal bearing of arms, and in preparation for his creation as Prince of Wales later that year, he used his father's established team of Jonson and Jones to design the masque which would give expression to his aspirations. Henry wanted his festival to have a military character, ending not with the protracted dancing of the revels, but in a passage at arms. Such a conclusion was definitely not to the taste of King James, who was notoriously averse to the sight of cold steel. Nonetheless, it was Henry's show. Henry caused a challenge to be issued at the Christmas feast to all worthy knights to contend for their honour at a combat at court, a challenge issued in the name of Moeliades, Lord of the Isles, Henry's chosen *nom de guerre* based on the anagram Miles a Deo, a Soldier for God, indicative of his militant zeal in the Protestant cause. On 6 January 1610, Prince Henry's *Barriers* took place, preceded by a masque set in the world of Arthurian romance. (Jonson usually scorned this subject area as outdated and exhausted, so we may assume that Prince Henry had imposed it on him.) The *Barriers* masque is in effect the prince's manifesto, and the text is unusually detailed and informative, full of statements about the prince's place in British history. The theme is the revival of chivalry under Prince Henry, coupled with an advocacy of the classical style in architecture which is presented as the proper accompaniment to this renewal of ancient virtue.

Presiding over the scene is King Arthur, 'discovered as a starre above', who approves Meliadus (the prince's pseudonym is variously spelt) and tactfully draws attention back to King James by hailing him as his greater successor. Arthur urges the prince on to acts of renown:

> Let him be famous, as was Tristram, Tor,
> Launc'lot, and all our list of knighthood, or
> Who were before or have been since. His name
> Strike upon heaven, and there stick his fame!
> Beyond the paths and searches of the sun
> Let him tempt fate ... (lines 87–92)

but he adds a note of caution: these deeds must be done for the glory of Britain and for the honour of King James, 'and when a world is won, / Submit it duly to this state, and throne' (lines 92–3). Arthur furnishes him with a shield of destiny, bearing histories and moral precepts relevant to his future career: 'It is a piece, was by the Fates devis'd / To arme his maiden valour; and to show / Defensive arms th'offensive should fore-goe' (lines 98–100). In that last line one can almost hear Ben Jonson recommending caution to the prince, prudently toning down the zeal for action to something more acceptable to the king, blunting the prince's intentions with politic advice. The management of arms should be for defence, not attack. Now Meliadus and his knights are discovered in their Portico of St George, and Merlin, the prophet of Ancient Britain, appears to foretell the prince's fate and interpret the figures on his shield.

> His arts must be to govern, and give laws
> To peace no less than arms. His fate here draws
> An empire with it, and describes each state
> Preceding there, that he should imitate. (lines 169–72)

So, the lesson begins with a list of kings who were active in war yet mindful of their country's well-being, illustrating Merlin's sober advice

> That civil arts the martial must precede,
> That laws and trade bring honours in and gain
> And arms defensive a safe peace maintain. (lines 206–8)

Merlin sounds here much like an apologist for James. The rest of Merlin's very long speech is, however, of a quite different character, recounting 'the conquests got, the spoils, the trophies reared' by fierce medieval kings, followed by a bloodthirsty account of the victory over the Armada, all to incite the prince to valorous emulation. But then Merlin's speech veers round again to compliment King James, whose peaceful works of union and empire overshadow all previous royal achievements. Jonson's twists and turns in this speech witness the strains he was under when writing for Prince Henry. His primary allegiance was to the king, who was the main spectator at the masque; his commission from Prince Henry was to rouse the military spirit of young England, unpleasing to the king. The consequence is a series of contradictory signals. The prince's charge prevails: 'let your drum give note you keep the field'. The dormant figure of Chivalry awakens to greet the prince, and the Barriers (the combat at arms) take place: 'Every challenger fought with eight several defendants two several combats at two several weapons, viz. at push of pike and with single sword, to the great joy and admiration of all the beholders.'[9] But decorum also prevails, for at the end of the fighting, Merlin reappears to insist again that all this energy must be dedicated to the throne. Henry and also Prince Charles, who is now drawn in, may 'shake a sword / And lance against the foes of God and you' (King James) (lines 419–20), but the conclusion shows Jonson still reluctant to endorse the emerging militaristic mood.

Did this show of bellicosity have any relevance to contemporary affairs? In his book *Henry Prince of Wales*, Roy Strong proposes that the background to the Barriers was the diplomatic crisis in Europe over the succession to the Duchy of Cleves. This state occupied strategic territory along the Rhine where the interests of France, Austria, Spain and the Protestant German states all met. The dispute over the succession, an incident now almost forgotten, involved Protestant and Catholic claimants who threatened to draw in the major powers to a general religious conflict, as would eventually happen over the Bohemian succession in 1619. Henri IV was orchestrating the anti-Habsburg forces at the end of 1609, and pressure was being applied on James to join the loose Protestant alliance that was then forming. For once, James was inclined to get involved, at least to the extent of sending a force of English and Scots soldiers already serving in the Netherlands under the command of Sir Edward Cecil. It was rumoured that Prince Henry might join this expedition as his debut on the military scene.[10] If such was the case, it would give a particular sharpness to the Barrier scenes, which include many references to English military exploits on the continent; it would also help to explain the wavering view of James that Jonson gives, now all for peace and domestic ease, now half willing to permit the use of 'sword and lance against the foes of God' as long as the event strengthens his throne. It was an uncertain time, shot through with heightened expectations centred on Prince Henry, and the masque reflects all this.[11]

Henry's creation as Prince of Wales took place in June 1610. The masque for the occasion was *Tethys' Festival*, offered by Queen Anne and written by her household poet, Samuel Daniel. Daniel was not an inspiriting masque-maker, for his inventions rarely advanced beyond the pageant–procession model; nor were the dancing ladies who were the queen's companions the best foil for Henry's political coming of age, and beneath the festive honouring of Henry as Great

Britain's prince there is more than a hint that a policy of restraint and limitation was being conducted, reflecting the king's and queen's anxieties about their over-active son. The theme was the homage paid to the Prince of Wales by Tethys (Thetis), consort of Neptune, and her nymphs of the rivers of Britain. The motif of the river nymphs was derived from *Poly-Olbion*, which Daniel's friend Drayton was then writing, and behind *Poly-Olbion* lay Camden's *Britannia*, so the subliminal theme of the masque is the celebration of the glory of Britain, with Henry as the inheritor of that glory. The Neptune–Thetis line provided an opportunity for ambitious thoughts about the nation's power by sea. Thetis, personated by the queen, presents Henry, who is once again cast as Meliades, with a sword and scarf, the first symbolic of the justice in whose cause he will wield his arms, the latter a counsel of restraint on the sphere of his actions. On the ritual scarf 'he may survey / Infigured all the spacious empery / That he is born unto another day' (lines 143–5). That is to say, it bears an embroidered outline of the British Isles, 'Which, tell him, will be world enough to yield / All works of glory ever can be wrought. / Let him not pass the circle of that field ...' (lines 146–8). The advice coming from the queen is to stay within the limits of Great Britain: here is world enough for all your heroic strength. The scarf is more like a bridle. Worse is to come. For his maintenance and income, the prince is told to turn to fish. Daniel gilds the herring in fine verses, but cannot disguise the ignominy of the suggestion:

> For there will be within the large extent
> Of these my waves and wat'ry government,
> More treasure and more certain riches got
> Than all the Indies to Iberus brought:
> For Nereus will by industry unfold
> A chemic secret, and turn fish to gold.　　(lines 150–5)

The decoration on the proscenium arch of 'Nereus holding out a golden fish in a net, with this word "Industria"', now disclosed its significance: the prince was to fish in home waters. Forget the plantation of Virginia, the assaults on the Spanish plate fleet or the far-ranging schemes of intervention and war, and encourage the fishing industry instead. A more lowering scheme could hardly have been devised for this ambitious prince.

The other figure on the proscenium arch besides Nereus with his fish was Neptune 'holding a trident with an anchor' and the words '"his artibus", that is "regendo et retinendo", alluding to this verse in Virgil "Hae tibi erunt artes etc."' Neptune was the persona of King James, the trident the symbol of his power by sea, the anchor the sign of the stability of his rule. The lines from Virgil were the king's motto, a declaration of government upholding peace and law. It was to Neptune-James that the rest of *Tethys' Festival* was directed after the Prince had been presented with his sword and scarf. After the revelation of the masquers (Tethys and her nymphs), in a glorious marine grotto decorated with much Italianate detail by Inigo Jones and running with fountains and cascades, they 'descended out of their caverns one after another, and so marched up with winding meanders like a river, till they came to the Tree of Victory', where they offered flowers in golden urns, accompanied by a chorus praising James. The Tree of Victory is not an emblem of Prince Henry's future conquests, but of James's achievements. The action of the succeeding dances leads to more honouring of James. One of the dances is followed by the beautiful reflective lyric 'Are they shadows that we see?' which concludes

> Glory is most bright and gay
> In a flash and so away
> . . .
> When your eyes have done their part,
> Thought must length it in the heart.   (lines 300–6)

The thoughtful spectator who lengthened out the brief splendour of *Tethys' Festival* in his heart would feel that there was a conspiracy to deny Prince Henry the glory of his day: Daniel and Queen Anne had turned the masque into a tribute to King James, and the prince's aspirations had been slighted. Did Queen Anne share her husband's wariness of the rising sun of the court? Arthur Wilson, the historian of the reign, observed 'how far the King's fears (like thicke clouds) might afterwards blind the eye of his Reason, when he saw [Prince Henry] (as he thought) too high mounted in the people's love, and of an alluring spirit'. These fears, Wilson believed, caused him 'to decline his paternal affection to him'.[12] The masque appears to have been influenced by these royal fears, and written in some measure to help the king strengthen his authority against the prince.

The next occasion when the delusive lights of the masque played around Prince Henry was New Year 1611, when he presented his masque *Oberon, The Fairy Prince*, at court. The masque is an act of homage to King James, but in Jonson's hands it almost becomes an

act of submission as well. Jonson was after all the king's man, and
was not interested in losing favour nor in making a transition to the
prince's service. As a poet, he was committed to the rhetoric of peace
and golden age Augustanism that saturated the Jacobean court; this
commitment made it difficult for him to sympathise with the military tendencies of the prince. *Oberon* derives from the Spenserian
genealogy in *The Faerie Queene* Book II that traces the British-Welsh
descent of Elizabeth and the House of Tudor. As such it was
appropriate to the Prince of Wales, whose right to the throne went
back to the Tudors and who also affected a British origin. After an
anti-masque of 'Silenus ... with some dozen satyrs and fauns who
had much to say about the coming of a great prince',[13] Oberon and
his knights were revealed in a translucent palace. Oberon himself,
impersonated by the prince, was clad in antique costume and rode
in a chariot. 'To loud triumphant music he began to move forward',
not to initiate some grand design, but to make a respectful bow
before his father. The songs and speeches rapturously acclaim James
and his virtues, ignoring Oberon. The thrust of the spectacle, that is,
the display of heroic youth in Prince Henry and his attendant lords,
is checked by the power of the words defending James. 'This is a
night of greatness and of state ... / A night of homage to the British
court / And ceremony due to Arthur's chair.' The 'knights masquers', like the creatures of Prometheus, are represented by Jonson
as owing their very existence to the king,

> To whose sole power and magic they do give
> The honour of their being, that they live
> Sustained in form, fame and felicity,
> From rage of fortune or the fear to die.   (lines 263–6)

Then follows the most exalted panegyric yet offered to James in a
masque. Prince Henry may be apparelled as a Roman emperor, but
he is in the presence of Jove. James's divinity is invoked and
worshipped in words that make him the first cause in nature, the
Platonic source of virtue, and the archetype of good government.
The masquers engage in ritual dances in honour of this god, and the
scene finally closes.

   This 1611 masque, the prince's own, seems to mark a willingness
on his part to restrain his desires to advertise his independence of
mind and spirit by his dutiful role in *Oberon*. It may be that as a
result of the murder of Henri IV and the defusing of the large

European conflicts that followed, Prince Henry's impetus to embark on some idealistic project of godly war or colonisation diminished, and *Oberon* is the expression of a heroic youth temporarily becalmed.

For the New Year masque of 1612, Jonson wrote one of his least memorable pieces, *Love Restored*. The prince did not participate in it, though the masquers appear to have been gentlemen associated with his court. The anti-masque deals with Anti-Cupid, 'that imposter Plutus, the god of money, who has stolen love's ensigns; and in his belied figure, reigns in the world, making friendships, contracts, marriages and almost religion'. The main masque of Cupid drives out the imposter and installs his graces, embodied by the masquers, in the court. It is a lightweight affair that prefaced a year dominated by negotiations for the marriage of Princess Elizabeth and also Prince Henry. Spain, Savoy and Tuscany were all unsuccessfully sounded out, and the question of dowries was an obsessive matter with James, financially hard pressed as he was after the failure in 1610 of the Great Contract that might have rescued his chaotic monetary situation. As Roy Strong has pointed out, the anti-masque to *Love Restored* had some barbed points to make about the sacrifice of love to pecuniary advantage,[14] and this was perhaps the first occasion on which Jonson was willing to shoot a few critical darts in James's direction under the cover of an anti-masque. If Henry sponsored *Love Restored* (for it appears in the Revels Accounts as 'the Princes Mask'), then the central triumph of Love may well be a declaration of his intention to marry where it pleased him, not where pragmatism directed. We know that he was nursing the idea of going off to Germany to find a bride of his own choosing about this time.

Marriage then was in the air, and by the autumn of the year Princess Elizabeth was promised to Frederick the Elector Palatine, who arrived in England in October 1612. According to contemporary accounts, Prince Henry took charge of the festivities for the betrothal and the wedding.[15] The marriage was the most significant international event to touch England since the signing of the peace treaty with Spain in 1604. It was the first serious commitment to the idea of a pan-Protestant alliance made by James, and it was a move entirely to the liking of Prince Henry. Elizabeth's marriage put England in line for a possible confrontation with the Habsburg powers which dominated Germany, always eager to reduce Protestant influence. The position excited strong-line Protestants, from the men who clustered around Prince Henry to the preachers who pounded their pulpits, urging the truth of the Protestant religion and confusion to papists. The festivities devised for the occasion, presumably with the approval of the prince, naturally had a strong political character, exploiting the event and sometimes becoming a vehicle for prophecy. It was in the course of these preparations that Prince Henry fell ill and died, amidst universal lament. His father decreed only a short period of mourning at court, so that the wedding might go ahead on St Valentine's day 1613.

The inventors of the masque for the wedding night were Thomas Campion and Inigo Jones. Ben Jonson had been in France as tutor to Sir Walter Raleigh's son during the spring of 1612, and so was off the scene during these eventful months, but, in any case, Henry may not have wanted Jonson to prepare a wedding masque, since Jonson habitually celebrated the king at the expense of those he was commissioned to honour. Campion, in professional life a medical doctor, was gifted with a delicate expressiveness in music and poetry, both of which arts drew him to the court, where he found patronage in the Howard circle. That he had formed some connections with Prince Henry is evident from the *Songs of Mourning* he composed on the prince's death, set to music by Coperario and filled with an intimate sense of Henry's presence. Campion's festival, known as *The Lords' Masque*, was lengthy and complicated ('more like a play than a masque', complained one spectator); Inigo Jones devised a sequence of magical effects, of aerial movement and transformation that exceeded in technical virtuosity all his previous displays. The theme was divine creativity in poetry and in marriage. It opens with Orpheus releasing Entheus, the embodiment of *furor poeticus*, from the Cave of Madness, where he has been mistakenly confined. This scene permits an anti-masque of fantastics and melancholiacs to cavort awhile until Orpheus calms their disorder before extricating Entheus, 'whose rage ... is all divine / Full of celestial rapture'. His release has been ordered by Jove (James?), who commands him 'to create / Inventions rare, this night to celebrate'. Only the most high-reaching conceits will fit this occasion, so Entheus immediately proposes the feat of Prometheus when he enkindled the clayey forms with divine fire to make men, the very act of human creation. Entheus calls up Prometheus with his fires, which appeared as 'eight starres of extraordinarie bignes', flaring in the heavens amid coloured clouds tinged with silver and fire. The star-fires moved in mid-air 'in an exceeding strange and delightfull manner' to novel music before vanishing suddenly among the clouds, being replaced by the masquers, fire-made men, who blazed in the upper air in igneous attire, formed 'of massie cloth of silver, embossed with flames of embroidery: on their heads they had crownes, flames made all of gold-plate enamelled, and on the top a feather of silke, representing a cloud of smoake.' (lines 194–6). They appeared in 'an element of artificiall fires, with several circles of lights in continuall motion, representing the house of Prometheus'. After a celebratory divertimento danced by pages dressed as fiery spirits, the masquers descended to earth, where, after a scene change, they moved towards a most elegant architectural screen all in gold in which four female statues stood. The Promethean men brought the women to life through the desire of love, and repeated the miracle with four more women who replaced them, all then joining in a dance of courtship and love which first drew in the newly married pair, then opened out into the general revels. So it was an evening of delight and wonder and music which glorified the court and revealed in fable to Frederick and Elizabeth the mystery of the quickening power of love. Into this heightened atmosphere at the end of the revels, Campion and Jones projected one final tableau which reminded everyone of the political dimension of the marriage.

After Orpheus, Entheus and Prometheus, another figure appeared, whose powers were beyond a mortal's reach: Sybilla, presumably the Cumean Sybil, who gave to Aeneas (in book VI of the *Aeneid*) the vision of the political greatness of Rome. From this happy moment of conjunction between Frederick and Elizabeth, a new perspective opened, showing, as in Virgil, the possibility of future empire. Sybilla drew forward an obelisk whose peak touched the clouds, an emblem whose significance was the Glory of Princes and their immortality; on either side of the obelisk was a golden statue, the bridegroom and the bride. The Sybil then began to prophesy in her native Latin. In translation, her words to Elizabeth run thus:

The mother of kings, of emperors. Let the British strength be added to the German: can anything equal it? One mind, one faith, will join two peoples, and one religion and simple love. Both will have the same enemy, the same ally, the same prayer for those in danger, and the same strength. Peace will favour them, and the fortune of war will favour them; always God the helper will be at their side.[16]

One understands why the Spanish ambassador declined to attend the wedding.

The next evening, 15 February, the court reassembled at Whitehall to watch the masque offered by the Middle Temple and Lincoln's Inn that George Chapman had devised. The masquers processed from Fleet Street along the Strand to Whitehall, riding in chariots, surrounded by musicians and torchbearers and a large entourage of magnificently dressed gentlemen of the Inns. Chapman had been amongst the most devoted of the artists patronised by Prince Henry. He had been working on his translation of Homer for the prince, who had also shown a favourable interest in his tragedies of modern French history. For his *Memorable Masque* Chapman proposed a fable of the New World, the masquers personating the princes of Virginia, who have voyaged on their floating island to Britain, the seat of Honour, so that they may 'do due homage to the sacred nuptials / Of Love and Beauty celebrated here'. The fable was simple yet dense, its outlines uncomplicated, though its implications were elaborate; as such it made a good subject for a masque, offering facile pleasure or moral commentary or political suggestion, according to the capacity of the spectator. Chapman astutely mixes congratulations to the married couple, praise to the king and honour to the country with a topical exotic theme of American adventure. The masque glorifies the court by asserting that this is where Honour has chosen to raise her temple and where Fortune, hitherto so mobile and unpredictable, has decided to bestow herself forever. (This motif would have had credibility in Prince Henry's lifetime, for it must have alluded to him, but his death made Fortune's fixture here painfully ironic.) So powerful is Honour's attractive force, that even Plutus, the god of riches, has been drawn to admire her, so wealth in Britain is now devoted to virtuous ends.

The Virginian princes are discovered in a mine of gold, their appropriate display-case, and as gold is their metal, so they worship the golden orb, the sun. As their priests the Phoebades make their devotions on this wedding night (in terms which make the sun's descent to bed a most erotic declension), Honour intervenes to correct their 'superstitious hymn'. In the climate of truth which prevails in Britain, the Virginians must see that the real sun god is King James,

> this our Briton Phoebus, whose bright sky
> (Enlightened with a Christian piety)
> Is never subjected to black error's night. (lines 599–601)

The king is portrayed in the manner of a god, as is customary in the
Jacobean masques, and in harmony with James's own claims for the
divinity of kings; at the same time his divinity is declared to be a
means of mediating with the ineffable God of heaven. The Virginian
princes undergo a conversion to the god of Britain, and so purified
they begin their dances in honour of the bride and groom, whose
perfections, when intermingled, will bring about a new golden age.
Thus the masquers enact a fable which announces that they have
moved from a land where gold is abundant but unserviceable, and
where devotion is misdirected, to one where gold is in the service of
honour, where true religion reigns, and where the age of gold is
dawning again. Britain is where they truly belong.

The Virginian theme had a particular relevance in 1612–13.
Prince Henry was an active supporter of the Virginia Company, and
had designs to plant colonies there, for trade but also, as Chapman
wrote elsewhere, to 'let thy sovereign Empire be increased / And
with Iberian Neptune part the stake'.[17] As well as contesting Spain's
grasp on the New World, the spread of the Protestant religion and
the conversion of the heathen were prime aims of the governors of
the Company. Spain was irritated by these activities, and entertained plans for destroying the Company's settlements: the des-
patches from the English ambassador in Madrid, Sir John Digby,
are full of references to Virginia during this period. Backing for the
Virginian venture was strongest in Prince Henry's circle, whereas
the king was wary of its policy of provoking Spain. Chapman, by
linking the Palatine marriage with Virginia, was in effect trying to
draw the Elector Frederick (and behind him the German princes of
the Protestant Union) into an anti-Spanish grouping. This would be
in line with Prince Henry's thinking, and a measure of how far
Chapman's masque was working out the prince's design in festival
form. In addition, as D. J. Gordon has pointed out, in his picture of
the Indian princes, Chapman seemed to have Guiana in mind more
than Virginia.[18] English descriptions of Virginia had stressed the
simplicity and agricultural nature of the people. The preoccupation
with gold, the worship of the sun, the feather decorations of the
princes seem to derive from some confused account of the Aztecs or
the Incas. In terms of English experience, they point back to
Guiana, the land reputed to be full of hidden gold, and that in turn
evoked the name of Raleigh, who had led an expedition there, and
who had also made the first settlement in Virginia.[19] Although in

prison in the Tower of London on charges of high treason, Raleigh had been befriended by Prince Henry, and had been making strenuous pleas in 1611 and 1612 to James and Cecil to be released so that he could return to Guiana to search for the gold mine he believed in so steadily.[20] Prince Henry supported his requests, but James denied them, not wishing to have the fervently anti-Spanish Raleigh stirring up trouble in the New World. *The Memorable Masque*, written, one assumes, under the supervision of Prince Henry, must have evoked the captive figure of Raleigh for many of the spectators, and the whole subject of Virginia and Guiana cannot have been very pleasing to the king: it was very much the Prince's masque.[21]

Overstressed by masques and incessant entertainment, King James dismissed the masquers of the third successive wedding fête when they arrived at Whitehall on the night of the 16 February 1613. To their intense chagrin, the men of Gray's Inn and the Inner Temple had to return home after a brilliant and expensive river crossing that had revealed their costumes and devices to the world; they were ordered to present themselves another day. Their masque had been written by the playwright Francis Beaumont, with some assistance from Sir Francis Bacon. Its subject was unremarkable, the marriage of the Thames and the Rhine, attended by the gods. In honour of the nuptials, Jove had decreed that the Olympian Games should be renewed after a long lapse. The masquers were the Olympian knights, discovered in their pavilions surrounded by their military furnishings; their dress was starry armour counterfeited in satin and silk, and they were attended by priests in white robes who played lutes. One might have expected the knights to engage in martial combat after the dances, and had Prince Henry lived they might have done so, but they appear to have performed mimic games in dance instead, in honour of Frederick and Elizabeth. By all accounts it was a lavish masque, but slight in invention. But was this the masque that the two Inns had originally intended to put on? Reports survive of a far more startling and provocative masque that seems to have been designed for the wedding, a propagandistic religious piece, that could well have been Prince Henry's trump card, a clear declaration of what this marriage was about in the context of religious history.

The unperformed masque, which has been called 'The Masque of Truth' by David Norbrook in his account of it,[22] depicted Atlas relinquishing the support of the world to Aletheia or Truth, who now dwells in Britain. Truth was represented as a large statue with radiant head, holding a globe and reading a great Bible. The Muses act as the presenters of the masque: they bring Atlas to England and then summon the nations of the world to pay homage to Truth, to Frederick and Elizabeth and then to King James, who is the patron of all. Europe, Asia and Africa send forth their princes and princesses to dance their tribute. The Muses call upon all nations to cease their ancient quarrels in religion and recognise the light of Truth as it shines in England under the protection of King James. Then the great globe itself dissolves to be replaced by a paradise guarded by an angel with a flaming sword. Truth is now seen surrounded by stars and angels. Celestial music plays as Truth invites the princes of the nations, moved by repentance, faith and love of Christ, to enter into paradise. The masque concludes with their entry, and paradise closes around them.

The argument of the masque as explained in the account printed in Heidelberg in 1613 proposes that the old Virgilian trope about Britain being a world divided from the world is now invalid, for the world must join itself to Britain because true faith resides there, protected by the wisdom of the king. Only in the Palatinate is true religion elsewhere known, and now that the Elector has been drawn to Britain in marriage, an invincible power for good has been forged that will compel all nations to enter into the right way of salvation that leads to paradise. The scenario is frankly apocalyptic. It represents a striking shift in the conventions of masque, away from the mythologised fable designed for the glorification of the monarch to an explicitly religious parable that aims to stir religious zeal. As Norbrook comments, 'The Masque presents the real meaning of the marriage as a decisive advance towards religious reformation rather than just a dynastic union.'[23]

It is easy to imagine that this 'Masque of Truth' might have been sponsored by Prince Henry, for it expresses views current in his circle. A concession made to the king's more peaceful ideas is that the nations will be persuaded to recognise true religion by example rather than by force. The feeling in the masque as we have it is of triumphant Protestantism of a kind associated with the court of Prince Henry,[24] and its cancellation must have been due to his death, which suddenly raised great doubts about the ways of God towards England. The anodyne masque of the Olympian Games was presumably rapidly designed as its replacement.

Eventually, after many delays, Frederick and Elizabeth sailed off to Holland and made their way to Heidelberg where more celebrations had been prepared for them. Then they settled down to princely life on one of the fault lines of European politics. Frederick's acceptance of the elective crown of Bohemia in 1619 would precipitate the long-anticipated conflict between Catholic and Protestant powers that would convulse the continent for thirty years.

The Palatine marriage was not only the high point of festivity in the history of the Jacobean court, it was also the most positive international move that James made in his reign after his initial agreement of peace with Spain in 1604. For the remainder of his reign he would be entangled in the toils of Spanish diplomacy as he tried to promote a marriage for Prince Charles that Spain did not want; the eventual rebuff of Charles's courtship would lead to war in 1624. James's indecisiveness over the Bohemian crisis and its aftermath would be a source of continual tribulation to him. Only with Elizabeth's wedding did he carry off a design which had the approval of most Englishmen, and which placed him tactically at the head of the Protestant states, a position he lost through inertia and muddle.

After 1614, Ben Jonson became the regular masque writer and gave up writing for the playhouse after *Bartholomew Fair*. From now on his livelihood depended on the court. Early in 1616 he was granted an annual pension of £66 by the king, and, while no duties were specified, it was evident that masque-making was expected. Masques had to be affirmative of royal power, whatever the national circumstances, and under Jonson the supportive nature of these festivals was assured. As part of the court, he had no desire to spoil his chances by displeasing James in any way. But Jonson could also be used by other courtiers to please the king: for example, the Twelfth Night masque of 1615, *The Golden Age Restor'd*, seems to have been used by the Pembroke faction (to which Jonson was indebted) as an opportunity to launch the court career of George Villiers as a counter-attraction to the current favourite, Somerset. Jonson's fiction on this occasion was that Jove had decreed that the time had come at last for the restoration of the Golden Age. The quarrelling martial characters of the Iron Age anti-masque are routed by Pallas, who prepares the way for the descent of Astraea (Justice) together with the personification of the Golden Age. They choose to dwell in the happy isle of Britain. They are welcomed by the spirits of old

English poets, for the arts will flourish in this new era. The race of
blessed spirits that once occupied the earth 'that for their living
good, now semi-gods are made' return to serve as the defenders of
Justice. These were the masquers, discovered in their Elysian bower,
chief among them George Villiers, who danced his way into royal
favour from this moment. The fable certainly held good for him, for
he became the Jacobean semi-god and lived on the milk and honey
of the court. In other respects, the proclamation of the Golden Age
revived under James proved ill-timed as the sordid events of the
Overbury case emerged later that year, bringing the whole court
into disrepute. However, Jonson's view as official masque-maker
would no doubt have been that the Overbury affair was the stuff of
anti-masque, corrupt humours that would be banished by chords of
regal music. Jonson steadily enlarged the god-like and beneficent
powers of King James over the final decade of the reign, and *The
Golden Age Restor'd* marks the beginning of a series of masques that
concentrates on presenting James as a just god presiding over
Britain's destiny. Queen Anne was no longer personally involved in
the masques, Prince Henry was dead, Prince Charles was still of
unformed character. James was completely at the centre of Jonson's
attention in the fables. In the dancing, Villiers, now Buckingham,
was the chief performer, soon accompanied by Prince Charles.

The curious title of the 1616 masque, *Mercury Vindicated from the
Alchemists at Court*, covers another fable of royal perfection. The
alchemists of the title appear to relate obliquely to those courtiers
who sought to make 'new men' out of base material to populate the
court.[25] Mercury, the spirit of transformation, refuses his assistance,
whereupon the alchemists under the guidance of Vulcan produce
only a race of 'imperfect creatures, with helms of lymbecks on their
heads', who dance an anti-masque. Mercury exclaims that his
creative powers are abused by the low designs of the court alchemists, and vows to be the servant of King James, who combines in his
majesty 'the excellence of the Sunne and Nature'. The scene now
changes to 'a glorious bower' where the twelve masquers stand
illuminated, with Nature and Prometheus at their feet. These perfections of nature are the king's true creations, the members of his
court whom he has made by the divine power of his majesty; he has
even renewed Nature: 'How young and fresh am I tonight', she
sings. This is another version of the Golden Age restored, with
Vulcan's anti-masque a variant of the Iron Age that is succeeded by

a new creation. *Mercury Vindicated* is a resounding affirmation of James's court after the embarrassing investigations into backstairs plotting, procuring and murder that would lead to the indictment of the Earl and Countess of Somerset a few days after the performance of the masque. As James gazed on the choicest members of his court, with young Villiers presumably prominent among them, he must have welcomed Jonson's theatrical act of confidence. It was in fact a time of renewal at court: just before Christmas, James had appointed a new Lord Chamberlain, William, Earl of Pembroke, to supervise the court, the Duke of Lennox had been made Lord Steward, the competent Sir Thomas Lake had just been made principal Secretary to carry the burden of state affairs, Pembroke's protégé Villiers was on his way up, having been made Master of the Horse a few days before *Mercury Vindicated* was performed, and the Somerset clique was on the way out.[26] James no doubt looked at his new creation and found it good.

At the close of the Christmas season 1617, James created Villiers Earl of Buckingham. The next evening Jonson and Jones's masque *The Vision of Delight* was danced, with Buckingham as the cynosure. After Fantasy had brought out her anti-masque of oddities and whimsical emanations, Wonder took over to induce the miracle of spring in the midst of winter. The Bower of Zephyrus opened to reveal the masquers as the Glories of the Spring. The god who had commanded this miracle looked on approvingly from beneath the canopy of state; Fantasy recognised his true creative power which outshone her own imperfect inspirations: 'Behold a King / Whose presence maketh this perpetual Spring.' *The Vision* was a gay and happy masque, without shadows, one which by its total concentration on the miracle of royal power and on those unblemished perfections it could create was beginning to sound chords of absolutist adoration.

The next new year brought an even stronger sense of springtime renewal at court, as Prince Charles made his debut in the masques. Although he had been created Prince of Wales in November 1616, his general physical weakness seems to have kept him out of court festivities until now. Jonson was entrusted with the making of a masque to bring him out, and contrived *Pleasure Reconciled to Virtue*, in which, either on his own initiative or at the prince's urging (probably the former, given Charles's self-effacing tendencies at this stage) Jonson made an attempt to impose his notions upon the court.

The fable of the anti-masque shows Hercules, the conventional exemplar of heroic virtue, fresh from the defeat of Antaeus, now subduing the drunken gourmand Comus, then scattering the pygmies who represent anger, spite and detraction, all these enemies of Hercules being undesirable aspects of Jacobean court life.[27] After his victory, Hercules is invited to rest from his exertions. Mercury announces that the time has come when it is decreed that virtue shall no longer fight against self-indulgent pleasures but shall be reconciled with them: the pledge of this reconciliation is the modest Prince Charles, who embodies this desirable equilibrium of court manners, to know pleasure yet to live with virtue. For once, the masquers have no specific denomination. Charles and his companions have been bred on the hill of knowledge, and have come to express their youthful maturity through the medium of dance. These masquers were the younger generation of courtiers who seemed to promise reformation in court morals. The masque was not much appreciated: more hostile comments about it survive than for any other.[28] Was it thought too moralistic, too improving in tone, a covert criticism of the well-established indulgence of the court? At any rate, when it was repeated for the benefit of the queen, who had been indisposed for the first showing, Jonson replaced the contentious anti-masque and the self-righteous introduction of the masque with an amusing parody of Welsh pride and loyalism which was much more happily received.

Masques could serve as a prism for refracting the white light of authority, making it visible at times of state celebrations in colourful displays that drew attention to the components of power, imaginatively understood. However, to use the masque as a critical apparatus for raising the question of the court's deficiencies was not acceptable, for the court was the precinct of majesty, and its character was contingent on the king, so after Jonson was rebuffed over *Pleasure Reconciled to Virtue*, he turned back to unqualified admiration of the monarch in his next entertainment. *News from the New World Discovered in the Moon* (1620) wittily brought forth the masquers as a race of lunar beings, 'a race of your own, formed, animated, lightened and heightened by you, who, rapt above the moon far in speculation of your virtues, have remained there entranced certain hours with wonder of the piety, wisdom, majesty reflected by you on them from the divine light, to which only you are less'. Chief of this bright race is Prince Charles disguised as Truth, an emanation of the divinity of the king, who leads his fellow spirits in a dance of adoration, so 'that all their motions be formed to the music of your peace and have their ends in your favour'. There was a kind of preposterous glory about this fiction, which ends with the chorus pronouncing the name of James, the name 'of all perfection'.

Exceptionally, in 1620, a masque was staged in midsummer to celebrate James's birthday, a tribute from Charles and his companions, it would seem. Jonson composed with Jones *Pan's Anniversary*, the most adulatory of all the Jacobean masques. James is typed as Pan the god of nature; the setting is completely pastoral, a genre that permits the presentation of absolute power in its most benevolent aspect, for Pan is essentially creative and life-sustaining.[29] The mode of the masque is worship. The masquers are attired as the priests of Pan, and they are discovered seated about the Fountain of Light, a neo-Platonic image expressive of the source of creativity in the universe, from which all life flows. Pan is also the creator of Arcadian society – the court in all its perfection: he has taught 'the rites of true society / And his loud music all your manners wrought, / And makes your commonwealth a harmony'. The songs of the Arcadians are described as hymns, and their praise reaches its height in the words that echo the familiar prayers to God the Father: 'Pan is our All, by him we breathe, we live, / We move, we are.'

The next shift in Jonson's strategy for elevating the court and amplifying royal authority was to turn to the full dignity of a Roman scene. Not since *Hymenaei* of 1606 had Jonson and Jones presented an entirely Roman masque: now the opportunity was given by the reconstruction of the Banqueting House by Inigo Jones after the fire of 1619. Jones had based his design for this key building of Stuart ceremony on the scheme for a Roman basilica out of Vitruvius, modified by Palladio, a design which carried imperial, judicial and religious associations. Given the thoroughgoing classicism of the Banqueting House, Jonson's choice of theme for his Twelfth Night masque in 1622 had a most appropriate decorum. In ancient Rome, the College of Augurs used to officiate at the opening ceremonies of great buildings to ensure good fortune for these works; so, *The Masque of Augurs* was devised by Jonson to inaugurate the new Banqueting House. Inigo Jones provided architectural scenes of great formal gravity and costumes of classical correctness, as Romans from the court of the British Augustus filled the Whitehall stage. The masquers are 'A college here / Of tuneful Augurs, whose divining skill' is particularly in request on this important occasion. They first recognise the sublimity of the king's wisdom and the felicity of his rule; then after their dances they proceed to read the omens of state, foreseeing in all the signs an auspicious future for the Stuart dynasty. James's wise government is praised, as are the security and peace which his wisdom gives to his realm. In fact, the mood in parliament during 1621 had not been so appreciative of the king's lofty self-possession: MPs had been clamouring for military intervention on the continent to save the Protestant cause from extinction after the defeat of Frederick and Elizabeth in Bohemia, and at the end of the session, the House of Commons had made a protestation affirming their rights and privileges to debate all matters relating to church and state in England, leaving nothing to the sole discretion of the king. Just before *The Masque of Augurs* was performed, James had torn this protestation from the journals of the House, and ordered the dissolution of parliament.[30] Jonson, as the king's servant, ignored the critical mood, which had been building up while the masque was in rehearsal, and continued in his role as the justifier of royal policy. The ritual decorum of the masque, consolidated as it was by firm images of Roman authority, excluded all sounds of dissent as it ratified James's policy of non-intervention and peace, going so far as to suggest that European states could desire no higher fortune than to be subjected to James's placid rule: 'Thy neighbours at thy fortune long have gazed, / But at thy wisdom stand amazed, / And wish to be / O'ercome, or governed by thee' (lines 381–4).

The 1623 masque, *Time Vindicated* actually used a view of the Banqueting House as a backdrop, and the masquers, 'The Glories of the Time', were revealed in a noble classical structure of commanding authority. These imposing settings, with their glamorised inhabitants, were in themselves a vindication of the time, an assurance offered by art that all was well in the state. The final acts of confidence in the king's rightness in his conduct of affairs were the two related masques to welcome back Prince Charles after his unsuccessful venture into Spain to court the Infanta. *Neptune's Triumph for the Return of Albion*, planned for Twelfth Night 1624, was not acted, in response to complaints from the Spanish ambassador. Its reworked version, *The Fortunate Isles and the Union* was presented a year later. The first reconstructed Charles's diplomatic discomfiture as a triumph of British enterprise, the latter proposed a reassuring fantasy: the time has come when that island of classical renown, the Island of the Blest, has been ordered by Jove to attach itself to the Fortunate Isles of Great Britain, to form a commonwealth where peace and the arts may flourish in perpetuity under a Stuart king. The final tableau showed the fleet, ready to enforce the isolation of these islands from all the strife and complexities of the continent. That outside world was always a source of trouble for King James, who would have liked nothing better than to live in a fortunate isle enjoying his own blessings of union and peace and watching the arts flourish – as long as there was time to hunt. The frequent formulas of Jonson's masques ('The time has come', 'It is decreed that ...') suggest how much both poet and king wished that some providential force would superimpose an ideal order over the vigorous confusion of national and international politics. The conventions of masque as they developed under Jonson and Jones encouraged the most extravagant demonstration of royal power in their glorious devices, where the king's poet and the king's surveyor contrived to make everything move smoothly to project the king's effortless authority. These demonstrations, however, were made only to the élite of the court, who had an interest in the status quo; to be present in an overstuffed Banqueting House on a winter's night was a good way of escaping from the unpleasantness of the season outside.

It is worth pausing to reflect on how much of a masque's political message got across to an audience. No contemporary reactions to masques make reference to political content: they are always concerned with spectacle, noting the success or failure of mechanical effects, appreciative of the dancing above all, making comments on other members of the audience. The general impression of the performing conditions of a court masque that one gets from the Jacobean letter-writers and diplomats is something like this: the hall was always vastly overcrowded, with people packed so tight that it was difficult to make a passage for the king's entry and to clear the dancing space in front of the stage. Members of the audience dressed as lavishly as they could: opulence was the order of the evening. The air was stiflingly hot and heavily perfumed by the spectators. It was very dim inside the hall ('the twilight of dusk' is how one spectator reported it[31]) because Inigo Jones's lighting effects needed to work against a surrounding darkness. There must have been an immense amount of chatter. Music played when the king entered and continued thereafter with breaks only for the speeches, and the music was often loud in order to impose itself on the audience, and to cover the creakings of the scene changes. In contrast, the songs were hard to hear, and lute accompaniments virtually inaudible. Several masque descriptions note that singers went up close to the chair of state so that the king could hear the words. All eyes were on the masquers when they appeared, for they were the well-known lords and ladies of the court in the most amazing costumes, showing themselves before a highly fashion-conscious audience. Many reports mention with approval the comic antics of the anti-masque, which were evidently much appreciated, a fact which explains why anti-masques became longer and more varied as the years went by. What gave most delight and appealed to the connoisseurship of the audience was the dancing: after all, the high point of a masque was the revelation of the masquers followed by the new dances they had rehearsed for weeks or months. Dancing must have occupied three-quarters of the time of a masque. The general revels that followed, involving the most prominent members of the audience (it is hard to believe there was enough room for everyone to join in), went on for two or three hours or longer. Finally there was the stampede for refreshments, which often resulted in the buffet tables being over-thrown. In all these reports, the actors and their words received little attention and few commentators said anything about the main fable. Who cared who Entheus was? 'Where are the masquers? Let's have a dance!' seems to have been the general mood. In fact, it must have been very hard to follow the intricacies of poetry and under-stand the significance of mythological figures in the distracting atmosphere of a festival at court. Moreover, the acoustics of the hall at Whitehall were probably very poor. Today, in the empty Banqueting House, it is hard to project a speech more than ten paces without blurring. It was for this reason that the poets printed the texts of their masques, and that Inigo Jones provided detailed descriptions of his architecture, his special effects and his costumes. What the audience could not hear or see properly could be recovered in print, when their minds were clearer. Jonson's pained assertion that his fables and learning and symbols were the soul of the masque that endured when Jones's magic had evaporated, or Daniel's resigned acceptance that his words were insignificant as far as the audience was concerned in contrast to the magnificence of Jones's staging, both indicate that the spectators did not pay much attention to the words of a masque. Certainly the festive atmosphere of the Banqueting House on one of these social occasions was the last place to contemplate the learned and philosophical inventions of the poets. Political nuances might well have gone unheeded too.

Yet, the masques were occasions of state. The presence of foreign ambassadors emphasised the sense of the court being on international display, and the ambassadors' dispatches often included reports on the latest masque. Courtiers were politicians too, and a court audience was factionalised into various interest groups. But a masque had to entertain the whole court and to associate everyone with the glory of the occasion and with the celebration of the monarch, so the political innuendoes, which could be divisive, had to be unobtrusive. Magnificence was the prime requirement of a masque, for that quality expressed the splendour of the court in the most undeniable way. Almost all Renaissance festivals turned on some mythological construct, which was in one way or another a statement about power and authority. Many of the educated men and women of courtly rank could be expected to decipher these mythologies with some ease, for the language of mythology was widely current, and courtiers would be aware that a masque had a political subtext, even though it might be well set back in the overall spectacle. Both James and Charles felt the masque to be indispensable to their concept of state, for they continued to fund these shows well beyond their means. They must have calculated that their value as advertisement outweighed their cost to the exchequer, for they knew that 'to induce a courtly miracle' was to vindicate the mysterious power of majesty that still held men in awe. In the final count, a masque was a display of political magic, and would last as long as the divinity of kings was credible.

NOTES

Unless otherwise indicated, all quotations from masques are cited from Stephen Orgel and Roy Strong, eds., *Inigo Jones and the Theatre of the Stuart Court*, 2 vols. (Berkeley and London, 1973).

1 'The Description of a Maske' in *The Works of Thomas Campion*, ed. Walter R. Davis (New York, 1970), p. 229. Campion's published text contains an ambiguous note that leaves unclear whether the song was actually performed on the night, but he describes it as 'a song used in the maske', and its sentiments are central to the praise of royal policy that is part of the masque's intention.

2 See the speeches printed in C. E. McIlwain, ed., *The Political Works of James I* (Cambridge, Mass., 1918).

3 These dedicatory poems are printed in *The Works of Thomas Campion*, pp. 207–10.

4 Samuel Daniel, 'The Vision of the Twelve Goddesses,' ed. Joan Rees, in T. J. B. Spencer and Stanley Wells, eds., *A Book of Masques* (Cambridge, 1967), p. 25. (Letter of dedication to Lucy, Countess of Bedford.)

5 *Ibid.*, p. 26.

6 *Ibid.*, p. 32.

7 The comments of contemporary spectators have been usefully included in the introduction to each masque by Orgel and Strong, eds., *Inigo Jones and the Theatre of the Stuart Court.*

8 Costumes were now designed specifically for the masques by Inigo Jones, whose fanciful inventions heightened the exotic splendour of the dancing courtiers, and also allowed symbolism of colour and emblem to be incorporated in the costume. Daniel's masquers had worn dresses taken from Queen Elizabeth's wardrobe.

9 John Stow, *Annals* (1615), p. 857. Quoted in Orgel and Strong, eds., *Inigo Jones and the Theatre of the Stuart Court*, I, p. 159.

10 Roy Strong, *Henry, Prince of Wales and England's Lost Renaissance* (London, 1986), pp. 76–7 and 151. For an account of the Cleves crisis, see S. R. Gardiner, *A History of England from the Accession of James I . . .* (London, 1883), II, pp. 93–101.

11 Shortly after the Barriers masque, Henri IV was assassinated, and a general conflict was averted; but James did allow the English force to participate in the siege of Juliers, with success and subsequent acrimony.

12 Arthur Wilson, *The History of Great Britain* (1653), p. 52. For a wider reading of *Tethys' Festival*, see John Pitcher's article in D. Lindley, ed., *The Court Masque* (Manchester, 1984), pp. 33–46.

13 William Turnbull, quoted in Orgel and Strong, *Inigo Jones and the Theatre of the Stuart Court*, I, p. 206.

14 Strong, *Henry, Prince of Wales*, p. 175.

15 See *ibid.*, pp. 176–7.

16 Translation from *The Works of Thomas Campion*, p. 260. The prophecy was surprisingly accurate, given the descent of the Hanoverian kings from Frederick and Elizabeth, and the rule of Victoria and her successors over the British empire.

17 George Chapman, 'De Guiana, Carmen Epicum'.

18 D. J. Gordon, 'Chapman's Memorable Masque', in Stephen Orgel, ed., *The Renaissance Imagination* (Berkeley, 1980), pp. 201–2.

19 Chapman knew the difference between Virginia and Guiana. He had written his poem 'De Guiana' as a preface to Lawrence Keymis's book *A Relation of the Second Voyage to Guiana* in 1596, and had addressed a

poem to his friend Thomas Herriot who had lived in Virginia and had written the first account of the colony in 1590.

20 See Robert Lacey, *Sir Walter Ralegh* (London, 1975), pp. 374–7.

21 The Venetian ambassador believed that the Inns of Court masques were prepared under the supervision of Prince Henry: 'Over and above the preparations for barriers, tourneys and ballets, the four colleges in which are five hundred of the wealthiest gentlemen of the kingdom are, in obedience to the Prince's orders and at great expense, preparing jousts, banquets, liveries and other sumptuous entertainments', *Calendar of State Papers, Venetian, 1612*, pp. 446–7.

22 See David Norbrook, 'The Masque of Truth' in *The Seventeenth Century* I, no. 2, (1986), 81–109. The article includes the detailed account of the masque published in French at Heidelberg in 1613. See also Strong, *Henry, Prince of Wales*, pp. 181–2.

23 Norbrook, 'The Masque of Truth', 87.

24 See Graham Parry, *The Golden Age Restor'd* (Manchester, 1981), pp. 82–4, and Strong, *Henry Prince of Wales*, pp. 71–85.

25 David Riggs in his recent biography of Jonson detects allusions here to the corrupt layer of court parasites exposed by the Overbury affair and to the accusations of illicit alchemy practised below stairs. See *Ben Jonson: A Life* (Cambridge, Mass., 1989), pp. 218–20. For further discussion of *Mercury Vindicated*, see Jonathan Goldberg, *James I and the Politics of Literature* (Baltimore, 1983), pp. 60–2, and Douglas Brooks-Davies, *The Mercurian Monarch* (Manchester, 1983), pp. 90–1.

26 See *The Letters of George Lord Carew to Sir Thomas Roe*, ed. John Mortean, Camden Society (London, 1860), pp. 18–23, for details of changes at court over the Christmas season 1615–16.

27 Commentators made much of the growth of extravagant and wasteful feasting at court in the year or so preceding this masque, and of the king's excessive drinking.

28 See the collection of opinions gathered in *The Works of Ben Jonson*, ed. C. H. Herford and P. and E. Simpson, 11 vols. (Oxford, 1925–52), x, p. 576, and examined in Riggs, *Ben Jonson*, p. 252.

29 Stephen Orgel gives an interpretation of the politics of the pastoral mode in masques in *The Illusion of Power* (Berkeley, 1975), pp. 49–56.

30 See Gardiner, *A History of England*, iv, pp. 261–5. For a helpful discussion of Jonson's late masques, see Sarah Pearl's essay, 'Sounding to Present Occasions: Jonson's Masques of 1620–5', in Lindley, ed., *The Court Masque*, pp. 60–77.

31 A phrase from the highly informative account of the performance of *Pleasure Reconciled to Virtue* (1618), by the chaplain to the Venetian embassy, quoted in Orgel and Strong, eds., *Inigo Jones and the Theatre of the Stuart Court*, I, p. 282.

CHAPTER 5

Reform or reverence? The politics of the Caroline masque

Martin Butler

I

Of all early Stuart cultural forms, the court masque was the one most closely tied to the institutions of government, and at no time more so than during the 'personal rule' of Charles I. So as revisionism and post-revisionism amongst political historians have raised the temperature of debate about Charles's government, it is no surprise that attention should have been redirected towards the Caroline masques. Situated as these masques were at the point of intersection between politics and the arts, their revaluation is a process which cuts two ways. The modest ascendancy of Charles's political star may now permit the masques' aesthetic qualities to be seen in a less prejudicial light. Conversely, political historians now have more than a passing interest in assessing how successful the Caroline masques were in promoting the confidence of England's political elites in their monarch's ability to govern.

Recent changes in the perception of early Stuart politics have left the old orthodoxy on the Caroline masque looking distinctly vulnerable. For a long time, writing on the masques was dominated by the gravitational pull of that magic date 1642. Overshadowed as they were by the knowledge that Charles's attempt to rule without parliamentary finance did indeed end in calamity, the masques have suffered a kind of guilt by association, and have often been described as if they were evanescent fantasies of power, always fighting a hapless rearguard action against inevitable disaster. Even in the work of Stephen Orgel and Roy Strong, compelling though it has been in establishing the masques' intellectual sophistication and formal complexity, the masques of the 1630s tend to be written off as distractions from the serious business of government, occasions for facile 'self-congratulation'[1] in the teeth of the relentless and unstoppable march of history. In large measure, this problem in Orgel and Strong's position is due to the historical model within which they work, which interprets the period as a simple and accelerating divide between court and country. Since in this view the real material politics (as it were) is seen as going on elsewhere, the masques are always understood as politically marginal, and Orgel and Strong are prevented from attributing to them any significant politics of their own.

Since the late 1970s, the assumption that Charles I was the victim of an inexorable slide into catastrophe has no longer been automatic. Historians have come to allow that his strategies of government were not in themselves without some prospect of success and that as long as men and women continued to co-operate and to respond to his demands for money his power was not a mirage. Charles may have used that power to implement policies that were divisive and sapped loyalty amongst the nation at large, but it is not now assumed that virtually any royal government would have been destined to fall. And as the most potent and ambitious images of princely power constructed within the period, the masques stand to gain considerably by being liberated from an encompassing teleology. Of course the masques idealised Charles's rule and represented it as better than it was, but if we understand them as part of the machinery of government rather than as substitutes for it then their functions will emerge more clearly. In 1630, in the wake of his recognition that he could no longer govern effectively with parliament, Charles needed to realise the value of his own resources, to instil a climate of ready obedience to the royal will, and to cut off activity that hindered the efficient operation of the organs of power. The masques offered one means by which this programme might be advanced, and in the best recent account of the Caroline masques, R. Malcolm Smuts treats them as the necessary cultural counterpart to the new political initiatives on which the crown embarked.[2] Performed before the same political elites on whom Charles was dependent to channel his authority into the nation as a whole, the masques were used to endorse the political and ideological priorities of Caroline monarchy, and to persuade of its rightness and endurance. An image-making machine of a distinctly superior kind, they proclaimed the justice, wisdom and authority of Charles's court, propounded the values by which Charles deemed his rule to subsist, and promoted an attitude of deference towards his all-competent kingship. In this view, the function of the masques after 1630 was not to provide escapism from unpalatable political realities, but to invest a regime intent on living off its own resources with the needful moral force and political conviction. Advertising a style of government focused on the person of the monarch, instilling reverence towards his authority and outlawing dissent as subversive and anarchic, the masques were designed to promote Charles's credibility, and to foster confidence in him as a ruler amongst precisely those spectators whose co-operation he needed for his government to be a success.

It seems likely that this view will become the consensus on the masque for the coming generation. But can revisionism go any further? In the most extensive single study of the Caroline masques to date, Kevin Sharpe has claimed for them a political function that goes significantly beyond that of mere support for Charles's initiatives in government.[3] In Dr Sharpe's account, not only are the masques exonerated from the charge of courtly sycophancy, they emerge as the voice of criticism from within. He represents the masques as political festivals in which Charles's rule was celebrated and praised, but also as forums in which the king was content to be counselled and advised. In his view, the masque poets were men of moderation and detached observers of the political scene who shared a common faith in a polity balanced between king and people. Consequently, although their masques are full of compliment for Charles's policies, they also set up a kind of debate about them. Alongside the overt praise (and particularly in the anti-masques which proliferated notoriously in the Caroline period) Dr Sharpe construes a range of arguments, rebukes and critical sentiments designed to police the excesses of Caroline power, and to instil in the king a recognition of the limits of his authority, the responsibilities of kingship, and the need for a consensual relationship between king and people (in parliament if necessary). In this perspective, the masques are seen as sounding-boards for criticism, a means of talking back to the king which redeems the Caroline court from the damaging charge of imperviousness to criticism. Far from accelerating the court's distance from the rest of the nation, Dr Sharpe argues, the masques were a channel of exchange between the crown and those with reservations about royal policies.

Kevin Sharpe has been recuperating Charles I for some years now, and it has to be said that he takes a view of Charles's staying-power more sanguine than that of most other historians. His case about the masques is part of a larger argument which, amongst other things, is seeking to rebut the image of Caroline Whitehall as narrow, exclusive and dominated by a limited and ideologically partisan range of attitudes. The danger of his case is that in his eagerness to exonerate the Caroline court he attributes more to the masques than they were capable of delivering. Nonetheless, the issue has to be addressed that some kind of counselling function was anticipated from court panegyric. As (for example) the radical pamphleteer Thomas Scott put it in 1624, 'Wee see sometimes Kings are content in Playes and Maskes to be admonished of divers things.'[4] Monarchs expected to be advised as well as praised, and the humanist tradition of *laudando praecipere* licensed panegyric as an arena in which counsel might be offered, in which discreet criticism could be advanced, or in which analogy and oblique allusion could be employed to insinuate a commentary on topical events. And yet the risks were considerable and the advice was unlikely ever to be unconstrained by the limits of tact. Thomas Scott's remark is a tribute to the survival of assumptions about what ought to have been possible, but it is fraught with ironies of its own: Scott himself was writing from exile in Utrecht whither his outspoken commentary on contemporary politics had banished him, and where he was eventually to be assassinated. Of course, Scott was no masque poet but an inflammatory pamphleteer unprotected by the conventions of licensed criticism to which he alludes, but neither had the masque poets themselves had a comfortable time of it recently. In 1623 Jonson was said to be 'like to heare of yt on both sides of the head' for having represented the radical satirist George Wither in *Time Vindicated* in an extremely unfavourable light;[5] and the anti-Spanish edge which in 1624 he gave to *Neptune's Triumph for the Return of Albion* was sufficient to make that masque totally unperformable. Jonson's experience suggests that in the fraught circumstances of the mid-1620s the attempt to address contemporary politics within panegyric, far from functioning as allowable counsel, could turn out to be *counter*-productive, and it raises the question for the masques of the next generation of how free they were to retail advice which the king did not wish to hear. To what extent was the desire to counsel likely to be overwhelmed or subordinated by the obligation to praise?

In the 1630s there certainly were occasions on which masques were hijacked by critics of the crown to political ends. In 1634, gentlemen of the Inns of Court presented *The Triumph of Peace* to the king as a gesture of apology for the offence he had been given by William Prynne's *Histriomastix*, but they found space in the anti-masques to satirise abuses amongst the granting of monopolies, and they used their main fable to instruct the king on what they took to be the proper relationship between his power and the law.[6] In 1636, during the visit to England of Charles's nephews, the exiled Palatine princes, whose diplomatic aim was to induce Charles to enter into an anti-Spanish alliance and help them regain their lands by force of arms, two substantial entertainments were presented to them, at the Middle Temple and at Richmond (the court of the crown prince). In these entertainments, the enthusiasm of Charles's subjects for war with Spain was strongly canvassed, and an old-style Elizabethan iconography of militarism and international solidarity was revived.[7] And in 1640, as part of the aftermath of the English defeat in the first Bishops' War, and during the run-up to the Short Parliament, Davenant sought to use *Salmacida Spolia* to articulate the need for a loving accord between king and people and to situate the king in postures of humility and patience.[8] All of these are clearly masques in which a sort of talking-back to the crown took place, in which the opportunity was used to accommodate differences between court factions, or even to lobby in support of policies that ran counter to the king's.

Yet none of these masques is without its special circumstances or problems, and none quite conforms to what structurally we would expect from a court masque: the changes in their political agendas have consequences in terms of the masque forms which they employ. Neither the Middle Temple *Triumphs of the Prince d'Amour* nor the *Entertainment at Richmond* took place at Whitehall, and neither fulfils the customary requirements of the form: one was part of the Inns of Court revels in honour of a Christmas prince, and the other is more in the nature of a pageant or a show than a court masque. *The Triumph of Peace* was performed at Whitehall, but it was presented to the king and queen rather than by them, and it too breaches the normal decorums of the occasion by introducing into the main revels a surprising and belated anti-masque involving people of the sort that were usually excluded from the rarified masquing air (or represented only as caricatured types). The common people who run on here pretend actually to be breaking in from the world outside the fiction; their presence disrupts the event and calls the self-sufficiency of the courtly games into question. And in *Salmacida Spolia*, as I have elsewhere argued at length,[9] the political accommodations which the masque is attempting to make can only with difficulty be contained within the orthodox complimentary form. In this masque the king is presented as a figure of patience and conciliation, but everywhere the pose of humility is hedged around with contradictory emphases on his power, and these strain the controlling structure of the masque to its limit. In *Salmacida Spolia* the impression of fracture within the form is hard to overlook and seems clearly related to the intractable problems of the moment to which the masque is addressed, but the underlying point is that for each of these masques it was difficult to encompass points of view divergent from the dominant Caroline ideology within the form of the court masque as it stood. The masques which are politically adventurous were presented on the fringes of the court, or were danced to the king rather than by him, or are problematic in the way they handle the customary expectations of the genre. For the Whitehall masques to function as vehicles of criticism as well as compliment, it was likely that they too would have had to devise strategic ways of subverting the ideological closure which was powerfully built into them as a form.

And the evidence suggests that in the 1630s the space for criticism was becoming less open, not more. Charles took a greater personal interest in the masques than his father had done, as he and his wife were regularly the main masquers. While royal participation might raise the masques' status as political festivals, it must ultimately have worked to diminish their freedom of manoeuvre. The royal presence might have the desired effect of legitimising whatever criticism the anti-masques presented (by dancing after them in the main masque Charles could be construed as allowing and acknowledging their advice), but it would plainly not be possible to make the king dance a role which expressed advice he was unwilling to take. Similarly, while Charles from time to time danced with men who were known to be critical of aspects of his rule, and while audiences are known sometimes to have included severe critics of royal policy, the stricter entry regulations that Charles introduced, such as admission by invitation and the employment of turnstiles to control entry, point in the direction of the masques becoming increasingly exclusive in character.[10] It is true that anti-masques proliferated markedly during the 1630s, and Kevin Sharpe reads this as a sign of increased

space for the contesting of ideological positions, but it is not the
number of anti-masques but what is done with them that counts.
Certainly the multiple anti-masques that preface *The Triumph of
Peace* enabled a complex scrutiny of the 'corruption' of the times,[11]
but the twenty anti-masques which in *Salmacida Spolia* were expressly
given over to detailing the 'People's folly'[12] can hardly be said to
have been allowing opposition to Caroline policies to speak with an
unprejudiced voice. While anti-masques sometimes presented criticism that cut against Charles or projected concessions that it would
have behoved him to make, there was a limit beyond which they
could not go if the masque form was to remain intact, and often
when returned to their context in the masque's structure their
function is seen to be that of dissent which the ensuing main masque
dispels or overcomes. On the whole, Caroline masques were constrained by expectations that royal authority would not be represented except as ultimately subordinating resistance or emerging
transcendent.

So to Kevin Sharpe's argument that within the ordinary form of
the Caroline masque there was a continual exchange between
criticism and compliment my response would be that if so, it must
have been a matter not of open assertion but a difficult transaction
limited by rules of tact, and that there is considerable doubt about
whether criticism could be made to bite without seriously modify-
ing the form. What is at issue here is the way that we negotiate the
complex entanglements of politics and hermeneutics which the
masques involve. In order to understand the masques' politics,
assumptions about the way that they make meaning have to be
advanced; conversely, interpretation of their meaning cannot
proceed without addressing their involvement in history. In the
past, interpretation of the masques has rediscovered their formal
complexities but has canonised assumptions about their politics
which are now becoming unstable; on the other hand, the desire to
uncover a more engaged politics risks extrapolating one element of
the masques at the expense of the formal priorities of the genre as a
whole (the hierarchy of discourses by which plebeian anti-masque
is subordinated to aristocratic main masque). What has to be
worked towards at the present is a general view of politics and
form which is responsive both to the way that masques make
meaning and to the circumstances within which that meaning is
made.

II

Though the political culture of the early Stuarts before 1630 was always coloured with a respect for order, stability, and the sanctity of kingship, it had usually coexisted with a broadly agreed consensus on the value of parliaments, the Calvinist temper of the church, and the importance of England maintaining a major role in Europe. But after 1630 these three priorities became severed from the crown's political agenda. The military catastrophes of the 1620s, Charles's preference for an ordered and ceremonious church, and the parliamentary fall-out of these things in the disastrous session of 1629, all combined to confirm Charles's emerging distrust in parliament as an institution unsuited to his purposes and whose criticism he came increasingly to take for subversion. In the 1630s, Charles eschewed parliamentary finance and turned instead to such sources of support as were available from the prerogative powers of the crown. Meanwhile, the gentry were encouraged to return to their duties as governors in their localities, the church courts were active in enforcing conformity, and a peace was made with England's European neighbours which was maintained throughout the decade, despite Charles's residual desire to play some kind of kingly role in Europe. The logic of this stance was to liberate the crown from its financial dependence on parliaments from which it had become increasingly estranged. By avoiding expensive military commitments to ideologically motivated causes overseas, Charles could divest himself of a damaging and largely deadlocked relationship with parliament and secure the nation in deferential obedience to an authoritative kingship whose rule was distinguished by its achievement of peace and conformity.[13]

The changed political emphases of the personal rule were directly echoed in changes of emphasis in Charles's masques. Charles's masquing continued to occupy much the same ideological framework that had been devised for his father: it is still the king's presence that calmed storms, changed hell to heaven and brought order out of chaos. But the masques written for Charles were focused more immediately than James's had been on the person of the king, and were harnessed more visibly to the initiatives of the Caroline peace. Since Charles liked to participate actively in his own ceremonial, the masques acquired a dimension of confrontation and vindication which their Jacobean predecessors had largely avoided:

dissent came to be presented not simply as a transgression against generalised notions of order but as an affront to the will of King Charles himself. At the same time, Charles liked to be seen in the posture of a reformer, presiding over actions in which the forces of turbulence were reduced to a decent obedience. This was overtly a rebuttal of the contentious and explosive politics of the late 1620s: in contrast to wars and parliaments, Charles's masques celebrated a dignified renovation, headed by a wise king and motivated by the desire for stability and prosperity.

The values to which Charles's government was repeatedly assimilated were those of discipline, enforcement and control. Charles could be situated as a paragon of kingly virtues with more plausibility than his father ever could, and his moderation and self-restraint were figured as the qualities which legitimated his power and modelled the government of the nation at large. At the same time, the power and coherence of his regime were proclaimed by drawing attention to their concrete manifestations in building programmes and public works: even as the masques collated and proclaimed the aesthetic beauty of the England emerging under Charles, they crystallised visually the value of its latent political symbolism. In *Albion's Triumph* (1632), the final scene was a prospect of London dominated by the imposing presence of the royal palace at Whitehall. In *Coelum Britannicum* (1634), the opening prospect of ruined imperial buildings was answered by a concluding image of Windsor Castle, which had been developed by Charles as the home of his Garter ceremonials and the cult of peaceful chivalry associated with them. And in *Britannia Triumphans* (1638), a view of London overlooked by St Paul's Cathedral, the national shrine of Laudianism, was yoked with a picture of a serene sea on which the fleet paid for by ship money tacked winningly to and fro. Some Jacobean masques had occasionally invoked the architectural monuments of Stuart kingship as part of their myth-making, but never before had there been so concerted an attempt to give cultural prestige to a political agenda. Charles's public works, the institutional environments of his power, were orchestrated as concrete symbols of an order that was harmonious both politically and aesthetically.

On the other hand, the masques' concurrent emphasis on reformation suggested that Charles's power was not just freely self-determining but was bound by acknowledged ideals of government. Repeatedly Charles's masques are focused, directly or indirectly, on the programme of reform by which he hoped to enforce his will on the nation. In *Coelum Britannicum* in particular, the fable – in which the corrupt signs of the zodiac are purged from the heavens and replaced with more ideal constellations provided by the Caroline court – takes its rise directly from the economies and reforms which Charles was seeking to introduce. In this masque Jove is represented as emulating in the heavens the superior government of King Charles on earth, and this is supported by allusions to a whole series of economic and social measures published after 1630: new rules for the order of the court, controls over monopolies, taverns, tobacco and foodstuffs, proclamations that the gentry should return to their estates. No other masque is quite so overt in its representation of Charles's strategies of government, but in *Love's Triumph through Callipolis* (1631), *Albion's Triumph* and *Britannia Triumphans* the idea that Charles's presence purges or reconstitutes the environments through which it moves remains a principal trope, and it is clearly related to Charles's attempts outside the world of the masque to reinforce his power by promoting a general reformation in court, church and society.[14] As Kevin Sharpe argues, this emphasis on reform in the masque carries considerable educational potential, articulating as it does an idea of what Charles's rule ought to be like: with Charles as reformer of the kingdom, his rule is validated not simply by its imperial force, but by the qualities of civility, kingly responsibility and care for the subjects which it displays. Charles's government is enthusiastically welcomed as a new thing, which reconstitutes the state in a better, more decent order, but it is a rule which has itself learned from the ethical values which the masques promulgate.

So reverence and reform – the power of the king and the education of that power – constituted the two poles on which the Caroline masque moved, and the structure of the masque consisted in the dialectic between them. As a cultural form mediating on behalf of the king to his potential elites, one function of the court masque was clearly to inculcate respect for the programme and achievements of Charles's government. Contrariwise, the masques might contrive to reinforce trust by implying that Charles could be influenced by reasoned criticism, by building bridges to the king's critics (some of whom might have been dancing in the masque),[15] or by affirming areas of consensus. The interpretative and political problem, however, is to know how successful the masques were in keeping the two poles separate. The validity of Kevin Sharpe's position depends on the masques being able to bridge the latent contradictions underlying these divergent objectives without one pole collapsing into the other. But under pressure this was always likely to be a danger, and the difficulty of criticising the king was always going to be that of squaring the desire to counsel with the ideological work which the masque was supposed to be performing on the king's behalf. The problem of restricting advice to parameters consistent with the masques' ideology of enforcement and control can readily be seen in the character of the reformation which Charles is conventionally depicted as leading. For all its newness, the reformation which Charles heads invariably has a strongly conservative element. It is always represented as a purging away of dross, or as a leading-back of society into a state of discipline and uniformity. As Davenant puts it in *Britannia Triumphans*, Charles had 'reduced the land, by his example, to a real knowledge of all good arts and sciences' (lines 21–3):[16] what seems to be implied is renewal without revolution, as the verb 'reduced' carries strong overtones of 'containment' or of 'reform controlled by powerful leadership'. What does *not* seem to be envisaged, here or anywhere else in these masques, is change that might be construed as puritanical or icono-clastic. Any more radical reform is always distinctly excluded, and appears only in the guise of disruptiveness or downright sedition.

The ideological limitations on the masques' freedom of address are seen even more clearly over issues of foreign policy. There is a striking contrast in this area between Charles's masques and those of his father, which had often carried a dimension of statement about Britain's posture towards Europe. By contrast, Charles's masques had very little to say about continental affairs, in spite of the fact that the 1630s was one of the busiest decades of international diplomacy. Occasionally ambassadors are mentioned (though usually in a joking fashion),[17] but the 1630s masques concentrate almost exclusively on domestic politics, and if Europe appears at all it is always in tropes elaborating on the contrast between shipwreck abroad and peace at home. This notable change in the masques' agenda projects the paralysis of the will which overtook British foreign policy in the 1630s. The survival of Charles's personal rule was premised on the maintenance of peace, or at least of a very minimal participation in the European wars. Charles still nurtured ambitions about restoring his brother-in-law to his hereditary realm in Germany, the Palatinate, but he hoped that this might be achieved through diplomatic pressure, or through alliance with Spain. The alternative, actively to back the Protestant powers and to wrest the Palatinate from the Habsburgs by force, would have involved him in alliances with international Protestantism which were ideologically unpalatable, and in a dependence on militant, war-mongering parliaments which he could ill afford. So, despite his goodwill towards his sister's family, Charles's inability to work with parliament or to countenance a confessionally motivated European line left him hamstrung and incapable of generating a creative foreign policy. The consequences for the masques were either disparaging allusions to the war-torn state of Europe, or silence about it altogether.

As the entertainments devised for the Palatine princes in 1636 at Richmond and the Middle Temple show, it *was* possible in the right circumstances for the court culture to accommodate a militant, confessionally determined line on Europe, and to revive the neo-Elizabethan iconography that went along with it. This visit, during which expectations were raised amongst many outside Whitehall and some within that Charles might be induced to take the lead in Europe and call parliament in support of a foreign policy that would have been truly popular, was perhaps the moment at which Charles had the safest opportunity of using his culture to focus and appropriate the hopes of international Protestantism in his own service. However, the masques in which these hopes were voiced were neither promoted by Charles, nor had Charles in them as a masquer. He did not sponsor any major court masque of his own in welcome to the princes, and his willingness throughout the decade to discourage the ambassadors of foreign powers from attending his own masque performances suggests how unconcerned he was to develop his political culture in this direction (despite the public prestige which these events carried, the official diplomatic presence at their performances under Charles was astonishingly slight).[18] And yet Charles had been active in continental politics in his youth and he still hoped to cut an honourable figure in Europe, a factor which the masques acknowledged by continuing to devise for him roles which hinted at aspirations towards military grandeur – a Roman emperor, an ancient hero, the British Hercules and so forth. These images were insisted upon, but they sit uneasily with the tropes of peace and restraint which were equally obligatory. This contradiction, which recurs in masque after masque, points to limits in Charles's ideological posture which were not negotiable and which had to be accommodated, with difficulty, by successive masque poets. Charles may have wished to be seen as warrior king, but any warfare could only be on his own terms, and it was left to the poets to make this persuasive. Not surprisingly, one legacy of the Caroline masques was a substantial contribution to the impression that Charles cared little for international commitments, whether to religion or to kin.

III

It seems to me that the sequence of masques written for Charles to dance in the 1630s falls into two halves. In the masques down to 1634 there exists a certain space for debate, in which voices that carry possibilities for criticism are raised, though in a carefully circumscribed way. From 1635, though, the masques acquire a character more of defence and vindication. This could well be because all the later masques were written by the same poet, William Davenant; but since no masque was the product of a single mind but was always a collaboration, it is more likely that this change in their character corresponds to conflicts becoming crystallised in Charles's England.

Ben Jonson's *Love's Triumph through Callipolis* (1631) is a good example of the kind of tact and restraint which was still current in the masques of the early 1630s. Jonson's fable develops a neo-platonic contrast between Heroic Love (= Charles, who comes in quest of the divine beauty of Henrietta Maria) and its grotesque opposite, sensual love in all its forms, and the fable is prefaced by anti-masques which involve the purging of Callipolis, the city of beauty, of all those humours and depravities which are inimical to the royal triumph of Love. These anti-masques have a literary source, Giordano Bruno's *De gl' Heroici Furori*, but it is not difficult to perceive a representation of the mechanisms of Caroline power and social policy, and a delicate compliment to Charles's relations with his real-life metropolis veiled in the respectful language of myth. Behind the masquing motif of a city purged of its humours lay a series of social initiatives which was an important element in the consolidation of Charles's political authority. Though James had sought to impose limits on London's worrying expansion, Charles was the first monarch to entertain planned schemes for urban development. Under his encouragement, the commissioners for building (led by Inigo Jones, the designer of this masque) endeavoured not merely to control London's rate of growth but also to influence its aesthetic character and propriety. At the same time, Charles's political interventions in London's affairs culminated in the 1632 proclamation commanding gentlemen to return to their country residences, and in the 1636 Incorporation of the suburbs, which brought all the unregulated craftsmen, labourers, aliens and criminals who had attached themselves to the City's margins (but who were outside the boundary of civic jurisdiction) within the control of a new instrument of government. One manifestation of Charles's personal authority would be a capital city properly regulated and architecturally of increasing uniformity, and in the masque Charles triumphs through a purified City very much as outside the masque his proclamations attempted to impose standards of control and planning on London's development.[19]

Jonson's masque makes no direct reference to London. It offers, rather, a moral and philosophical programme in which figures who embody values of restraint, reasonableness and poise are set in opposition to figures who are distempered, turbulent and chaotic; the clearing away of the grotesques by the heroes is made emblematic of the process of refinement by which the king, as Heroic Love, achieves his union with Divine Beauty, who is the queen. Moreover, the sensual lovers of the anti-masque are not directly identified as English citizens but are dressed in costumes 'of the foure prime *European* nations' (line 33).[20] Yet the anti-masque is so contrived as to enact a contest between the centre and the margins, the king and those inimical to the power of the royal will, which replicates the ideological substructure of the personal rule. King Charles reduces his metropolis to a decent order exactly as Heroic Love casts the plague of uncontrolled passions out of the suburbs of Callipolis:

> *Loue, in perfection, longeth to appeare,*
> *But prayes, of fauour, he be not call'd on,*
> *Till all the suburbes, and the skirts bee cleare*
> *Of perturbations, and th'infection gon.*　　　　　(lines 74–7)

This is not dissimilar to the way that in yesterday's London Mrs Thatcher validated her government by urging people to keep the streets clean and set an example by picking up specially scattered

bits of litter in Hyde Park – though Jonson's mythologising of
Charles's political ideology at least had the advantage of a political
underpinning that related the outward pursuit of order to an inward
ideal of rational control in self and state.

Beneath Jonson's ideological formulae a political contrast is
latent, though not fully disclosed. Jonson's thinking about the nature
of the threat to order on the city's margins emerges in the prose
narrative of the masque, when he describes the depraved lovers
whose confused energies have to be disciplined as 'certaine Sectaries'
(line 23). Opposed to their 'continew'd *vertigo*' (line 27) stand not
only the king and his fellow perfect lovers but a chorus carrying
censers who, in an action reminiscent of the ceremonial innovations
introduced into the Caroline church, ritually process about the
dancing-space and fumigate it. This antithesis between priest-like
celebrants of the king and oppositional 'sectaries', extremists or
fanatics, brings strongly to mind the political divide that was to
develop between Charles's Laudian loyalists and his militantly
Protestant critics: if Jonson was not helping to crystallise the conflicts
of the coming decade he was at least sensitive to their emergence.
And yet if this political contest is latent in Jonson's fable, it is handled
so as not to inhibit the masque's appeal to most sections of an
audience of courtiers and gentlemen. Whilst employing an iconography that was to be current in the political controversy of the
decade – sectaries, ceremonials, cities – Jonson dwells more emphatically on the social dimensions of the contrast between masquers and
anti-masquers. The figures who disturb the peace of Callipolis are
mean and vulgar: they are '*slaues to sense*' who scarcely qualify for the
'*degree of brute*', a '*weake diseased race*' that are more '*cattell*' than '*men*'
(lines 86–96). By contrast, the heroic lovers led by the king are
notable for their grace, civility and courtesy. Their social pre-
eminence is coded into their bearing as lovers; led by '*the noble appetite
of what is best*' (line 55), their intellectual superiority is premised on
their status as aristocrats. It is difficult not to feel that whatever
reservations some of Charles's spectators or fellow masquers might
have had about the tendencies of his policies,[21] the ideological frame
of the masque was one that a court audience would have found
comfortable. Jonson represents Charles as disciplining figures of
sedition that recollect the political divides of the 1630s, but he
accommodates their purgation within a more generalised antithesis
between aristocratic order and plebeian contumacy.

With *Albion's Triumph* by Aurelian Townshend (1632), the situation is much the same, though the problem of how to retain a margin for dissent from the king's view is confronted altogether more openly. Townshend's masque pointedly raises the possibility that what it says may not be the truth about Charles at all, though the issue is handled in such a way that it can be folded back into the masque's structure of compliment. In this masque, Jones and Townshend glorified Charles's power by staging a full-scale reconstruction of a Roman triumph, discovering the king in the guise of an emperor attended by his consuls, and parading him against stupendous and archaeologically exact scenes of classical architecture. Though making no direct reference to Charles's social reformation, the masque's visual language alludes to the cultural reformation that went alongside it. Charles had recently purchased Mantegna's series of canvasses *The Triumph of Caesar* from the Duke of Mantua, and his interest in this kind of iconography was as much political as aesthetic: *Albion's Triumph* co-ordinated the cultural prestige of the Whitehall art collection with the trappings of imperial power that such cultural icons served. By 1632 the dominant priorities of the personal rule were well established, and Townshend's masque articulates the self-image of a monarchy confident of its ability to survive on its own resources. Its architectural frame makes Charles's government seem quite literally monumental: in the final scene a prospect of Whitehall is revealed, resplendent under figures symbolising innocence, justice, religion, concord, peace, and affection to the country, while the climactic song eulogises the values of a sound defence policy and of prosperity in trade and agriculture. At the same time, what validates this self-confidence are suggestions of an educative side to the masque, and gestures in the direction of restraint and the responsible exercise of power. In the fable, Charles, as Albanactus, is on a quest for Alba (= Henrietta Maria), by the love of whom his conquering power is moderated; this argument seems to be implying that though Charles's authority is absolute it is not simply free, since it is controlled by his love for Alba and the queenly restraint which she embodies. '*Subdu'd by* ALBAS *eyes*' (p. 84),[22] his aggression is fearful, but safely bridled under the management of virtue. Charles is made at one and the same time godlike and understandable on a human scale.

Between the first appearance of Albanactus's triumph and the

entry of the Roman anti-masquers Townshend inserts a long dialogue in prose between a common man, Publius, and a philosopher,
Platonicus, and it is here that he establishes a space for resistance to
the idealising procedures of the masque form and for scepticism
about uncritical identification between the participants in the
masque and the roles which they play. Both Publius and Platonicus
refuse to allow the persuasive strategies of the masque, though from
opposed perspectives. Publius, the common man, is an experiential
materialist. He assumes things say what they are and nothing more,
so when Platonicus tells him there is a moral under every stone he
picks a stone up and is disappointed to find nothing there. Consequently, he is entirely unresponsive to whatever moral or allegorical meanings can be read off from the spectacle. To him, the
triumph is a glorious parade and nothing more, and the message
that it shadows about the conquest of vice (which Platonicus
endeavours to expound) is entirely lost. Platonicus, on the other
hand, is (as his name indicates) the philosophical idealist. He is
adept at glossing the spiritual meaning of the material show, but
with his sophisticated awareness that it is necessary to expound and
interpret a most significant distinction is introduced. While Platonicus's interpretation of the triumph for Publius is entirely complimentary to King Charles (he tells Publius that the triumph
symbolises Albanactus's command over his passions), his acknowledgement of a space between the concrete existence of the image
and the moral or ideological meaning which is read into it allows
Townshend to insinuate a scepticism about whether the images
really do correspond to the values they are supposed to embody.
Platonicus asks Publius to describe the triumph:

> PUBLIUS: ALBANACTUS CAESAR from his
>   sumptuous Pallace, through the
>   highstreets of ALBIPOLIS rid
>   Triumphing, on a Chariot, made –
> PLATONICUS: Of wood, perhaps guilt, perhaps
>   gold. But I will save you all
>   those charges, if you will goe
>   on to the Persons, and let the
>   Pagents alone.
>
>   (p. 80)

For Platonicus, the real triumph is not these outward trappings but
the triumph of the mind; he tells Publius he can understand the

triumph perfectly even without having seen it. This is immensely
flattering to Charles, as it allows Platonicus to identify Albanactus
with the idealised conqueror, whose victories are more than mere
feats of physical strength. But it also introduces a problematic
perception that the triumphs of the masque are not simply embodi-
ments of Charles's inner qualities but strategic representations of
what those inner qualities are supposed to be. In reality they are
nothing more than wooden chariots, 'perhaps guilt, perhaps gold'.

The Platonicus–Publius dialogue is of central importance to discussions of the Caroline masque as it shows the very considerable
difficulties that an author like Townshend faced in writing panegyric. Of all the masque poets of the 1630s, Townshend is the only one
who has some claim to being ideologically distanced from the
Caroline monarchy. It was he who was the author of the elegiac
epistle on the death of Gustavus Adolphus – the Swedish king who
until his death in 1632 was the champion of European Protestantism, and whose victories had seemed to be unpicking the Habsburgs'
grip on Europe – to which Carew famously replied by saying that
'Tourneyes, Masques, Theaters' are subjects better fitted to English
pens than the German drum, bellowing 'for freedom and revenge'.[23]
Townshend's poem on Gustavus Adolphus is not quite the radical
document it is sometimes made out to be: Townshend is enthusiastic
about the godly heroism that Gustavus showed, but his enthusiasm
is restrained by the assumption that it is always up to monarchs to do
the leading. Notwithstanding, this is a remarkable poem to have
come from a Caroline masque-poet, and it is not the sort of thing we
ever find Jonson, Davenant or Carew writing.

And if we glance sideways at Townshend's other masque, *Tempe
Restored*, there are suggestions there too of a discomfort with the
formal prescriptions within which other Caroline poets were happy
to work. Like *Albion's Triumph*, *Tempe Restored* is full of praise for
Charles and Henrietta Maria, but it problematises that praise by
admitting the perception that it's not always possible to tell whether
there's a direct fit between the idealised images which the masques
propound and the court to which those images are applied. The
masque begins by drawing attention to that gap between ideal and
actuality which makes panegyric very tricky, as it opens with a
gentleman in flight from a 'sumptuous Palace' in the Vale of Tempe
(p. 96). The gentleman explains that although the palace looks like
a courtly elysium, there are dangers hidden beneath the perfect

surface: since vice can assume the outward characteristics of virtue, it is never possible to know certainly whether the glamour that is seen corresponds to the moral state within. Of course all this is contained within a reassuring framework by Townshend, who will identify Charles and Henrietta Maria with the true court of virtue in opposition to Circe's false Tempe, but this tactic disturbs the comfortable celebration of an easily identified courtly virtue at the outset. These are not perceptions which commonly get into the 1630s masques, in which idealised palaces usually turn out to be what they seem. Indeed, this is the only court masque from this period to share much common ground with Milton's *Comus*.

So Townshend is a masque-poet for whom the idealising strategies of the masque were from time to time a source of anxiety: he manifested a perception that such images do not always correspond to a reality, and he was not whole-heartedly in favour of the policies they were used to underwrite. In this perspective, the Platonicus–Publius dialogue in *Albion's Triumph* lays down a significant benchmark: the poet provides flattering icons for his political master but draws attention to the fact that these are wood and paint and do not have a guaranteed correspondence with actuality. It is rather like Jonson's complaint that Jones's images were merely 'shows, mighty shows',[24] only this time the scepticism is expressed from within.

And yet having dwelt upon this episode in which Townshend lays down what is, as it were, the limit to his faith in the Caroline monarchy, it is still difficult to conclude that his masque as a whole is significantly disrupted by its educational thrust, or that Townshend's scepticism seriously disturbs the masque's formal serenity. Having opened up a space for reservations about the correspondence between the masque's idealisations and the reality to which they refer, Townshend at once elides the gap by having Platonicus allegorise the show. Ultimately it doesn't matter that Charles's chariots are only gilded wood, since the inner actuality as Platonicus glosses it (and teaches to Publius) transcends *all* material representations. Given the obligation to restrain the sentiments of the masque within a convention of compliment to Charles, Townshend has no way out of his dilemma other than by a double vision that is unresolved and unresolvable – on the one hand Platonicus's transcendentalist glosses, on the other Publius's literal-mindedness. And in other respects the educational edge of this masque gets blunted.

The fable may imply that Charles's power is policed by a respect for virtue, but inevitably it's a self-policing that is imagined. Albanactus submits his power to the restraints of Alba, but since Alba is Henrietta Maria, and since her presence is so awe-inspiring that even Mercury gets the feathers on his feet burned (p. 78), these restraints don't seem to have a great deal of practical force: Charles is only promising to conduct himself according to the political standards which he and his queen adjudge to be best. Townshend even refrains from using the other anti-masques to elaborate on the political advice which might be given to Charles; rather than anatomising the limits of rule, the anti-masques copy entertainments used at Roman triumphs, and bear little relation to any discussion of Charles's use of his power. Within the form of a reconstructed imperial triumph, there was presumably little more that Townshend could do to give his anxieties any greater purchase. With its acknowledgement of doubt and its containing of that doubt within a structure basically reverential to Charles, *Albion's Triumph* is a revealing indication of the limits to negotiation within which the masque-poets had to work.

In *Albion's Triumph*, this issue remains on the margins of the text; but with Carew's *Coelum Britannicum* (1634) it moves to the centre. In Carew's masque, the dialectic between reverence and scepticism is fundamental to what is the most substantial set of anti-masques in any Caroline masque. Carew's fable is the archetypal Caroline fiction: Charles has reformed his nation so impressively that at last Jove is shamed into removing all the naughty constellations from the sky. Once the bad old stars have been pulled down and the heavens left lightless, four candidates for stellification put themselves forward: Plutus (Money), Poenia (Poverty), Fortune, and Hedone (Pleasure). Each of these claims to have the greatest power in the world, but each proves deficient in some way or other, and the prize of stellification is given to the worthies of England, led by the king. But in advancing this, the most flattering of all flatteries, Carew introduces Momus, the scoffing and satirical god, as co-presenter with Mercury, Jove's messenger. The combination of Momus with Mercury gives *Coelum Britannicum* a double vision like *Albion's Triumph*, only more extended. It is by no means clear whether the dignity of Charles's performance survives the coarsely cynical commentary of this 'Vniversall Calumniator' (line 138).[25]

A great deal has been written about Momus, and virtually all of it assumes that he punctures the pretensions of the Caroline masque. He even appears on Kevin Sharpe's dust-jacket as a symbol of courtly criticism. His impact on *Coelum Britannicum* is undeniable. At the very least, he projects Carew's sense of saving distance from the courtly ceremonials he is involved in celebrating. As Joanne Altieri conceptualises it, Mercury and Momus promote contrary perspectives on the courtly festival, one idealising, the other satirising. The basic project is to praise the personal rule, and indeed at the end Momus leaves and Mercury remains, but Momus has gone without conceding any ground to Mercury and his voice has permitted more than a passing glance at the mundane realities that the Caroline masque dresses up as myth. The effect of *Coelum Britannicum* is thus neither quite that of worship nor of subversion. It is, rather, 'a rational interpretation of a cultural necessity', a strategy by which the king may be praised but the courtier retain his right to think otherwise in private.[26]

Probably *Coelum Britannicum* goes as far as the Caroline masque could go in the direction of scepticism without shattering the form outright. No other masque finds so much space for the play of ironies, or allows them to resonate without clear signals of their containment. But what precisely does Momus mean for the politics of the masque? How could Charles have danced in a masque that seems so playful about initiatives that were fundamental to the conduct of his government? Everything hangs on what we suppose a court audience would have made of Momus. In Joanne Altieri's very exact account, 'What Momus sees is the mundane world stripped of its abstract pretences'. His presence inhibits 'excessive solemnity' and prevents the idealisations of the masque from being simply automatic; he renders the masque's idealisations visible as idealisations, but does not thereby disallow them altogether.[27] Kevin Sharpe, though, takes a more radical line. His Momus is overtly subversive and corrosive of the priorities of Caroline rule: he is sceptical about the political value of royal decrees, whether Jove's or, by implication, Charles's, and his interventions expose and hence disparage 'the reality behind the masque'.[28]

It certainly is true that Momus's irreverence can cut against decrees that Charles had made, for example his remark (lines 241–6) that though Jove has prohibited families from frequenting the metropolis the women are still coming up on their own (though this is as much a joke against women as it is a joke against the proclamation to the gentry). More daring, though rarely noticed, is his account of himself as 'a Woolsacke god' who, though he has 'no vote in the sanction of new lawes, [has] yet a Praerogative of wresting the old to any whatsoever interpretation' (lines 146–9), a comment that clearly responds to anxieties about Charles's manipulation of the law and the judges. Charles had resurrected obsolete statutes against (for example) encroachments on royal forests as a means of raising hard cash; doubtless those courtiers in the audience who had paid large punitive fines calculated on the basis of a sylvan geography, forgotten since the reign of Edward I, would have been pleased to hear this particular joke. Such satiric thrusts clearly do police some of the more blatant shortcomings of Charles's government, but it is less evident that Momus is in the business of encouraging disrespect for the personal rule as an enterprise in itself. Momus's insults are not directed at Charles (that, patently, would have been extremely tactless); rather, he has fun with the imagery in which idealising masque poets (whose projection in *Coelum Britannicum* is Mercury) dress up Caroline government. He reduces Mercury to speech-lessness by reminding him that he is a god of thieves as well as a divine messenger; he is rude to the audience, whom he insults as 'gay people' (line 126); he provides an undignified worm's-eye view of Parnassus; and he is hilariously ribald about the attempts, only partially successful, of Jove in heaven to match Charles on earth. His cynical, scoffing reiteration of Mercury's message reveals the masque for the fiction that it is, but it is an exaggeration of Carew's strategy to suppose that it undermines the legitimacy of the personal rule itself. Momus's ability to be playful about Charles's style of government is an important step in the direction of self-criticism, but it does not damage the masque's underlying confidence in the rightness of personal rule. As will become apparent in the long ethical speeches which Momus and Mercury introduce, jokes at the expense of royal dignity are possible because the ideology of personal government on which they are premised remains substantially intact.

In introducing four pretenders for stellification, the presenters define an ideology of self-rule which is not inimical to Charles's power, even though it does incorporate a significant critique of it. Previous discussions certainly have overlooked the element of critique in these ethical debates, not least in the satire on court pastimes and pleasures which Carew is careful to include. Momus makes fun of the vogue for court poetry with erotic mythological themes (lines 306–26), and the last candidate for stellification that the presenters consider is the courtly figure of Pleasure who, as Mercury explains, looks like happiness but is in fact the root of all the vices being here outlawed (lines 809–35). The censure of Pleasure enables Carew to emphasise that the court which is about to be stellified does take its responsibilities seriously, and it reassures spectators that even amidst its festivals the court understands pleasure for the transient, frivolous thing that it is. Plainly, this cuts potentially against some sections of the Whitehall audience;[29] on the other hand it does not undermine the authority of a king renowned for his chastity and piety, and it has been the function of the other pretenders to contrast unfavourably with Charles's perfect self-rule. Unlike Riches, who is worldly, mean, competitive, contentious and sacrilegious (lines 499, 519, 530, 558), Charles's virtue is active without being self-seeking. Unlike Poverty, who looks unworldly but is in fact lazy, passive and stupid (lines 645, 654, 656), his virtue is contemplative without being abject. And unlike Fortune, who is reverenced only by the 'giddy superstitious crowd' (line 755), the Caroline heroes owe their eminence neither to mere caprice nor to the whims of vulgar popularity; their heroism is inner wisdom, not mere outward contingency. In reviewing these figures, Mercury and Momus are marking out criteria which Charles's heroism fulfils and which disqualify the challenge of any competitors as illegitimate; the programme for which they legislate is not at odds with the ideology of the personal rule. On the contrary, the vices which are removed from the heavens are consigned to that ultimate exile reserved for the puritanical troublers of Charles's peace – Momus thinks they should be sent 'to the plantation in *New-England*, which hath purg'd more virulent humors from the politique body, then *Guacum* and all West-Indian druggs have from the naturall bodies of this kingdome' (lines 387–90).

So although Momus problematises the certainties of the Caroline masque and enables the ethical framework which polices royal power to be foregrounded more assertively than was customary, his disparagement does not finally displace the legitimating functions of the form. He does permit attitudes to be voiced which usually lay beyond the masque's tonal range, but he does not speak for an outside 'reality' which discredits the enterprise of Caroline kingship; rather, his scepticism about the whole ceremonial side of govern-

ment still remains bounded by an ethos of aristocratic privilege. He
registers a necessary sense of the distance between the use of power
and the images with which power is dignified, but his perception of
events from a more down-to-earth position does not prevent him
from providing his own validations to the masque's affirmations. His
voice may dismiss the portentousness of court ceremonial, but he still
joins Mercury in purging the heavens and adjudicating the candidates for stellification. He is clearly amused by the inflated claims of
Caroline kingship, but he can hardly be said to be opposed to its
survival.

Coelum Britannicum is the most impressive Caroline masque, and of
all Charles's poets it is Carew whose work is most intellectually
demanding and participates most vigorously in the play of cultural
influences competing at the Caroline court. Yet for all that Carew
has been stereotyped too readily as a 'Cavalier', it is equally simpli-
fying to recruit him as a voice of courtly 'opposition'. His earliest
significant step at court had been to enter the employ of Sir Dudley
Carleton, the statesman and diplomat who in the 1620s emerged as
one of the leading spokesmen for the Protestant interest at
Whitehall. His second memorable act was to get himself dismissed
for writing what seems to have been a scurrilous character of
Carleton and his wife. Subsequently, that culture and brilliance
which recommended him to the king (who made him carver and
gentleman of the privy chamber) also led to friendship with such
men as Clarendon and Selden. On the other hand, the associates
who figure in his verse tend to be men closer to the centres of power:
there are two epitaphs on Buckingham and several other poems to
members of the Villiers clan, while the Lord Chief Justice for whom
Carew wrote a courtship poem was Sir John Finch, a man closely
involved in many of the crown's least-loved prerogative measures
and who fled the country in 1640 before parliament could impeach
him. It was Carew who urged Townshend not to eulogise Gustavus
Adolphus, and whose mildly pornographic verse did much to
damage Whitehall in the eyes of those outside who were anxious
about the moral character of Charles's servants; in 1640 he achieved
the dubious distinction of being the only court poet complained of
by name in the petitions presented by the English counties to
parliament.[30] By this time Carew's discomfort with the way things
were had become overt, and in his 1639 epistle 'To my friend G. N.
from Wrest' he reflects in a melancholy way on the king's current

problems and redeploys the iconography of *Coelum Britannicum* with renewed insistence on its inappropriateness. But whereas the masque had dealt playfully with the confident promise of the personal rule, the poem's response to its collapse is to invoke nostalgia for fast-disappearing ways of hospitality and deference, and to imagine a private Elysium which is radically separate from the world of war with which Charles struggles.[31] The turn away from politics in this poem recapitulates the problems of individual perspective and public commitment which in *Coelum Britannicum* are broached but not finally resolved. The poem's difficulties in finding a viable public response to the crisis of 1639 could not have been predicted from the masque; but given the masque's unease about its own ceremonial forms, it is not entirely unexpected either.

IV

Revisionism has taught us to avoid speaking of the 1630s in terms of neat polarisations, and it would be misleading to situate Davenant's masques in a context which was simply that of accelerating 'opposition' to the personal rule. Nonetheless, the years 1635–40 did see Charles's search for finance increasingly running into the sand or provoking constitutional objections (as in the ship money case, 1637), and if these years did not produce a concerted opposition they still saw the creation of anxieties on a number of fronts which would eventually feed into the overall case against Charles's government in 1640. The consequences for Davenant's masques are two-fold. First, the trope of reform and the critical dialectic which that enabled virtually disappears from Davenant's masques, either because the masques had more urgent priorities to turn to, or because the parade of reforming intention at court was itself turning into a scramble for hard cash. Second, the quantity of sheer apology and vindication in the masques increases correspondingly. These masques no longer operate on the assumption that the ideological framework of the personal rule was uncontentious, and they turn increasingly to pontification on the values which Charles's rule upholds, for the sake of an audience now overtly acknowledged to be, in part at least, hostile and unconvinced.

The *Temple of Love* (1635), which was sponsored by the queen and engages with preoccupations specific to her entertainments, does not really belong with the main sequence of Charles's masques. Its exotic theme and concern with Platonic love doubly distinguish its proceedings from masques written for the king. The masque is set in the Indian kingdom of Narsinga, to which a company of noble Persian youths has come in search of the true temple of love. The way, though, is blocked by a 'tribe' of magicians who are enemies to chaste love and who use their powers to seduce men to sensual and intemperate desires. The intervention of Henrietta Maria as Indamora, Queen of Narsinga, supported by Orpheus and Divine Poesy, dispels the mists that hide the Temple of Love, and establishes Charles and his queen as, together, the emblem of true chastity. This is a long way from the imperial imagery associated with Charles, though as a double masque *The Temple of Love* involved the participation of male courtiers who customarily danced with the king, and some of its features connect with the earlier masque sequence.[32] In a general way, the emphasis on remoteness and strangeness is conducive to a magical conception of kingship. Resolving cabbalistic battles and dissolving fogs, errors and misconceptions, the transcendence of royal power is affirmed, a power which scarcely deigns to stoop to topicalities.

Two things are particularly remarkable about this masque. The first is the quantity of explanation involved, the exegesis of Whitehall's Platonism. If we take away the magicians who oppose Indamora, everything that remains is given over to expounding Henrietta Maria's ideas about love: her adorers, whether poets or lovers, are led into decent, purified and ceremonious friendships that convert sensual couplings into virtuous unions of the mind. Davenant is very precise in defining Henrietta Maria's Platonism, including, before the entry of the male masquers, a speech from a page who jestingly deprecates any cult of souls that forgets the claims of the body, in order to establish what the queen's Platonics are not. In the past the page's speech has sometimes been taken as ridicule of the royal Platonism, criticism from within, in Kevin Sharpe's terms. But, as Erica Veevers has shown, the queen repudiated Platonic preciosity and held that the proper end of love was physical union in marriage: the aim was to subordinate body to mind but not to erase the body altogether.[33] Consequently, Davenant's page is there not to satirise the queen but as a figure complementing the magicians in a single, two-pronged definition of love: the magicians are demonised versions of sensual intemperance, while the page affirms that the body still has claims even on convinced Platonists. The remainder of the masque celebrates the royal union as the prototype for relationships which 'keep love warm, yet not inflame' (line 449),[34] thus rendering the Platonic motifs serviceable to the praise of Caroline kingship. But the consequence of this procedure has been to shift the emphasis of the masque from the validation of kingship to its bare affirmation. In effect, the exegesis of purified love and its exemplification in the royal pair substitute for what in Townshend and Carew constituted the masque's reforming or educative thrust. There is little suggestion here that Charles has much to learn from or about love. Indeed, Divine Poesy reassures him at the outset that 'So much thou art beloved in heaven / That Fate hath made thy reign her choice / In which Love's blessings shall be given' (lines 121–3). Charles is aligned with chaste love by the bare fiat of Poesy's command, and such instruction as is on offer is directed less at him than at the masque audience, his subjects. Fewer questions are being asked about how his kingship actually embodies this purified love, and more of the masque's energies are involved in its promulgation.

The other remarkable feature concerns the figures who constitute the threat to the rule of love. It is, of course, entirely customary for the ideals of the masque to be opposed by figures who are spurious, sensual, intemperate, plebeian and generally inimical to the aristocratic ethos of the main masque. What is new here is that the threat to Charles's government is identified overtly and provocatively for the first time with Puritanism. The magicians who challenge chaste love are not themselves Puritans, but adepts who possess sovereign powers of their own, and which are embodied in the elemental spirits which they raise, as well as in the alchemists and witches who are their followers. In overcoming the challenge of these false 'sovereign princes' (line 167), Henrietta Maria demonstrates the stronger royal magic which she wields, but as the climactic entry in their train of subversive followers, the magicians offer the masque's only – yet critical – topical allusion:

> To these I'll add a sect of modern devils,
> Fine precise friends, that hear the devout close
> At every virtue but their own, that claim
> Chambers and tenements in heaven as they
> Had purchased there, and all the angels were
> Their harbingers: with these I'll vex the world.   (lines 273–8)

The references to preciseness and to sects, not to mention the association of these 'modern devils' with fanaticism, self-righteousness and bigotry, are clearly designed to announce this entry as an extremely unfriendly representation of the Puritanical sects, and Davenant's prose account of the dance makes it clear that the unflattering likeness was even more insistent in performance. The seventh anti-masque, he writes, '*was of a modern devil, a sworn enemy of poetry, music, and all ingenious arts, but a great friend of murmuring, libelling, and all seeds of discord, attended by his factious followers: all of which was expressed by their habits and dance*' (lines 300–3). It doesn't take much effort to realise that Davenant's primary target here was William Prynne, whose *Histriomastix* had appeared in 1633, and who had paid for it with his ears in 1634. And it is equally evident from Davenant's handling of him as leader of a sect or faction that Prynne was being offered not as an isolated case of lunatic dissent from the perfect royal rule but as the symptom of a malaise that went wider and deeper. Says the third magician, if they fail to uphold the cause of sensual love, they can still 'infect the *queasy* age / With blacker sins' (line 267). This is a momentous remark: in acknowledging the 'queasiness' of the times, the masque is on the verge of admitting that there was a bad fit between the image of the masque and the actuality. In effect, this is the first masque that faces up to the possibility that Charles's England might be something other than serenely untroubled.

Crystallising on the margins of this masque, then, was an acknowledgement of manifestations of hostility to Caroline rule which weren't being easily dispelled. Prynne was the outstanding individual case, but Davenant could hardly have been unaware of the resistance that had been encountered to the Book of Sports, to the metamorphosis of communion tables into altars, to the Scottish Prayer Book, and to Laud's suppression of lectureships. There might still be a case for reading this masque as endeavouring a kind of conciliation, especially as several of the masquers dancing were men known to have been concerned about preserving the Calvinist faith;[35] possibly the masque set out to solicit the assent of those who were worried about Laudianism but who were equally averse to Prynne's type of confrontational response. But on the whole the masque doesn't seem very accommodating. It doesn't so much conciliate as legislate, and it constructs Puritanism not simply as an aberration to be disciplined but as an obstacle and a threat to royal power itself. In so doing, Davenant disclosed both the political implications of the masques' ideological programme, and the contradictions which were calling the survival of that ideology into question. In the masque, Charles stands as a transcendent and untroubled figure of reasoned self-control, opposed to energies of disruption, turbulence and sedition which are identified with Puritanism and offered up as forces which have not merely to be controlled but to be cast out. At the same time, however, the ideology of transcendence and effortless control is troubled by intimations that its activity is not, after all, effortless but requires enforcement and corresponding vigilance. Consequently, the second half of *The Temple of Love* repeatedly exhibits an ambivalence which exposes the masque's own uncertainty about the programme it pursues. Despite situating king and queen as figures extrinsic to the turbulence which modern devils create, the songs for the main masque constantly dwell on the processes of reconciling, soothing and subduing by which that supposed extrinsicality is in fact sustained (lines 389, 390, 423). The final song institutionalises this ambiguity by claiming that they rule 'by example as by power' (line 513), a formulation which sounds confident, but which on examination proves deeply undecided about the justification for Charles's power. Is Charles powerful because he is good or good because he is powerful? Davenant's masque comes close to eliding the categories and in so doing to undermining the whole educative basis of the masque form altogether, the dialectic of which depends on power and goodness being seen to be distinguishable.

There was a three-year gap before the performance of Davenant's next masque, *Britannia Triumphans* (1638), and the interim can be said to have aggravated rather than dispelled the problems which *The Temple of Love* tried with difficulty to contain. Specifically, the occasion for this masque was the legal and constitutional controversy over ship money, which came to a head around Christmas 1637–8. Hampden's case was being argued in the Exchequer Chamber in November and December 1637, and at the time of performance the judges' opinions were still tensely awaited. Davenant's masque sets to work propagandising on behalf of the royal position with a will. The proscaenium to the stage featured figures who symbolised Naval Victory and Right Government, the one with a rudder and a garland, the other with a sceptre, sword and book. Below were representations of bound captives, above were 'maritime fancies' (line 52), including tritons and children riding seahorses and fishes. The subject, said the text, concerned Britanocles, whose 'wisdom, valour, and piety' secures not only his own nation's defences, but even clears the 'far distant seas infested with pirates' (lines 20–1). This alludes to the double purpose which the fleet, financed by ship money, was supposed to be serving: the protection of English fishing vessels against Dutch privateers, and the securing of Mediterranean trade routes against Moroccan piracy (a measure which dovetailed neatly with Charles's friendship towards Spain and the encouragement of Anglo-Spanish trade).[36] Fable and proscaenium alike linked a show of strength on the high seas with a firm grip on recalcitrant mutterings at home, a theme which was to be powerfully reiterated at the masque's climactic moment, Britanocles's appearance, called forth by Fame:

> *What to thy power is hard or strange?*
> *Since not alone confined unto the land,*
> *Thy sceptre to a trident change,*
> *And straight unruly seas thou canst command!*   (lines 523–6)

Judges who were not convinced by the arguments of Solicitor General Lyttleton might still be impressed by a persuasive statement of the international prestige which the ship money fleet would attract, as well by a royal insistence that the collection of ship money was bound up with the survival of stability and good order in the nation at large. Davenant's iconographic version of the ship money arguments underlines the increasingly dominant preoccupation of the masques with the strength of royal government: Charles is represented as a vigorous and militaristic prince whose presence *compels* his people's obedience.

Before we reach Britanocles, however, Davenant provides an elaborate and densely argued series of anti-masques which develop an ideological justification for the political apotheosis to follow. These anti-masques have received surprisingly little attention,[37] yet they are exceptionally revealing of the formal consequences for the masque of a time of narrowing political options. Davenant's recognition of the difficulty of the times and of the need to address the problem of dissent is writ large in the opening dialogue between Action and Imposture which is an extended treatment of the nature of virtue, heroism and right. This conversation occupies the space which in earlier masques constituted the educative element in the occasion, and it appears to have something of the receptiveness to other ways of seeing which we have noted in other masques: Kevin Sharpe calls it a 'debate'.[38] Yet it is clear only moments into the dialogue that the conversation is not open, and that it has the ideological function of underpinning the authority of Charles's government. Action and Imposture are so clearly labelled as good and bad that any opportunity for the anti-masque to allow an exchange of attitudes is dead at birth. Action, who speaks for reason, truth and magnanimity, voices the position that will be underwritten by poet and king. Imposture, who is involved with fantasy, scepticism and contempt, is labelled as self-serving and untrustworthy, so any criticism which issues from his mouth is devalued in advance. In particular, Davenant discredits Imposture's politics by assimilating them on the one hand to an anarchic libertarian populism and on the other to a gloomy and corrosive fanaticism.

Imposture's first point against Action is the pyrrhonist one that everything is mere pretence. Whatever appearances are to the contrary, all men 'even from / The gilded ethnic mitre to the painted staff / O'th' Christian constable' are in pursuit of pleasure and self-satisfaction (lines 103–5). The moral is: any action that pleases is good (lines 116–21). Action then objects to another variety of imposture, which is that 'rigid sect' of 'sullen clerks' (lines 171, 179) who hold that goodness can only be achieved through denial, that pleasure is worthless, wisdom is a cheat, and man's life no better than a beast's. This prong of attack involves more than a sideways glance at Calvinism and its beliefs about providence and human nature: these particular impostors 'impute / A tyrannous intent to heavenly powers, / And that their tyranny alone did point / At men' (lines 159–62). On the one hand, pleasure-seeking anarchy, on the other fanatical self-denial; in both perspectives virtue is impossible, 'a mere name' (line 184). What these attitudes mean in terms of the ordering of the state Davenant then illustrates in his anti-masque entries, all performed against the backdrop of 'a horrid hell' (line 231), which dwell on the chaos that follows when men are allowed to pursue what they want unchecked. The satire makes a show of evenhandedness by including four old-fashioned parasitical courtiers, but the overwhelming bulk of these entries depicts the foolish and mindless pursuit of pleasure by ordinary vulgar citizens – a group of poor musicians, a ballad-singer and his miserable audience, some street traders and a mountebank with an old charwoman and two wenches. The climactic entry is reserved for 'rebellious leaders in war' (line 262), the spectre of popular anarchy as symbolised by those great bogeymen, John Cade, Jack Kett and Jack Straw, with their soldiers whose apparel 'showed their base professions' (line 266). Jones's costume designs further include sketches for Knipper-dolling and John of Leyden, the Anabaptist 'kings' of Munster. These two are not mentioned in Davenant's text, but Jones's designs suggest that in performance this section of the anti-masques culmi-nated with figures whose presence would have alluded to hysterical fears of popular communism and apocalyptic millenarianism.[39]

In antithesis to this nightmare of populism and revolt, Davenant makes Action the spokesman for an ideology of virtue and heroism focused on a courtly elite. Action derides Imposture for being 'most cheap, and common unto all' (line 77) and he laments the childish-ness and stupidity of most men, but he puts his faith in the reason-able remnant, 'a few whose wisdoms merit greater sway' (line 180):

> there are some few 'mongst men
> That as our making is erect, look up
> To face the stars, and fancy nobler hopes
> Than you allow, not downward hang their heads
> Like beasts to meditate on earth, on abject things
> Beneath their feet. (lines 143–8)

Who these 'few' are it's not hard to guess, but Davenant delays their apotheosis in order to define more precisely the heroism which they represent. This is done in the mock romansa, a kind of counter-masque which Davenant inserts between the anti-masque entries and the appearance of the main masquers, and which parades a debased version of courtly heroism to which Charles and his mas-quers will be situated as superior. The mock romansa is staged by Imposture as a rebuttal to Action's valorisation of heroic virtue. He asks Merlin to conjure up a ridiculous episode in rhyming couplets that involves a knight, squire and dwarf rescuing a damsel from the clutches of a giant, and which purports to debunk the pretensions of chivalric honour by showing what it amounts to. But the mock romansa is easily dismissed by Action. It is self-evidently ludicrous, 'noise and shows' that pose no real challenge to 'Our intellectual strength' (lines 329–30), and such triviality is swept unavailingly from the stage at the arrival of Charles's solid heroism, heralded by Fame. There may indeed be in the mock romansa a gesture of reservation about too easy an acceptance of Charles's virtue on its own terms, but the figures that are set against Charles are straw men whom no audience could possibly respect – Action can call the unquestionably heroic figure of Bellerophon to his aid, whereas all Imposture has in his party is Merlin, a figure tainted with 'superstitious rites' and prophetic enthusiasm (lines 210, 193). The suggestion of an ideological contest between conservative elitism and puritancal fanaticism is built deeply into the structure of this masque. Indeed, by making the mock romansa a pastiche of Spenserian chivalry, Davenant takes the opportunity of disparaging a set of literary conventions that had become closely associated with the militant and iconoclastic tendencies of Protestantism.[40]

So on this account, *Britannia Triumphans* discloses a significant hardening of attitude in the political climate of 1637–8, and its consequence for the masque is the loss or at least the marginalisation of the possibilities within the genre for accommodating criticism or seeking out consensus. This masque was patently an attempt to generate credibility for a regime which was anxious about the emerging lack of reverence for the crown as worn by King Charles. Except that it wildly overestimates the likely success of Charles's fleet at sea, the masque is not yet a text in which the ideal pretence is belied by the reality, but it is a text which is becoming nervous about the possibility. At the same time, its response to dissent is not that of exploring alternative ways forward, but of insisting on the authority of the king and the illegitimacy of resistance to his perfect government. The anti-masques which Merlin conjures up are dismissed for being 'the great seducers of this isle' (line 225), and Bellerophon objects to Imposture that he plays 'tunes to which the numerous world / Do dance (when your false sullenness shall please)' (lines 310–11). True virtue, and by implication loyalty, are seen as surviving only in a few trusty breasts whereas the 'prosperous, brave, / Increasing multitude' pursue the steps of Imposture (lines 188–91). There is a glaring confusion here between the king's supposedly undeniable and transcendent virtue, and the anxious overkill lavished on those who continue to be unimpressed by it. As the summary of the fable puts it:

These eminent acts [of the king's] Bellerophon in a wise pity willingly would preserve from devouring time, and therefore to make them last to our posterity gives a command to Fame, who hath already spread them abroad, that she should now at home, if there can be any maliciously insensible, awake them from their pretended sleep, that even they with the large yet still increasing number of the good and loyal may mutually admire and rejoice in our happiness. (lines 23–31)

This double-edged summary is trapped uncomfortably between saying that the king's virtue is visible to all and his critics are of no account, and that his virtue is plain to only a few loyal worthies and his public unpopularity is a real problem. Davenant's difficulty is that he is reluctant to acknowledge the emergent crisis, but he cannot bring himself to ignore it, and in failing to create a language for analysing it which allows the possibility that any fault might lie with the king he is prevented from imagining any other way that things might be. On the contrary, dissent is demonised as rebellion, criticism is depicted as imposture and lies, and the authority of the king is not so much validated as whitewashed. The only version of government which Davenant has to offer is that of the aristocratic few bridling the insolence of the plebeian many. It is hard to feel that this is a constructive response to the problems of 1638. It seems instead like a recipe for galloping polarisation.

V

The epilogue to *Britannia Triumphans* is Davenant's *Salmacida Spolia*, a masque written in the very middle of crisis and which attempted to develop the form in the direction of conciliation, accommodation and the finding of consensus. But as I have argued elsewhere, Davenant's modifications of the form in *Salmacida Spolia* were neither effective nor coherent.[41] Here Charles posed as a patient and forgiving ruler, dancing in the arena with courtiers who were known to favour concessions to the king's critics; yet the masque continues to insist that the real fault is the stubbornness of Charles's subjects, and to subvert its gestures of love with sabre-rattling and intimations that the king's power may not always be held in check. *Salmacida Spolia* was haplessly shipwrecked on the contradictory imperatives of a royal policy that wanted at one and the same time to posture as loving father and to have its children well-schooled in obedience; but this is a tension which, I have been arguing, emerges to a greater or lesser extent in all the earlier masques.

And yet the Caroline masque ought to have been able to function in a more productive, creative or enabling way. The spectacle of king and subjects dancing together in a loving accord and graciously acknowledging their mutual dependence should have been a forum in which symbolic exchanges could be made, a relationship of trust established, and bridges built between the crown and those with reservations about Charles's government, yet who had no desire to plunge England into crisis. And as *The Triumph of Peace* and the entertainments devised for the Palatine princes showed, the court's ceremonial forms could be used to accommodate different kinds of iconography and to initiate exchange and debate (albeit in a circumscribed way). But on the whole, Charles's principal masques did not seize effectively on these opportunities. Townshend and Carew did make some attempt to set the reverence of their masques in dialectic with a critique of Charles's rule, but as I have argued that project was constrained by the governing imperative of the court masque, to dispel criticism; and analysis of the masques of Davenant reveals their employment of the reform/reverence dialectic to be painfully compromised. It cannot really be said that the Caroline masque-poets made good use of their opportunity for influencing the politics of their day: their masques do not propound viable answers to the problems to which they are purportedly addressed. Working within an ideology that opposed enthusiasm and turbulence to discipline and control, they were prevented from inventing a language that expressed a more consensual style of rule, and their inability to do so worked to reinforce rather than to ameliorate their society's tendencies towards polarisation. Ultimately, they may well have helped unwittingly to precipitate that catastrophe which they had every intention of resisting.

Of course, no one had any answers to the problems of the 1630s; that is (in part) why the Civil War happened. There is no point in berating the masque poets for a conflict they could not avert, nor in overestimating the functions of counsel and advice which the masques were capable of performing. In this regard, the masques were victims of ideological rifts which were already pulling apart within the period and which no form of discourse may have been able to bridge; their formal limitations which seem so glaring in retrospect are manifestations of the ideological blind spots (so to speak) of their day. Yet one may still legitimately feel that there was a failure of initiative here on the part of the court culture which, in combination with other, more material factors, helped to bring on the crisis which ended the decade. Charles clearly understood and sought to develop the political potential which the masques offered, yet for all its gestures in the direction of points of view divergent from that of the crown, the court culture which he was interested in sponsoring was not permitted to reform itself sufficiently for a genuine exchange of trust to take place; nor was the political agenda which it promoted sufficiently flexible to accommodate the adjustments which he eventually needed to make. So the masques represented neither a retreat from politics, nor a fund of constructive criticism which Charles was failing to take; rather, they were used politically by Charles but in such a way as to write him into a corner which was without the space he needed to re-negotiate his options. When the crisis came in 1640 and Charles found himself without those resources of goodwill and personal prestige which a different monarch might have achieved, it was partly due to the masques which had failed to inspire that confidence; and it was Charles's failure to use his culture to more constructive political ends that prevented the masques from liberating themselves from the aesthetic contradictions in which they had become embroiled.

NOTES

1 S. Orgel, 'Plato, the Magi, and Caroline Politics: a Reading of *The Temple of Love*', *Word and Image*, 4 (1988) 663. I have developed my critique of Orgel and Strong's account of the politics of the masque more fully in the article cited at note 6 below.

2 R. M. Smuts, *Court Culture and the Origins of a Royalist Tradition in Early Stuart England* (Philadelphia, 1987).

3 K. Sharpe, *Criticism and Compliment: The Politics of Literature in the England of Charles I* (Cambridge, 1987). I have developed my reservations about the argument of this book in detail in 'Early Stuart Court Culture: Compliment or Criticism?' *The Historical Journal*, 32 (1989) 425–35.

4 T. Scott, *Vox Regis* (London, 1624), p. 34.

5 *The Works of Ben Jonson*, ed. C. H. Herford, P. Simpson and E. Simpson, 11 vols. (Oxford, 1925–52), x, p. 648.

6 See my essay, 'Politics and the Masque: *The Triumph of Peace*', *The Seventeenth Century*, 2 (1987) 117–41.

7 See my essay, 'Entertaining the Palatine Prince: Plays on Foreign Affairs 1635–37', *English Literary Renaissance*, 13 (1983) 319–33; reprinted in A. F. Kinney and D. S. Collins, eds., *Renaissance Historicism* (Amherst, Mass., 1987), pp. 265–92.

8 See my essay 'Politics and the Masque: *Salmacida Spolia*' in J. Sawday and T. Healy, eds., *Literature and the English Civil War* (Cambridge, 1990), pp. 59–74.

9 *Ibid.*

10 For example, when *The Triumph of Peace* was presented at Whitehall, the members of the Inns of Court who attended included Sir George Croke, a Justice of the Common Pleas who would disallow ship money on constitutional grounds, and the future Presbyterian MP Sir Simonds D'Ewes. See T. Orbison, 'The Middle Temple Documents Relating to James Shirley's *Triumph of Peace*', *Malone Society Collections*, 12 (1983) 41; and S. D'Ewes, *Autobiography and Correspondence*, ed. J. O. Halliwell, 2 vols. (London, 1845), II, p. 105. But for turnstiles and ticket entry, see A. J. Loomie, ed., *Ceremonies of Charles I: The Notebooks of Sir John Finet 1628–1641* (New York, 1987), pp. 27–8, 32, 148, 150, 196, 241; and J. Orrell, 'Amerigo Salvetti and the London Court Theatre 1616–1640', *Theatre Survey*, 20 (1979) 12.

11 J. Shirley, *The Triumph of Peace*, ed. C. Leech, in S. Wells and T. J. B. Spencer, eds., *A Book of Masques* (Cambridge, 1967), pp. 275–313, line 329.

12 W. Davenant, *Salmacida Spolia*, ed. T. J. B. Spencer, in Wells and Spencer, *A Book of Masques*, pp. 337–70, line 179.

13 The most recent account of the personal rule is by L. J. Reeve, *Charles I and the Road to Personal Rule* (Cambridge, 1989). For some conflicting views, see also E. S. Cope, *Politics without Parliaments 1629–1640* (London, 1987); D. Hirst, *Authority and Conflict: England 1603–1658* (London, 1986); C. M. Hibbard, *Charles I and the Popish Plot* (Chapel Hill, 1983); and K. Sharpe, 'The Personal Rule of Charles I' in H. Tomlinson, ed., *Before the English Civil War* (London, 1983), pp. 53–78.

14 On this topic, see Sharpe, 'The Personal Rule of Charles I' and 'The Image of Virtue: The Court and Household of Charles I, 1625–1642', in D. Starkey, ed., *The English Court: From the Wars of the Roses to the Civil War* (Harlow, 1987), pp. 226–60; and L. M. Hill, 'County Government in Caroline England 1625–1640', in C. Russell, ed., *The Origins of the English Civil War* (London, 1973), pp. 66–90.

15 In these masques we not infrequently find Charles dancing beside men who were eventually to fight him. I have explored this topic in detail in 'Politics and the Masque: *Salmacida Spolia*'.

16 All references to *Britannia Triumphans* are taken from S. Orgel and R. Strong, *Inigo Jones: The Theatre of the Stuart Court*, 2 vols. (Berkeley, 1973), II, pp. 662–7.

17 See *Coelum Britannicum*, in T. Carew, *Poems*, ed. R. Dunlap (Oxford, 1949), lines 108–22, 404–20; and *Chloridia*, in *Ben Jonson*, ed. Herford and Simpson, VII, lines 120–64.

18 See Loomie, *Ceremonies of Charles I*, pp. 98–100, 240–2.

19 N. G. Brett-James, *The Growth of Stuart London* (London, 1935), pp. 105–26, 223–47; H. M. Colvin, ed., *The History of the King's Works*, III, part 1 (London, 1975), pp. 129–60; V. Pearl, *London and the Outbreak*

of the Puritan Revolution (Oxford, 1961), pp. 9–42; R. Ashton, *The City and the Court 1603–1643* (Cambridge, 1979), pp. 163–71.

20 All references to *Love's Triumph through Callipolis* are to the edition in Herford and Simpson eds., *Ben Jonson*, VII.

21 At least three of the leading masquers in *Love's Triumph through Callipolis* – the Earls of Pembroke, Holland and Newport – were men who held religious views significantly to the left of the king's. Their participation alone is enough to establish that this masque addressed itself to a significantly diverse group of spectators or participants.

22 All references to *Albion's Triumph* are to the text in C. C. Brown, ed., *The Poems and Masques of Aurelian Townshend* (Reading, 1983).

23 T. Carew, *Poems*, ed. R. Dunlap, p. 77.

24 Herford and Simpson, eds., *Ben Jonson*, VIII, p. 403.

25 All references to *Coelum Britannicum* are to the text in Carew's *Poems*, ed. R. Dunlap.

26 J. Altieri, 'Responses to a Waning Mythology in Carew's Poetry', *Studies in English Literature 1500–1900*, 26 (1986) 107–24, p. 113. See also Altieri, *The Theatre of Praise* (Newark: University of Delaware Press, 1986), pp. 79–87; Annabel Patterson, *Censorship and Interpretation* (Madison, Wis., 1984), pp. 107–11; and K. Sharpe, *Criticism and Compliment*, pp. 232–43.

27 Altieri, *The Theatre of Praise*, pp. 81, 84.

28 Sharpe, *Criticism and Compliment*, p. 238.

29 There is, of course, an in-joke here for those who knew Carew's poetry. In making Momus censure erotic poetry, Carew was having ironic fun at his own expense (and this tends to tell against the seriousness of Momus's critique).

30 See L. B. Larking, ed., *Proceedings, Principally in the County of Kent* Camden Society (London, 1862), p. 32.

31 On this poem, see (with a somewhat different emphasis from mine) M. Parker, '"To my Friend G. N. from Wrest": Carew's Secular Masque', in C. J. Summers and T.-L. Pebworth, eds., *Classic and Cavalier: Essays on Jonson and the Sons of Ben* (Pittsburgh, 1982), pp. 171–92.

32 For example, its foregrounding of a hermaphroditical Mary-Charles figure, which is developed from Townshend. It should be added that there is another politics at stake in this masque (and in *Love's Triumph* and *Tempe Restored*) which is the occasion's possible significance as a moment of public negotiation between king and queen. Reasons of space discourage me from introducing this theme in the present essay, but see my *Theatre and Crisis 1632–1642* (Cambridge, 1984), pp. 29–30.

33 E. Veevers, *Images of Love and Religion: Queen Henrietta Maria and Court Entertainments* (Cambridge, 1989), pp. 33–47.

34 References are to the text in Orgel and Strong, eds., *Inigo Jones and the Theatre of the Stuart Court*, II, pp. 600–4.

35 For example, the Earl of Newport, whose disgust at his wife's conversion to Catholicism amounted to maltreatment (Hibbard, *Charles I and the Popish Plot*, p. 55).

36 See Reeve, *Charles I and the Road to Personal Rule*, pp. 206–7.

37 The main exception is Joanne Altieri, *The Theatre of Praise*, pp. 109–15. Sharpe also discusses them (*Criticism and Compliment*, pp. 247–51), but his view of them is quite the reverse of mine. There is an interesting early account of this masque in *The Stage Condemned* (1698), published anonymously in the wake of the Collier controversy. The author misunderstands many aspects of the masque, but he is highly sensitive to (and upset by) its features which are hostile towards Protestant sects. He is also well aware of how provocative the court was being by dancing the masque on a Sunday.

38 Sharpe, *Criticism and Compliment*, p. 248.

39 Orgel and Strong, *Inigo Jones*, II, pp. 696–7. Orgel and Strong assume that these designs were rejected before the masque performance, but, unlike other rejected designs, the one for John of Leyden is a fully worked-up fair copy, which would tend to suggest that he actually appeared in the masque. And even if he didn't, his appearance amongst the sketches tells us how Jones's and Davenant's minds were working.

40 This point is so widely discussed that it barely needs documentation, but see D. Norbrook, *Poetry and Politics in the English Renaissance* (London, 1984), pp. 195–234.

41 See my 'Politics and the Masque: *Salmacida Spolia*'.

CHAPTER 6

The Spectacle of the Realm: civic consciousness, rhetoric and ritual in early modern London

James Knowles

In May 1606 Sir Henry Wotton commented on the unusual magnificence with which the annual Venetian Corpus Christi procession was celebrated:

The reasons for this extraordinary solemnity were two, as I conceive it. First, to contain the people in good order with superstition, the foolish band of obedience. Secondly, to let the Pope know (who wanteth not intelligencers) that notwithstanding his interdict, they had friars enough and other clergymen to furnish the day.[1]

The procession offered a response to papal interference in Venetian religious affairs by glorifying ducal power and by pointedly citing Mark 12:17 ('Render unto Caesar ...') to emphasise the separation of ecclesiastical and civil powers in the Republic.[2] Wotton's description encapsulates the complex inflections available in Renaissance ceremonial forms: ritual encouraged obedience and propagandised the state; simultaneously it might criticise other states, contest a political position, or counsel an alternative political agenda.

Whilst current criticism of the court masque is alert to such complexity, analysis of the civic rituals associated with London remains relatively unsophisticated. Most work, as in David Bergeron's *English Civic Pageantry*, centres upon the development of ritual, especially the lord mayor's inauguration, as a dramatic form.[3] Where attention has been directed towards the social context of pageantry or its functions within the City, the models used and the historical research deployed have been outdated or have oversimplified London's complex social history.[4] We lack an account of London that locates civic ritual firmly within the cultural ethos that fostered an explosion in civic ceremony after 1603.[5]

The exclusive concentration upon the Lord Mayor's shows, rather than upon the variety of civic rituals that punctuated the ceremonial calendar, distorts our understanding of the place of the shows within the culture that produced them.[6] This calendar shaped London's governmental year, marking all its major events with a range of rituals that included processions to communion or to hear sermons, inter-guild feasts, visits to the estates of the corporation outside London, progresses to the conduit heads, arcane rituals, such as the swan upping, and a variety of oath-swearing ceremonials that preceded admission to civic office. Middleton's *Honourable Entertainments* (1621), largely neglected by critics, were designed precisely to celebrate such occasions. Equally, the familiar overemphasis upon the pageants distorts the nature of the Lord Mayor's show itself, in that it fails to consider the various signifying elements deployed, such as processional order, liveries, and guild symbolism.[7] To understand the function of civic ritual in Renaissance London, we need to relate the familiar mayoral pageants to other ceremonial forms, and to the wider contexts of civic rhetoric and urban consciousness.

I

In 'Ritual, Drama and Social Body in Late Medieval England' Mervyn James draws attention to the York Corpus Christi procession of the host in monstrance followed by members of the city's trade and religious guilds and the mayor and aldermen. The procession, he suggests, sought to unite the body politic through a symbolic resolution of the tensions between the guilds themselves and other sections of society. In particular, imagery and rhetoric constituted an efficacious 'symbolic thread' to 'bind together the social fabric of the townscape'. The power of the Corpus Christi imagery derives from the double significance in the corporeal language that 'provided urban societies with a mythology and ritual in terms of which the opposites of social wholeness and social differentiation could be both affirmed, and also brought into a creative tension, one with another'.[8] Body images represented both hierarchy and community, read on the one hand to support hierarchy, and on the other to encourage social integration.[9] In civic ritual both these readings are continuously present, simultaneously locking the citizen into a matrix of hierarchical (patronage and deference) and communal (neighbourhood and community) relations.

Like its earlier counterpart in York, London civic ritual integrates potentially conflicting social groups, and thus ceremonialises order

and stability. Mid-Tudor ceremony emphasised these two objectives. Stow commented, for example, on the Midsummer festivals,
celebrated with bonfires and feasts which 'were called bonfires as
well of good amity amongst neighbours that being before at controversy, were there by the labour of others, reconciled, and made of
bitter enemies loving friends'.[10] These festivities coincided with the
Midsummer watch, which represented the order of the City and
symbolically marked out the boundaries of its jurisdiction.[11] Order
was ceremonialised, with neighbourly amity to resolve conflicts, and
the force of the law to suppress disorder. Even after the main
ceremonial focus had moved from Midsummer to St Simon and St
Jude's day in October, and even after the religious changes occasioned by the Reformation, this double emphasis remained. In
direct continuity with its medieval antecedents, civic ceremony
propagated civic ideology, promoted the internal stability of the
City through the exhortation to and ritualisation of order, and
demonstrated that stability to the wider national audience.[12]

The civic ritual of London can be understood and evaluated only
through an interpretation of the capital's social structure in this
period, difficult though this is, given fragmentary evidence and
intractable interpretative problems.[13] Today's historians, following
contemporary commentators, agree that the central issue was
London's stability (or lack of it), but analyses of the evidence
diverge, with modern historians divided (again like contemporary
observers) into those who imagine London spiralling towards chaos,
and a more optimistic group who argue for the City's general
stability.[14] Both groups locate London's problems in population
growth, uncontrolled physical expansion, high prices, dearth, heavy
taxation and the resultant destitution, vagabondage and social
unrest. These were common phenomena in the rest of England, but
were exacerbated, it is claimed, by the capital's stark contrasts of
wealth and poverty.[15]

The major issue, both for contemporary observers and modern
historians, is the prevalence and significance of popular disorder in
the capital. Some historians have concluded that 'even when due
allowance has been made for the exaggerated fears of contemporary
authorities, the rioting which intermittently disturbed the peace of
early Stuart London and its suburbs constituted a problem of serious
proportions'. More recent studies have argued for the inherent
stability of the civic government, with high participation rates, and

a sense of belonging fostered by the large percentage of freemen of
the City.[16] Local surveys in particular have highlighted the strength
of neighbourhood and community ties which diminished the unsettling aspects of internal and external immigration and social mobility. While once it was common to argue that London's oligarchy
retreated in the face of disorder, some interpretations now envisage
disorder as a negotiating strategy and highlight the flexible and
sensitive response it drew from the urban elite.[17]

In a valuable study, Ian Archer has recently questioned 'the myth
of "urban anomie"', showing how the livery companies, parishes
and wealthier citizens of London instituted a social system which
locked the poor into 'a matrix of overlapping communities', and
how poor relief, despite its limitations, 'worked to promote stability,
because of the way the exercise of philanthropy served to invest elite
figures with reputations for charitable virtue, and because of the
way it could be manipulated to secure conformist behaviour'.
Archer suggests that London's inhabitants identified themselves
with the City (as the frequent use of 'citizen' affirms), but that the
primary site of identification was more local in nature. He demonstrates that several communities operated at different levels in the
City, some geographical and administrative, such as parishes, and
some occupational, such as guilds. In particular, Archer shows how
the language of civic duty, community and neighbourliness aided
the 'formation of community consciousness', and 'provided a set of
values to which the disadvantaged could appeal, because it shaped
popular expectations of their ruler'.[18]

Whatever the verdict of modern historians, the *perception* of crisis
in the capital was common. No argument is possible, furthermore,
over London's difficult relations with the provinces. Throughout the
sixteenth and seventeenth centuries merchants from the outports
railed against London's commercial hegemony, which threatened to
strangle their trade. In the social sphere, the expanding population
and nascent social season seemed to transform London into 'the
Spleene ... which in measure as it ouergrowes, the body wastes'.[19]
Equally problematic were the City's political relations with the
crown and its servants. Friction often developed over the exact
relationship between the City's privileges and its duty to the
monarch. The peculiar elective nature of London's mayoralty also
caused anxiety.[20]

Yet within these difficult circumstances a positive ideology was being developed. Stow, the most prominent of London's apologists, envisaged the City as the 'mystical body whereof Christ is the head', its wealth and power tending to social stability both within the metropolis and in the wider political life of the nation (as shown in its loyalty to the monarch). Cities, according to Stow, especially London, civilised and made men 'reasonable'.[21] The *Survey* belongs to the marked development of urban consciousness in the late sixteenth century, itself part of the growth of local and national consciousness in late Elizabethan England.[22] Chronicles, chorographies, topographical descriptions, maps and panoramas all fuelled this awareness.

The development of a stabilising urban consciousness in the period can be seen in the support offered by the livery companies to those who glorified the City or its guilds. In 1602 Stow was paid 10 shillings for research into previous mayors and aldermen drawn from the Merchant Taylors, doubtless to provide coats of arms for the shields carried in the Lord Mayor's inaugural procession. In the same year he was substantially rewarded for his *Survey* and his *Brief Chronicle*, patronage which continued for Munday's extensions of the *Annales*, with payments in 1617 and 1618, and further sums for his widow in 1634. Edmund Howe, another city chronicler benefited in a similar way, gaining £10 'the better to encourage him to proceed' in his abridgement of Stow's *Chronicle*.[23] The relationship between such chronicles and civic ritual is clear, not only in the overlap of personnel, but also in the office of Chronologer (held by both Middleton and Munday), which was 'to collect and set down all memorable acts of this City and occurrences thereof', as well as to be the 'inventor of honourable entertainments for this City'.[24] The underlying thinking for such patronage is attested in the Goldsmiths' accounts, where in 1610 a 'gratuity of £6 13s 6d' was paid 'to Anthony Munday for a book called *A Briefe Chronicle of the Successe of Times* wherein it is conceived he hath remembered the worship and antiquity of the Company'.[25] *A Briefe Chronicle* places London as the culmination of the history of other great cities of the world,[26] and explains its civic government, with due attention to the charitable activities of its citizens, and to the antiquity, dignity and justice of its governance.[27]

Much of the pro-civic writing directly responds to anti-metropolitan polemic, with its concerns with the over-rapid growth of London, with the City's disorder and the damage that its commercial hegemony does to the trading life of the nation. Stow emphasises the city's civilising nature – its promotion of *urbanitas* – and answers one of the main charges laid against London and its merchants, that they stored up wealth to the detriment of the rest of the nation. London, Stow protests, does not seditiously endanger the nation, since it 'consisteth not in the extremes, but in a very mediocrity of wealth and riches', and that although London's 'great multitude' might appear dangerous, 'yet the greatest part of them be neither too rich nor too poor, but live in the mediocrity'.[28] Other tracts, such as *The Merchants New-Royall Exchange* (1604) emphasise that commerce benefits all, even 'the blacke Indians', and encourages learning, exploration, pleasure, and most of all leads to a 'neighbourly borrowing and lending betweene Kingdomes'.[29]

Such emergent civic consciousness, manifested not only in formal panegyric, but also in pamphlets, plays and ballads on London life, and in acts of collective or individual patronage, or projects for edification of the City (such as the paving of Smithfield or the rebuilding of Aldgate) shaped the climate in which civic ritual was produced.[30] A further aspect of civic consciousness was the rhetoric of civic magistracy which developed through the early modern period. Essentially paternalist, rooted in the family as model for the state, it inculcated order, piety, charity.[31] 'An Ordinance for Nourishing and Relieving the Poor Members of the Merchant Taylors' Company' of 1571 notes:

Forasmuch as it is the duty of every Christian society to help and relieve every willing and labouring brother in the Commonwealth, and specially such as are incorporated, grafted together in brotherly society, remembering the scripture written [that] he which doth not provide for family and household is worse than an infidel.[32]

The language here reveals an expectation of the performance of duty on both sides. The magistrate or higher orders were to provide for the poor, whilst the poor were to be 'willing and labouring'. The promotion of 'Christian society' and guild solidarity, and the idea of the 'Commonwealth', point towards the reconciliation that both guild and magistracy rhetoric sought to foster.

Such a system has a double impact, providing a code of behaviour by which both governors and governed can operate. As with the medieval Corpus Christi imagery that brings differentiation and integration into creative tension, so this discourse integrates the whole parish, guild or city in the values of 'society' and 'Commonwealth'. Equally it promotes hierarchy and systems of patronage and deference. It does so by establishing mutual concepts of duty, including the duty of good governance for the elite (accepted by both the rulers and the ruled), and a duty to conform for the governed. London's ritual adopts this rhetoric, with the City depicted as ordered, and the potential damage of its commercial power minimised, whilst the benefits are dwelt upon. In particular, the City is naturalised through demonstrable relation to past communities, or accepted versions of history or mythology. Through civic ritual London is differentiated as being pre-eminent, but the dangers of that domination are limited by integrative strategies that mesh London into the national fabric, through historicisation, mythologisation and naturalisation. Internally, its citizens are involved in a 'process of social and cultural definition and identification' that locates them physically and socially in the City.[33]

II

A significant example of this identifying and defining process can be found in oath-taking ceremonies. Oaths marked all the major events in the citizen's life, apprenticeship, freedom of the company, office-holding both within the guild and in the wider civic structure.[34] In Coventry the oath-taking ceremony was the pivot of the civic calendar. During it, the incoming officers processed to meet the out-going officers, and the new mayor was obliged to doff his hat to the old mayor. The ceremony culminated in communion; by the seventeenth century the oath ceremony actually took place within the service, between the first lesson and sermon. These ceremonies 'invested office with solemn and social attributes over and above the practical demands of annual executive position'.[35]

In 1584 Lupold von Wedel reported a similar ceremony in London, on St Simon and St Jude's day, when the old mayor awaited the arrival of the new mayor in the Guildhall, both accompanied by guildsmen and liverymen in procession. Von Wedel continues:

When the council has reached the platform the present burgomaster and the one which is to come are seated behind a small table, and then the macebearer advises three times all present to pay attention. Then he takes down a book, and he and another gentleman, kneeling down on cushions placed on both sides of the table, they read the oath which the new megger has to swear. When this is done a book bound in red velvet with gilt edges is handed by another person, together with the seal, sword and sceptre, to the new megger. After this ceremony they all go out again, but now the late megger following the newly elected.[36]

Unlike Coventry where the out-going mayor awaited the newly elected incumbent, the London mayors symbolised the transition of power through the reversal of processional order before and after the oath. Although the ceremony does not stress the deference of the new official to the old in the Coventry manner, the location of the ceremony in the Guildhall and the reversed processional order would doubtless serve to remind the new incumbent of his obligations to the aldermanic elite, and exhort him to virtue comparable to that of past office-holders.

Oaths played an essential role in the enforcement of behavioural models. In London, oaths were ubiquitous, and specific 'oath-books' were established by some companies containing the relevant oaths and biblical extracts, which were then sworn upon to solemnise the oath.[37] The oath of the wardens of the Goldsmiths included promises to ensure true measures and not to deal in false gold, but also stressed wider social ends, such as the importance of the 'common profyt of the Company', 'feleshyp' and 'conscience' in all actions.[38] Similarly, the printed oaths of freemen, which appeared throughout the early modern period, enjoined the freeman to contribute to the City, obey all its rules on trade, measures and apprenticeship, as well as binding him to a wider loyalty to the crown.[39] The oath became the basis of all civic and political order: 'wee sweare by a greater then ourselues, to the end that such swering may be a present remedie against all strife and contention amongst vs'.[40]

The Lord Mayor's oath of loyalty to the crown was sworn in a ceremony that was preceded by a water-borne journey to Westminster (often marked by water pageants), and took place in the Court of Exchequer, before the monarch and court as well as the whole civic governmental elite. The oath-taking was accompanied by a speech from the Recorder of the City and sometimes by the monarch, after which the mayor would return by water. Then the pageantry on land would commence, climaxing in communion at St Paul's.[41]

A number of Recorder's speeches outlining the virtues of the civic magistrate survive from both the late sixteenth and early seventeenth centuries. In the 1607 speech at the installation of Sir Henry

Roe, the Recorder stresses the obedience of the mayor to the monarch:

This skarlett, by your Majesties indulgence, is the roabe wherin they triumph, or rather blush that they cannot doe your Majesties that servic wich with all alacritye they desier and owe.[42]

In addition to obedience the Recorder stresses the worth of the office and the worthiness of the recipient. He traces the origin of the procession to Roman antiquity, and emphasises the blessing bestowed by the 'Kingly Oracle'. Next he continues to highlight Roe's fitness for office:

his memorable father sometimes bore the same offic, so fertill hath this familie allwayes bin of good Cittizens; and that, as others his foregoers hav employed their laudable servic against the Plague and Infection, so this Gentleman hath with much vigor and industry against the cold and famin; whereof ... numbers of people must hav miscarried; but that God, the fortune of your Majestye, and the modesty of the people, by his equall and exemplary Government, the sam occured.

Once Roe's suitability was established, the sword that preceded him in procession and represented his magisterial powers was sanctioned by the king and symbolically handed over to the mayor. As in Coventry, the oath-taking invests the mayoralty with wider social significance, here linking the mayoralty to ancient forms of government to dignify it, and the city is confirmed in its pre-eminent role as the 'Presence [chamber]' of the kingdom.[43]

The significance of the oaths does not go unmarked in the pageants that followed the ceremonies. In *Triumphs of Loue and Antiquity* (1619), Sir William Cockayne was reminded during the water speech to use his mayoralty well:

> So the Iudicious when he comes to beare
> This powerfull Office, struck with Diuine feare,
> Collects his spirits, redeemes his howres with care,
> Thinkes of his Charge, and Oath, what Tyes they are,
> And with a Vertuous Resolution then
> Workes more good in one yeare, then some in Ten.[44]

The sense of duty (the 'Charge') and the expectations generated by civic ideology along with the oath are the 'Tyes' that impel the mayor towards good magistracy.

There were two oath-taking ceremonies, one at the Guildhall after the election, and the second before the king, thus marking the double position of the Lord Mayor within local and national government. Both show that civic ritual instils integration and differentiation simultaneously. The Guildhall oath integrates the mayor with his fraternity and the aldermanic elite. The Westminster oath-giving, marked by a symbolic use of location, where the mayor travels to the seat of national government, differentiates the mayor by placing him in a hierarchy of relations, and reminds the audience of the chain of government that descends from God to king to mayor. Similarly, the emphases of the two ceremonies, on fraternal loyalties and on justice, bring together the integration and differentiation which the office-holder must combine: love for his fellow citizens combined with impartiality in justice.

III

The oath-taking ceremonies belong to the inauguration of the mayor which, as the major event in the governmental calendar, was the focus of most civic ritual. The main vehicle was, of course, the land-pageants that accompanied the mayoral progress through the city, but even the lesser elements, such as the barge processions to and from Westminster, were not devoid of ceremony. The barge processions, for example, were ordered in the traditional hierarchy of the guilds, whilst the barges themselves were a matter of guild pride, and carried pennants and tilt cloths with the company arms and symbols.[45] The importance of these water-borne processions can easily be overlooked. The river, England's main trade route, was the source of the City's wealth, so the procession affirmed its significance. The water speech in *Trivmphs of Loue and Antiquity* imagines how '*Desert and Loue will be well matcht today*' (sig.A4[v]) and depicts the Lord Mayor's year of governance as a marriage between him and the City. Such marital imagery is developed by Webster in his *Monuments of Honour*, where Thetis asks Oceanus:

> What brave Sea-Musicke bids us Welcome, harke!
> Sure this is *Venice*, and the day Saint *Marke*
> In which the *Duke* and *Senats* their course hold
> To wed our *Empire* with a Ring of Gold.[46]

The allusion to Venetian practice highlights the importance of the river and the sea in London's life, and equates the London mayoral pageant, a wedding of the mayor to the City, with the Venetian sea-wedding.[47] The frequently used ship-devices offered another tribute to London's maritime dependence.

It was the land-pageants, however, that provided the major ceremonial form to present civic rhetoric. The central and linked strategies of mythologisation, historicisation and naturalisation are most clearly displayed in *The Magnificent Entertainment* (planned for 1603 but staged 1604), a royal entry that established a model for Jacobean mayoral entries by setting new standards of magnificence and sophistication.[48] Here, the 'Londinium' arch utilises classical mythology to dignify the City, relating London to Virgilian Rome, both in the use of the triumphal arch (as seen in Harrison's well-known engraving) and in many details, such as the allusion to Virgil's description of the Tiber (*Part of ... [the] Magnificent Entertainment*, sigs.A3^r–B1^r). Like Rome, London, another ideal city, is given a 'Genius Vrbis' to welcome James, supported by six daughters (Gladness, Veneration, Promptitude, Vigilance, Affection and Unanimity). The arch is designed to present the 'expression of state and Magnificence (as proper to a triumphall arch) but the very site, Fabricke, Strength, Pollicie, Dignities and Affections of the Cittie were all laide downe to life' (*Part of ... [the] Magnificent Entertainment*, sigs.B2^{r-v}). The mythologisation continues in the 'Hortus Euporiae' arch on Cheapside which linked London to classical pastoral, symbolising the natural plenty of the City. In the 'Temple of Janus' at Temple Bar the Virgilian overtones are developed, through the citation of Virgil's *Eclogue* 4, emphasising that the Golden Age has returned with the arrival of James I (*Part of ... [the] Magnificent Entertainment*, sigs.C4^{r-v}). Moreover, in the distribution of the arches, and the inclusion of the Italian Arch at Gracious Street and the Dutch Arch at the Royal Exchange, various segments of the City community are integrated into the triumph, each accentuating the centrality of London for overseas trade and the accumulation of wealth – a capacity embodied in the City's ability to mount this vast production (not once, but twice). Here, latently, the criticism of anti-metropolitan polemic is answered, and the city's trading position extolled and naturalised.

Concentration upon the wealth of the city, its benefit to both London and the realm, and the emphasis upon 'Vnanimity' and unity become the twin themes of many civic pageants. In the case of London's trading wealth, the importance of the Thames and the oceans is recognised, not simply in the water-borne barge proces-

sion, but through frequent references in the land pageants themselves.[49] In the 1605 pageant, Munday's *The Triumphs of Re-United
Britannia* we see a 'Shippe called the *Royal* EXCHANGE', loaded with
spices and manned by a Master and Mate, who celebrate the
election of Holyday (the supposed owner of the ship) to mayoral
office. As they progress through the crowds the crew 'liberally
bestow' their cloves, pepper and mace upon the populace to demonstrate the 'loue and bounty' of the company and Holyday.[50]
Moreover, the significance of the ship's name would not be lost on
the audience, as it recalls Gresham's Exchange, one of the
monuments of civic edification.[51] The pageant clearly suggests that
the trading wealth of London is not restricted to the oligarchy but
filters down to the whole populace: exploration and trade enrich
metropolis and nation.

If *The Magnificent Entertainment* provided the major impetus for
civic pageantry in the first decade of James's reign, the next major
development occurred with the work of Dekker and Middleton in
1612 and 1613, when both authors strove to increase the ideological
and dramatic coherence of the inaugural shows.[52] Dramatic coherence was improved through more developed plots, usually a battle
between vice and virtue drawn from morality drama, whilst ideological coherence was extended in the distinctly Protestant emphasis
of both the 1612 and 1613 shows. In *Troia-Nova Triumphans or London
Triumphing* (1612), Dekker develops a more complex use of the ship
image to demonstrate the access to wealth that the companies
provide. Here Neptune describes the ship battling against the seas of
misfortune, and eventually safely docking, guided by the pilot who is
true to his conscience. The vessel's arrival has been transformed into
an act of virtue, which equates steering the ship to safety with
governing the city.[53] Implicitly, it is suggested that good trading
skills are not only enriching, but the result of virtue and therefore
doubly beneficent. Indeed, *Troia-Nova Triumphans* transforms the
mayoral progress into a morality play battle between Envy and
Virtue, with civic virtue eventually triumphant. In the case of
Middleton's *Triumphs of Truth* (1613), announced by its title-page as
'redeem'd into Forme', David Norbrook has argued that the
pageant's focus upon Truth has specifically Protestant and apocalyptic overtones.[54] Perhaps its most notable feature, apart from its
elaboration, lies in the emphasis placed upon trade as a method of
conversion of native populations. One wagon features the arrival of

the King of the Moors in what he calls the land of '*true Religion*', to do homage to the country and the City which sent out the merchants '*Whose* Truth *did with our Spirits hold Commerse*' (sig. CI^r). London's trade is justified not simply in terms of its internal benefit to the City, but as a way to propagate the true faith.

Such markedly Protestant features point towards an important explanatory function in the pageants, as they justify the wealth and power of the mercantile elite by suggesting that all eventually share in the prosperity, and by transforming commerce into religion. So in *Troia-Nova Triumphans* Virtue explains Swinnerton's function as Lord Mayor:

> *Thou must be now*, Stirring, *and* Resolute;
> *To be what thou art* Sworne, (*a waking Eye*)
> *A farre off* (*like a* Beacon) *to descry*
> *What stormes are coming, and* (*being come*) *must then*
> *Shelter with spred armes, the poor'st* Citizen.
> *Set* Plenty *at thy* Table, *at thy* Gate
> Bounty, *and* Hospitallity: *hee's most* Ingrate
> *Into whose lap the* Publicke-weale *hauing powr'd*
> *Her* Golden shewers, *from* Her *his wealth should hoord*.   (sig. B3^v)

Here the importance of civic hospitality is stressed, and magistracy establishes a duty on the magistrate to return the benefit he has received, otherwise he will be labelled 'Ingrate'. Wealth is no longer simply material, it is now spiritual.

The City as the well-spring of Godly charity became an important theme, incorporating references to works beyond the City boundaries, for example in Webster's 1624 triumph for Sir John Gore. Good works during the mayoralty will result in an honourable memory; they will become, as the title has it, *The Monuments of Honour*. The fourth pageant, 'the *Monument of Charity*',

fashioned like a beautiful Garden with all kinds of flowers, at the foure Corners foure artificiall Bird Cages, with variety of Birds in them: this for the beauty of the Flowers, and melody of the Birds, to represent a Spring in Winter: in the middest of the Garden, under one Elme-tree, sits the famous and worthy Patriot Sir *Thomas White*; who had a dreame that hee should build a Colledge where two bodies of an Elme sprang from one roote. (lines 244–51)

The text goes on to describe the foundation of 'the Colledge of St *John Baptist* in Oxford' (line 263; see also lines 250–65). Next to White in his mayoral gown sits Charity with a pelican in her hand,

Learning on the other side carrying a book, and a model of the
Oxford college behind. Just to emphasise the message, the pageant
carries the models of twenty-four other cities at its edge – all
recipients of White's munificence (lines 280–3). Learning interprets
the spectacle for the new mayor, and emphasises the example that he
should emulate. We are told how White:

> Built Saint *Johns* Colledge – Truth can testifie
> His merrit, whilst his Faith and Charity
> Was the true compasse, measur'd every part,
> And tooke the latitude of his Christian heart;
> Faith kept the center, Charity walkt this round,
> Untill a true circumference was found;
> And may the Impression of this figure strike
> Each worthy Senator to do the like!   (lines 296–303)

The mapping imagery suggests how White's 'true compasse' that
'measur'd every part' literally inscribes the outer edge (the 'true
circumference'), and connects it with the centre. So charity connects
the margins with the centre, and the lines of 'latitude' are transformed into the lines of patronage that bind recipient to donor.

Continually the Lord Mayor's installation exhorts the incumbent
to the key civic duty of charity. In *Chrysanaleia* (1616), for instance,
the lemon tree pageant vehicle (punning on Sir John Lemman's
name) carries a lemon tree and a pelican. The bird represents 'an
excellent type of gouernement in a Magistrate, who, at his meere
entrance into his yeares Office, becometh a very father of the
Family: which though hee bred not, yet by his best endeuour, hee
must labour to bring vp'.[55] Such reiterated injunctions to protect
the poor remind us of other ways in which ritual sought to integrate
the poor into the economy of the City. For example, in the processional order given by William Smythe in 1575, some seventy or eighty
poor men, dressed in blue gowns with red sleeves and caps, follow the
leading standards bearing the arms of the City and the mayor's
company.[56] Their very presence in the procession demonstrates and
enacts the charity of the company and City, tying the poor into the
civic structure represented in the hierarchy of the procession.[57]

It is easy for the modern reader to overlook the significance of the
processional order and processional route. The absence of good
visual evidence for the processional order has led to neglect of the
manner in which the procession literally creates a model of the guild
and City government. The abundant continental illustrations, such

as Matteo Pagan's *Procession of the Doge on Palm Sunday* (1556–9), make very clear the importance of the processional order to an early modern society. As Edwin Muir remarks, the ducal procession in Venice *was* the constitution, its division into *cittadine* (officials) and noble magistrates respectively before and behind the Doge representing civic order.[58] In London the procession divides into guild brethren (from whifflers to livery), then the mayoral officials, then the mayor and the symbols of his office, followed by the aldermen and sheriffs. Despite this slightly different structure, the same basic pattern applies as the Venetian example, with hierarchy and relations of service and patronage in front, and those of more nearly equivalent rank behind.

Thus within the mayoral procession William Smythe described how the members of the mayor's company went first and then:

After them followe Sheriffes officers, and then the Mayor's officers, with other officers of the citie, as the Comon Sergent, and the Chamber-layne; nexte before the Mayor goeth the Sworde Bearer, having on his headd the capp of honor, and the sworde of the citie in his right hande, in a rich skabarde ... on his left hand goeth the Comon Cryer of the cittie, with his great mace ... [then] ... The Mayor ... and with him rydeth the olde Mayor also.[59]

This order reverses the processional order seen before the Guildhall oath ceremony and embodies the changeover of power, yet also its continuity.[60] In the post-Guildhall procession the order ties the new mayor to the institutions of his rule and to the previous incumbent, who, as he accompanied the new mayor, would represent his bond with the aldermanic elite. In this way the procession embodies the dual and simultaneous principles of hierarchy and integration. In one sense the whole civic structure is integrated in the entire procession; but the hierarchical relation of the ruler to his company is expressed in the ascending order of the first section, then the division that his office creates (the vaunted impartiality) marked by his staff and the symbols of his office, and finally he is linked to and integrated into the aldermanic elite through the crucial figure of the previous incumbent.[61]

Other elements also contributed to the integration of the social body. In particular, the heraldic elements in the processions and on the pageants themselves sought to integrate the company into the history of the country and the City. Thus, many of those processing would carry pennants or shields of past eminent members of the

company, or even the company's arms themselves. In 1602 figures of
a lion and camel were included on the ground that the former was
'parte of the Companie's Armes, and the Cammell the Companie's
supporters'; whilst in 1616 a model dolphin appeared on the double
grounds that it belonged to both the mayor's and the company's
arms.[62] Middleton's *Triumphs of Integrity* (1623) included an
'Imperial Canopy, being the ancient arms of the Company', which
appears to have accompanied (or possibly covered) the mayor on
the barge journey from Westminster.[63] The significance of the
combination of heraldry and history is represented in the same
pageant by the chariot of 'Sacred Memory' which,

> presents the never-dying names of many memorable and remarkable
> worthies of this ancient Society, such as were the[n] famous for state and
> government: Sir Henry Fitz-Alwain, Knight ... under the person of
> Government; Sir John Norman ... under the person of Honour; the valiant
> Sir Francis Drake, that rich ornament to memory ... under the person of
> Victory; Sir Simon Eyre ... under the figure of Charity; Sir Richard
> Champion and Sir John Milborne, under the person of Munificence or
> Bounty; Sir Richard Hardell and Sir John Poultney ... under the figures of
> Justice and Piety ... this Chariot drawn by two pelleted lions, being the
> proper supporters of the Company's arms; those two upon the lions
> presenting Power and Honour, the one in a little streamer or banneret
> bearing the Lord Mayor's arms, the other the Company's. (*Integrity*,
> pp. 388–9)

Memory, who speaks from the chariot, concludes that a good magistrate is not created by 'shows, pomp, nor a house of state / Curiously
deck'd', but by virtue and nobility, and who

> ... in his fair deportment there revives
> The ancient fame of all his brothers' lives.   (*Ibid.*, p. 391)

Through such heraldic and historical contexts the Lord Mayor
'became part of a historical continuum, a succession; in the living
union of past and present he acquired his immortality'.[64]

Civic virtues were fostered in an immediate and practical sense by
the magnificence of the processions. Alms were distributed and
clothing given to the poor, who were actively aided through the
amount of work the pageantry provided for the City's economy. As
Richard Mackenny has shown, the costs of the London pageant
were enormous (in 1604, £536 10s 5d, in 1613 a staggering £1,094
11s 11d), but the value to the economy was equally great. The 1604

show generated the equivalent of 10,000 days' work.[65] The conspicuous display that foreign observers such as Puget de la Serre saw (part of the queen mother's entry into London in the late 1630s), with all of the balconies and shops hung with rich silks and clothes, showed not only the variety of London's trade connections, but also practically primed the economy.[66] Some of this filtered down to the poor, mainly in the form of direct charity or the food and clothes they received for their participation, and probably in the form of menial tasks.[67]

The integration achieved through charity was not the only unity sought. For Dekker's *Troia-Nova Triumphans* a great variety of people (including the Elector Palatine) arrived to gaze on the Lord Mayor:

all the streames of *Nobility* and *Gentry*, run with the *Tide* hither. When all *Eares* lye listning for no newes but of *Feasts* and *Triumphs*: All *Eyes* still open to behold them: And all harts and hands to applaud them: When the heape of our *Soueraignes Kingdomes* are drawne in *Little*: and to be seene within the Walles of this City. (sig. A3ᵛ)

Here London epitomises the kingdom, as it did in the 'Londinium' arch; but the significance lies in the way the rhetoric of unity prevailing throughout the whole of *Troia-Nova Triumphans* links civic to national unity. The same occurs in *Triumphs of Re-United Britannia* where the unity of the people in celebrating the election of Holyday echoes the court's joy at the king's proposed union of England and Scotland, to be celebrated later with *Hymenaei*.[68] These extensions of the rhetoric are significant because they highlight the national dimension to the pageantry, linking capital and nation, City and court. The community of the guild generates the community of London, whose spirit in turn links City and court, and whose sense of unity informs the unification of the kingdoms.

Triumphs of Re-United Britannia weaves together guild, civic and national unity in its synthesis of mythologies. Both Britain and London (*qua* Troynovant), each founded by Brutus (a main speaker in the pageant) belong to a civilising process. Brutus explains that England was until his arrival:

> Peopled with men of inciuility,
> Huge and stearne Gyants, keeping company
> With sauage monsters, this was *Albion* then,
> Till I first furnisht thee with ciuill men. (sig. B2ʳ)

The connection between Brutus's 'ciuill men' and civic government would not be lost on a contemporary audience, especially given that the foundation of Troynovant is depicted as part of that civilising of Britain. This relationship is strengthened in the second pageant, which comprises a chariot accompanied by various speakers, who explain the antiquity and purpose of the guild, tying the Merchant Taylors to royal policy and dignity. In particular the guild charter is eulogised as granted by Edward III (a talismanic monarch) for 'preseruing peace and kinde societie' (sig. cɪᵛ). The 'peace and kinde societie', the values of civilisation, are now extended by the arrival of the second Brutus and in the re-unification of Albion and Scotland as Great Britain.

Such depictions of the City and its guilds as part of an ancient civilising process that embodies the values of 'society' or community are common in civic rhetoric and ritual. For example, they recur in *Troia-Nova Triumphans*, where the City's 'Ciuill, Popular govern-ment' is described as an ordered classical building, designed perhaps to recall classical republicanism:

> Twelue *strong* Pillars *it sustaine*;
> *Vpon whose* Capitals, Twelue societies *stand*,
> (Graue *and* well-ordred) *bearing chiefe Command*
> *Within this* City.
>   (sig. ʙ3ʳ)

This building concretises the civilised, ordered and well-founded nature of City- and guild-government, and elaborates a common-place of Renaissance political thought. In classical myth, cities were founded either by Amphion or Orpheus, who drew beasts, rocks and trees with their harmony; in Christian terms cities attempted to repair the damage of the Fall.[69] We might gloss this passage by citing Botero's treatise *Of the Magnificence of Cities* which explains, in 'Of the commodities of Conduct', that cities were founded to facilitate trade, which promoted amity both within the city and between nations:

For his diuine maiestie, willing that men should mutually embrace each other, as members of one body: diuided in such sort his blessings, as to no nation did he giue all things, to the end that others hauing need of vs, and contrary wise we hauing of others, there might grow a Communitie, and from a Communitie Loue, and from Loue an vnitie betweene vs. (*A Treatise*, sig. ᴅɪᵛ)[70]

Herein lies the ultimate justification for London's trade and position.

The appearance of Orpheus in *The Trivmphs of Loue and Antiquity* combines the idea of the City as a civilising institution with the reformation of abuses. Orpheus appears before a 'Wilderness' filled with beasts, which he interprets for Cockayne ('example is the crystall glass'):

> Behold, then, in a rough example here,
> The rude thorny ways thy care must clear;
> Such are the vices in a city sprung,
> As are yon thickets that grow close and strong; ...
> Just such a wilderness is a commonwealth
> That is undrest, unprun'd, wild in her health;
> And the rude multitude the beasts a' the wood,
> That know no laws, but only will and blood;
> And yet by fair example, musical grace,
> Harmonious government of the man in place,
> Of fair integrity and wisdom fram'd,
> They stand as mine do, ravish'd, charm'd, and tam'd:
> Every wise magistrate that governs thus,
> May well be call'd a powerfull Orpheus.   (sigs. $B2^r-B3^r$)

Here, in symbolic terms, are many of the concerns of anti-metropolitan writers, but transformed to the glorification of the magistracy. The pageant simultaneously exhorts Cockayne to resolve the abuses of the City, to become an Orpheus and exercise 'Harmonious government', whilst the allusion to the Orphic myth recalls the origin of the City as a civilising force.

IV

Civic feasts, like the pageants, were a frequent vehicle used to demonstrate the company's magnificence, whilst demonstrating hospitality to its guests. These often included the monarch or court, as in the Merchant Taylors 1607 feast for the election of a new mayor. They also provided ample opportunity for alms-giving. Such feasts might include entertainments in imitation of the court and aristocracy. The 1607 Merchant Taylors banquet featured a musical entertainment, the pageant of a ship suspended from the rafters of the hall, and a speech by Jonson for a child dressed as an angel of gladness.[71] Later in the century Middleton provided seven such entertainments (most included in his *Honourable Entertainments*) for various mayoral celebrations.

Triumphs of Re-United Britannia extols the significance of guild feasts, when Eros notes how Richard II 'To build this body on a stronger frame' instituted the authority of the Master and four keepers of the guild, granted a livery and ordained the annual guild feast on St John the Baptist's day (sig. ci^v). The imagery here points towards unification (the guild as miniature body politic), whilst in the same figure justifying the guild hierarchy. The hospitality offered for the patronal feast symbolises the double integration of the guild within itself, and within national power structures. Several pageants stress the numbers of the royal family or aristocracy who have either feasted with the company or become honorary members.[72]

As with other London rituals these entertainments seek to inculcate the virtues of civic magistracy. Middleton's Cockayne entertainment in particular praises the mayor's justice, and the exemplary lives of his guests, the aldermen. Moreover, it incorporates the unificatory qualities sought on these occasions, as the actual speech (given by a 'Sewer') celebrates the ritualised drinking of a toast (lines 32ff).[73] The feast expresses the concept of the company's

> Noble Welcome, turn'd into
> A Cup of Bounty, and t'adorne the Feast,
> Loaden with loue comes to each worthy Guest;
> And but obserue the manner, there's in that,
> Freenesse exprest, humility, yet State　　　　　　(lines 81–5)

Each of the aldermen were then to drink from a cup (given to the Skinners' Company) in the shape of a cock, which punned on the mayor's name and arms (lines 13–14 and 94–6). The song explains the reciprocal duties that this ceremonial drinking represents:

> *O pledge it round:*
> *The Ceremonies due*
> *Forget not as they were begun to you,*
> *When you are dranke to, y'are by duty led,*
> *First to kisse your hand, then take of the head,*
> *You cannot misse it then,*
> *To put it on and kisse it agen;*
> *The next to whom the Health doth flow,*
> *It taught to honour your Pledge so,*
> *So round, round, round, let it goe*　　　　　　(lines 103–12)

The ritual seeks to bind the mayor, the aldermen and the privy councillors present, and to instil order and harmony.

Other entertainments from the *Honourable Entertainments* dignify various events in the civic calendar and the virtues appropriate to them. Amongst these are military virtue (*Honourable Entertainments* iv, for the 'generall Training') and care for the civic environment and the provision of fresh water (*Honourable Entertainments* iii, for the renewal of visits to the conduit heads). In the 'Entertainment At the House of the Right Honourable Sir *Francis Ihones*' the qualities of hospitality and justice were celebrated. Comus ('the great Sir of Feasts') presented Jones with a dish representing two arms breaking through clouds to support a laurel wreath; the wreath symbolised the mercy and justice he should exercise as a magistrate, and also formed part of the Haberdashers' arms (*HE* vi, lines 3–11). Jones is exhorted to be just and not fear either malice or envy, since as a magistrate he is '*Apolloes* Tree', and so will not be uprooted or struck with malice's lightning (line 64).

The magnificence exemplified in guild feasts did cause anxiety, since they could be interpreted as expressions of the vast wealth and commercial dominance of the livery companies. To counter such charges the civic feasts often stress their temperance – what Dekker epitomised as '*sumptuous Thriftinesse*' (*Troia-Nova Triumphans*, sig. A3ʳ). *Honourable Entertainments* viii, the Christmas celebration for Sir Francis Jones, features a debate between Severity and Levity over the nature of Christmas feasting, which is resolved by Temperance, after both Severity and Levity have ceded precedence to her. She concludes:

> So, Thus things should haue thir becomming grace,
> For *Temperance* fits the Reuerence of this place.   (lines 88–9)

She summons Music, a 'modest Seruant', to 'Raise chast *Delight*' and 'grace' the season (lines 94–5). Such rhetoric carefully distances these aldermanic feasts from the charge of extravagance, and may even locate them as reformed entertainments within the Protestant tradition.

V

Religious observance provided another series of ceremonies designed to integrate community. To accept communion, the recipient was supposed to be in charity with his neighbours, and so the repeated appearance of the mayor and his brethren at communion could be seen as encouraging amity and providing an example

to the wider popular audience.[74] Norton's *Exhortation* to the Lord
Mayor, a guide to civic duties, reminds him of the need to support
preachers to educate the people. Public observance is recommended:

What a thing is the Communyon and incorporatynge of Christ into yow to
the strengtheninge of your owne conscience! What a thinge ys it to the
unitinge of yowr bretherne the Aldermens harts to joine with yowe, and to
quenche all stormes that maye sever the knot of yowr concord and godlie
confederacy together![75]

There were seven regular occasions on which the mayor, accompanied by the companies, processed to services, but other major
feasts were marked with joint communions or attendance at sermons.[76] Among the most important of these was the mayoral procession to the Spittle sermon, involving a procession of the mayor, his
wife, and aldermen, who wore special scarlet liveries to mark the
feast. This procession attracted an audience, and the sermon proper,
or rather the series of sermons preached in Easter Week near St Mary
Spittle in Bishopsgate Without, marked a major occasion in the civic
calendar. From Stow's description we know that sermons were
attended by the bishop and clergy of London, and members of the
court, as well as the civic dignitaries and their wives. They all sat in a
'fair built house', which may have resembled the sermon-house at St
Paul's.[77] Civic integration was furthered by the presence of the
Children of Christ's Hospital, the epitome of civic charity and
concern for the spiritual and physical welfare of London's poor
orphans.[78] The national dimension of civic ceremony is marked in
the attendance of the privy council, who were often invited to feast
with the Lord Mayor afterwards.[79]

The sermons particularly preached charity. Roger Fenton's *A
Sermon Preached at St Mary Spittle on Easter Tuesday 1613* builds on
Galatians 6:7 (*'whatsoeuer a man soweth that shall he also reape'*) to argue
the necessity of alms-giving.[80] The charitable citizens 'strong in
well-doing ... present themselues at this time like *Lazarus* in *Abra-
hams* bosome; a most heauenly ornament vnto this City' (sigs. c7[r–v]).
In an earlier *Sermon Preached at St Mary's Hospital* (1588) Lancelot
Andrewes urged the aldermen to recall their reputation for ordered
governance, celebrated in the suppression of Jack Straw, and to
silence their current detractors through beneficence. Such 'feeding,
clothing, visiting, harbouring, succouring ...' will count at the final
judgement.[81] Indeed Andrewes argues that London deserves defence
because of its famed charity:

Now to them in your just defence I say – for God forbid but while I live I should always defend this honourable city in all truth – to them whom the mist of envy hath so blinded that they can see no good at all done but by themselves, I forbid them, the best of them, to show me in Rhiems or in Rome, or in any popish city Christian, such a show as we have seen here these two days. To day but a handfull of the heap, but yesterday and on Monday the whole heap, even a mighty army of so many good works as there were relieved orphans, 'the chariots' of this city, I doubt not, and 'the horsemen thereof'. (pp. 36–7)

He urges that wealth should not be stored away for private use, but distributed as 'beneficial to society', or bestowed upon some common use, and concludes 'in a word, that you should be lords, knights, aldermen, masters, wardens, and of the livery in good works, as you be several wards and companies'. The sermons thus develop a 'moral economy', placing a duty on the wealthy to justify themselves through alms-giving.[82]

Middleton's two entertainments for the feast after the Spittle sermon express similar praise for the charitable values of the civic elite. The first, a masque of Flora, written for Sir Francis Jones, imagines a '*Garden* of those *Deeds*' (line 93), that is,

> Your Cares, your Charities, the holy Vse
> Of pious exercise. (lines 85–6)

The plants of this garden (markedly similar to Webster's Garden of Charity) are the orphans of Christ's Hospital, who become the 'Cities *Bancke* of *Violets*' (line 98). These horticultural images are then developed as the scent and curative properties of the flowers are presented as reputation or honour and the ability of the alderman to 'apply Ease to his Brothers griefe' (line 118). The colour of the violets is linked to the violet robes worn at the sermon, and the aldermen are hailed as in 'this latter Spring of your graue yeares' and exhorted to be 'greene in Vertues' (lines 175–6).

Whilst this entertainment pastoralises and naturalises the city with considerable sophistication, Middleton's Barkham *Invention* (1623) has Honour appear before the mayor and aldermen, carrying a sheaf of arrows, which are explained in a brief song and dialogue between Base and Mean as 'shafts of justice 'gainst impiety', but 'tied with Mercy's silken band'.[83] The piece has a Protestant emphasis, with '[Religious] conscience' as 'an armed man', and concludes with a specific application to the aldermen present:

For 'tis an emblem that concerns you all.
You of the honourable brotherhood,
Knit all together for the city's good,
In whose grave wisdoms her fair strength does stand,
You are the sheaf; the magistrate's the band
Whose love is wound about you. Witness be
His bounty and welcome, both most free.
And as this day you saw the golden sheaf
Of this bless'd city's works in the relief
Of the poor fatherless, may you behold
That sheaf of glory that makes dross of gold.
Th' Almighty's arrows on your enemies fall,
And Heaven's arm'd arms protect you all.   (*Invention*, p. 376)

This speech summarises the concerns of civic ritual in early modern London. The image typifies the interplay between integration and differentiation that has been traced throughout the civic rhetoric and ritual of the period. The idea of 'brotherhood' is played against the differentiating force of the magistrates, yet that apparent hierarchy is metamorphosed into another force for unity ('the band / Whose love is wound about') to produce a unified social body. Equally the emphases on piety, on charity, on honour ('the sheaf of glory'), on the transformation of commerce into religious vocation, and most centrally, the marked Protestant tone, all find their prefigurations and echoes in the other civic shows.

VI

Beyond the rhetoric of brotherhood the reality of inter-guild relations was more complex. Much civic ritual is designed to instil inter-guild amity precisely because competition between guilds was marked and there were frequent disputes over trade demarcation. Indeed, this competition might even extend into the ceremonial arena. For instance, in 1602 the Merchant Taylors, hearing that the Goldsmiths had acquired an elaborately decorated tilt cloth for the barge, ordered a similar cloth embroidered with their own company's arms.[84] Doubtless the high cost of the pageants was fuelled by this competition, as the Ironmongers' pageant *Campbell* (1609) dolefully suggests when it admits its meagre resources have failed to produce the requisite magnificence.[85]

In general, however, civic ceremony sought to minimise these inter-guild conflicts, as both *Chruso-thriambos* (1611) and *Chrysanaleia*

(1616) demonstrate.[86] These shows present images of past conflicts between the Goldsmiths and Fishmongers. The origin of or reasons for the historical precedence struggle remain unclear, but by the mid-fifteenth century the members of the two guilds exchanged liveries and feasted each other on St Dunstan's day to celebrate their amity, and the two companies symbolised this concord through the exchange of part of each company's coat of arms. In *Chruso-thriambos* one of the pageants consisted of an 'Orfery' to symbolise the Goldsmiths' craft, preceded by emblems of a merman and mermaid quartered with a golden unicorn, to recall the unity of the two companies.[87] In *Chrysanaleia* the pageant of the King of the Moors on a golden leopard echoes the leopards' heads in the Goldsmiths' coat of arms, whilst the Moor, as the prefatory epistle explains, alludes to guild mythology about the joint re-edification, first of two gates of Jerusalem and then Moor gate and Cripple gate of 'England's Jerusalem' (sigs. A4^{r-v}). Both pageants refer to the causes of current tension, the commercial rivalry and desire for dominance through display (hinted at in the suggestion of shared costs for the pageant) and banish them by the resurrection of past amity.

I have stressed the variety of strategies through which civic ceremony presents an idealised image of London and its civic ethos. There is, however, a double edge to much of the panegyric. The City is exhorted to further virtue through praise of its current strengths, an instance of '*laudando praecipere*, when by telling men what they are, they represent them what they should be'.[88] The manner is almost Jonsonian. This is particularly true of Dekker's *Troia-Nova Triumphans* and Middleton's *Triumphs of Truth*, both of which stress the temptations of office and the moral re-armament needed to achieve civic virtue. We should not forget that Dekker also criticised the City, as in *The Seven Deadly Sins of London*, or Middleton in his satire of citizen behaviour in his London comedies. In this respect both Dekker and Middleton function to the City as Jonson does to the court: they aim to produce virtue through an adroit mixture of praise and criticism.

In fact, several civic ceremonies voice criticism as well as deflect it. *Chruso-thriambos*, for example, appears to attack royal extravagance, even though the companies themselves were open to the same charge.[89] This kind of double reading of civic ritual was clearly available to contemporary Englishmen, as Wotton's reading of the 1606 Corpus Christi celebrations in Venice shows. Yet in general the civic ceremonies emphasise harmony and reconciliation with the court. Thus in *The Honourable Entertainments* Flora appears to justify obedience to the sovereign (*HE* ix). The context was a brawl between London apprentices and servants of the Spanish ambassador Gondomar, who regarded the punishment of the apprentices as insufficiently stringent.[90] The king agreed and appeared at the Guildhall, where he privately admonished the aldermen to 'looke better to the government'.[91] Flora explains that

> To chasten, where he loues, it is the Seale
> Of the *Almighties* fauor, *He* doth deale
> So with his *Chosen*, doe not languish then,
> Thou *Prince* of *Citties*, cause the *King* of *Men*
> Divinely did reproue thee, know, tis Loue,
> Thou art his Chosen *Cittie*, and wilt prooue
> (As thou hast euer beene) faithfull and free,
> The *Chamber* of his sweete Security.   (lines 59–66)

This 'need not be read as a craven acknowledgement of subservience to the Crown but rather as a pious hope for future harmony which mutual accommodation has revealed'.[92] The speech treads a careful line between the City as 'faithfull' and 'free', skirting the difficult issue of London's freedoms and the limits of royal jurisdiction that the case raised. The transformation of a source of potential conflict into an act of 'Loue' exemplifies exactly the way civic ceremony seeks to reconcile tensions, and to incorporate that solution in its moment of production.

Civic ceremony seeks to embody reconciliation and inculcate order, not simply in its explicit rhetoric, but in its very form, especially the processional element, which actually manifested the whole social body and constitution of the City for its citizens. It acted in its content, its imagery and its performance to provide models by which both governors and governed might behave, and understand their place within the urban structure. It is unsurprising, then, that when Aldgate was rebuilt between 1606 and 1609, the civic authorities presented London as a domain of brotherly love. The re-edified gate carried

two feminine personages, the one South-ward, appearing to be Peace, with a silver Dove upon one hand, and a guilded wreath or Garland in the other. On the North-side standeth Charity, with a child at her brest, and another led in her hand. Implying as (I conceive) that where Peace, and Love and Charity do prosper, and are truly embraced, that Citie shall be for ever blessed.[93]

NOTES

'Spectacle of the Realm' derives from a 1572 proclamation cited in M. Berlin, 'Civic Ceremony in Early Modern London', *Urban History Yearbook* (1986) 15–27, p. 23. Earlier versions of this chapter were presented at Leicester and Warwick Universities and I should like to thank those present for their constructive criticism, especially Ian Archer, Peter Clark and Lois Potter. As always thanks go to Julia Briggs, and also to Jeremy Gregory and Jan Hewitt. The faults are mine.

1 L. P. Smith ed., *The Life and Letters of Sir Henry Wotton*, 2 vols. (Oxford, 1907), p. 350; cited in E. Muir, *Civic Ritual in Renaissance Venice* (Princeton, 1981), pp. 229–30, p. 230.

2 *Ibid.*, p. 229.

3 D. Bergeron, *English Civic Pageantry, 1558–1640* (London, 1971). G. Kipling, 'Triumphal Drama: Form in English Civic Pageantry', *Renaissance Drama*, ns 8 (1977) 37–56, explores the continuity with medieval practice and emphasises the triumphal aspect of civic ritual. Bergeron himself updates his views on pageantry in D. Bergeron, ed., *Pageantry in the Shakespearean Theatre* (Athens, Georgia, 1985), pp. 1–16.

4 For example, G. K. Paster, 'The Idea of London in Masque and Pageant' in Bergeron, ed., *Pageantry*, pp. 48–64, and S. Wells, 'Jacobean City Comedy and the Ideology of the City', *English Literary History* 48 (1981) 37–60, both explore the interaction of court and City, but from rather rigidly dichotomous historical models. The most useful essays on civic pageantry remain M. C. Bradbrook, 'The Politics of Pageantry' in *Shakespeare in His Context; The Constellated Globe*, Collected Papers of Muriel Bradbrook, vol. IV (Brighton, 1989), pp. 95–109; and G. Kipling, 'Triumphal Drama' 37–56.

5 The most useful general works on London history are I. W. Archer, 'Governors and Governed in Late Sixteenth Century London, *c.* 1560–1603: Studies in the Achievement of Stability', unpublished D.Phil thesis, Oxford, 1988, and S. Brigden, *London Before the Reformation* (Oxford, 1989). I have also benefited from A. L. Beier and R. Findlay, eds., *London 1500–1700: The Making of the Metropolis* (London, 1986), esp. the introduction, 'The Significance of the Metropolis', pp. 1–34.

6 Berlin, 'Civic Ceremony', *passim.*, provides a useful survey. Compare C. Phythian-Adams, 'Ceremony and the Citizen: the Communal Year at Coventry, 1450–1500', in P. Clark ed., *The Early Modern Town* (London, 1976), pp. 106–28.

7 G. Wickham, *Early English Stages*, 3 vols. (London, 1959–81), II Pt 1, pp. 209–44, and Bergeron, *Civic Pageantry* pp. 245–72 and *passim.*

8 M. James, 'Ritual, Drama, and Social Body in Late Medieval England', *Past and Present* 88 (1983) 3–29, esp. pp. 4–5.

9 *Ibid.* 6–10. Compare T. Sorge, 'The Failure of Orthodoxy in *Coriolanus*', in J. E. Howard and M. F. O'Connor, eds., *Shakespeare Reproduced: The Text in History and Ideology* (London, 1987), pp. 225–41; A. Fletcher and

J. Stevenson, eds., *Order and Disorder in Early Modern England* (Cambridge, 1985), pp. 2–3 and p. 196.

10 J. Stow, *The Survey of London*, ed. H. B. Wheatley, rev. edn (London, 1987), p. 93. Hereafter *Survey*.

11 Berlin, 'Civic Ceremony', 19.

12 It seems to me that Renaissance civic ritual can profitably be compared to the type of 'aesthetic or narrative form' that is 'seen to be ideological in its own right, with the function of inventing imaginary or formal "solutions" to unresolvable social contradictions'. Ritual, in effect, enacts social unity, even in its movement through the city, which establishes a narrative thread linking the diverse sectors of the city. See F. Jameson, *The Political Unconscious* (London, 1983), p. 79.

   See also Kipling, 'Triumphal Drama', *passim*, on continuity with medieval antecedents; James, 'Ritual', 12, emphasises the importance of outsiders viewing civic ritual. Berlin, 'Civic Ceremony', stresses differences from medieval ritual forms, arguing that the secularised mayoral shows 'dwelt on the celebration of the office of lord mayor' (p. 19), and 'the privatized values of civic honour and pecuniary worth rather than the structural integration of contending social groups within communities' (p. 20). Berlin minimises the important integrative/differentiative paradox in civic ritual, and underplays the religious continuity, with patronal symbols retained even into the 1630s. The process is not so much one of secularisation, but rather one of adaption and reformation of the older religious modes to new ends – a typical strategy of English Protestantism. On London and Protestantism, see P. Collinson, 'The Godly Town', in *The Birthpangs of Protestant England: Religious and Cultural Change in the Sixteenth and Seventeenth Centuries* (London, 1988), pp. 28–59.

13 P. Clark, 'Devouring Capital', *TLS*, October 20–26, 1989, p. 1,162 (review of S. Rappaport *Worlds Within Worlds*), and Archer, 'Governors and Governed', pp. 11 and 21 on evidence.

14 Archer, 'Governors and Governed', p. 2. Archer, p. 10, cites Peter Clark's view that 'at certain times, as in London in 1595, it seemed as if the whole community might disintegrate'. Recent pessimistic interpretations can be found in M. Power, 'London and the Control of the "Crisis" of the 1590s', *History* 70 (1985) 371–85, and 'A Crisis Reconsidered: Social and Demographic Dislocation in London in the 1590s', *London Journal* 12 (1986) 134–45.

15 S. Rappaport, 'Social Structure and Mobility in Sixteenth Century London: Part 1', *London Journal* 9 (1983) 107–135, and 'Social Structure and Mobility in Sixteenth Century London', *London Journal*, 10 (1984) 107–34. V. Pearl, 'Change and Stability in Seventeenth Century London', *London Journal*, 5 (1979) 3–33, and 'Social Policy in Early Modern London', in H. Lloyd-Jones, V. Pearl, and B. Worden eds., *History and Imagination: Essays in Honour of H. R. Trevor-Roper* (London,

1981), pp. 115–31. E. Jones, 'London in the Seventeenth Century: An Ecological Approach', *London Journal*, 6 (1980) 121–33.

16 K. Lindley, 'Riot Prevention and Control in Early Stuart London', *Transactions of the Royal Historical Society* XXXIII (1983) 109–26, p. 126. Rappaport, 'Social Structure', *passim*, emphasises social stability through participation. Archer, 'Governors and Governed', pp. 9–28, esp. pp. 13 and 17.

17 Archer, 'Governors and Governed', pp. 28–106, esp. pp. 60–73. J. Boulton, 'Residential Mobility in Seventeenth Century Southwark', *Urban History Yearbook* (1986) 15–36. See also J. Boulton, 'The Limits of Formal Religion: The Administration of Holy Communion in Late Elizabethan and Early Stuart London', *London Journal*, 10 (1984) 135–54.

18 Archer, 'Governors and Governed', pp. 68, 3, 7, 60–73, 39.

19 James I, 'Speech in Star Chamber' (1616), in C. H. McIlwain, ed., *The Political Works of James I* (Cambridge, Mass., 1918), p. 343.

20 London's defenders, such as John Stow, trod a narrow line, on one hand at pains to stress both governmental stability and civic independence, on the other hand countering claims that London held too many rights. Stow's 'Discourse' stressed the rights of the City, suggested that cities were a bulwark against tyranny, yet still placed London 'in respect of the whole realm' as 'but a citizen and no city, a subject and no free estate': see *Survey*, pp. 482–500, esp. p. 491.

21 *Ibid.*, p. 485.

22 R. Helgerson, 'The Land Speaks: Cartography, Chorography and Subversion in Renaissance England', in S. Greenblatt, ed., *Representing the English Renaissance* (Berkeley, Calif., 1988), pp. 327–61.

23 *A Calendar of Dramatic Records in the Books of the Livery Companies of London 1485–1640*, ed. D. J. Gordon and J. Robertson, Malone Society Collections, vol. 3 (Oxford, 1954), pp. 60 (1602), 175 (1602 book), 177–80 (payments to Munday). Hereafter MSC 3.

24 R. C. Bald, 'Middleton's Civic Employments', *Modern Philology* 31 (1933) 65–78, p. 67; G. Bentley notes that Middleton wrote '*Annales*' of the City (now lost), *The Jacobean and Caroline Stage*, 7 vols. (Oxford, 1941–68), iv, p. 858.

25 MSC 3, p. 176. See also W. S. Prideaux, *Memorials of the Goldsmiths' Company*, 2 vols. (London, 1913), i, p. 114.

26 A. Munday, *A Briefe Chronicle of the Successe of Times* (London, 1611), sigs. A2[r]–A3[v].

27 *Ibid.*, sigs. 2N4[r]ff. Munday's book should not be seen in isolation, since it belongs to a general fascination with the antiquity of the city and its institutions, illustrated by the list of mayors, aldermen and City wards given in manuscript commonplace books and in printed pamphlets. Archer, 'Governors and Governed', p. 61, discusses the commonplace books of Richard Hill and John Collyns; see also W.I., *A View of All the right honourable the Lord Mayors of London* (London, 1601).

28 *Survey*, p. 490.

29 Anon, *The Merchants New-Royall Exchange* (London, 1604) [STC 16784], sigs. 12r–v.

30 Archer, 'Governors and Governed', p. 35; R. Ashton, 'Popular Entertainment and Social Control in Later Elizabethan and Stuart London', *London Journal*, 9 (1983) 3–19; A. Barton, 'London Comedy and the Ethos of the City', *London Journal*, 4 (1978) 158–80; P. Burke, 'Popular Culture in Seventeenth-Century London', in B. Reay ed., *Popular Culture in Seventeenth-Century England* (Beckenham, 1985), pp. 31–58; and L. Manley, 'Proverbs, Epigrams, and Urbanity in Renaissance London', *English Literary Renaissance*, 15 (1985) 247–76. See also Sir William Craven's donations to Burnsall, cited in C. M. Clode, *The Early History of the Guild of Merchant Taylors* II, pp. 206–31, esp. p. 306.

31 S. D. Amussen, 'Gender, Family and the Social Order, 1560–1726', in Fletcher and Stevenson *Order and Disorder*, pp. 196–217, esp. pp. 196–201.

32 Cited in Clode, *Early History*, I, p. 393.

33 Raymond Williams defines tradition not as 'an inert, historicized segment of a social structure', but as 'a *selective tradition*: an intentionally selective version of a shaping past and a pre-shaped present, which is then powerfully operative in the process of social and cultural definition and identification'. See R. Williams, *Marxism and Literature* (Oxford, 1977), p. 115.

34 Berlin, 'Civic Ceremony', p. 15; Phythian-Adams, 'Ceremony and the Citizen', pp. 108–9.

35 Phythian-Adams, 'Ceremony and the Citizen', p. 109.

36 G. von Bulow, trans., 'Journey through England and Scotland Made by Lupold von Wedel in the Years 1584 and 1585', *Transactions of the Royal Historical Society*, ns IX (1895) 223–70, p. 252.

37 S. Brigden, 'Youth and the English Reformation', *Past and Present*, 103 (1988) 67–112, pp. 87–93.

38 Bodleian MS Gough London 10, fol. 13^r, 'The Othe of the Wardens Off Goldsmyths'. Reference from Brigden, *ibid.*, p. 87.

39 *The Oath of euery Free-man of the City of London* (London, *c.* 1610) [STC 16764].

40 R. Fenton, *A Sermon Preached the 8. day of May 1615 in the Parish of S. Stephen in Walbrooke London. At an anniuersarie Solemnitie and assemblie of the Companie of Grocers of London. In commemoration of their ancient and first beginning to be a Companie* (London, 1615), sigs. A5^r, A7^{r-v}. See also sigs. B4^{r-v}.

41 R. T. D. Sayle, *The Lord Mayors' Pageants of the Merchant Taylors' Company in the 15th, 16th and 17th Centuries* (London, 1931), p. 4, and *The Barges of the Merchant Taylors' Company* (London, 1933), pp. 2–4; von Wedel describes the barge procession in detail: see 'Journey', p. 252; and compare Busino, 'the ships were beautifully decorated with ballus-

trades and various paintings. They carried immense banners and countless pennons' (MSC 3, xxviii r.2).

42 Sir Henry Montague, speech to James I, 29 October 1607. Cited in J. Nichols, *The Progresses of James I*, 4 vols. (London, 1828), II, pp. 155–7. Transcribed from BL MS Cotton Julius CXI fol. 178.

43 *Ibid.*, pp. 156–7.

44 Thomas Middleton, *The Trivmphs of Loue and Antiquity* (London, 1619), sig. B1^r.

45 Sayle, *Barges*, p. 49, gives the order for the 1610 procession for Prince Henry's installation 'accordinge to . . . place, device, and degree . . .'.

46 John Webster, *The Monuments of Honour*, in *The Complete Works of John Webster*, ed. F. L. Lucas, 4 vols. (London, 1927) III, pp. 311–39, lines 40–3.

47 Compare *The Trivmphs of Loue and Antiquity*, sig. D1^r:

> *You are by this the Cities Bride-groome prou'd,*
> *And She stands wedded to her best Belou'd:*
> *Then be, according to your Morning-Vows,*
> *A Careful Husband, to a Louing Spouse.*

48 Two texts of *The Magnificent Entertainment* survive, Jonson's *B. Jon: His Part of King James His Royall and Magnificent Entertainment* (London, 1604), and Dekker's *The Magnificent Entertainment* (London, 1604), and testify to disagreements about the purpose and approach to the entry. See Bergeron, *Civic Pageantry*, pp. 71–89; and J. Gasper, *The Dragon and the Dove: The Plays of Thomas Dekker* (Oxford, 1990), pp. 36–43, who emphasises the stylistic and ideological differences between the contributions.

49 Ships appeared in 1604, 1605, 1613, 1623; an ocean with moving mermaids and tritons in 1609; Neptune in 1612; a seahorse in 1606; and the Thames (as Thamesis) in 1603–4.

50 A. Munday, *The Trivmphes of re-vnited Britannia* (London, 1605), sig. A4^v.

51 Barton, 'London Comedy', pp. 176–8, discusses Gresham's role in civic myth.

52 On dramatic coherence, see Bergeron, *Civic Pageantry*, p. 71; for the politics, see D. Norbrook, '"The Masque of Truth": Court Entertainment and International Protestant Politics in the Early Stuart Period', *The Seventeenth Century*, 1 (1986) 81–110: esp. p. 93.

53 See esp. *Troia-Noua Triumphans. London Triumphing. . .* (London, 1612), sig. B1^v.

54 Middleton, *The Triumphs of Truth* (London, 1613), sig. A1^r; on 'reformation' see D. Norbrook, 'The Reformation of the Masque' in D. Lindley, ed., *The Court Masque* (Manchester, 1984), pp. 94–110, p. 96.

55 A. Munday, *Chrysanaleia: The Golden Fishing* (London, 1616), sig. B2^r.

56 Sayle, *Pageants*, p. 2, William Smythe's account (1572) from BL MS Cotton Vitellius LV. Compare the early seventeenth-century order given in appendix 1, p. 148.

57 In the seventeenth century 'Marshalling', above the poor the order
then ascends from whifflers, through bachelors, the livery, the officers of
the City, the mayor flanked by the common cryer with the mace, the
Sword bearer and the last Lord Mayor, followed by the aldermen, and
is rounded off with the sheriffs. Sayle, *Pageants*, p. 148. During the
procession the pageant joined the parade in front of the mayor,
although the exact position remains unclear from the accounts. See also
Kipling, 'Triumphal Drama', 49.

58 Muir, *Civic Ritual*, pp. 189–211 and plate 7 (A–D), esp. pp. 190 and 192.

59 Sayle, *Pageants*, p. 3.

60 Von Wedel 'Journey' 252.

61 Berlin, 'Civic Ceremony' 15.

62 Sayle, *Pageants*, p. 60; *Chrysanaleia*, sig. B1^v.

63 Middleton, *The Triumphs of Integrity*, in *The Works of Thomas Middleton*,
ed. A. H. Bullen, 8 vols. (London, 1885), VII, pp. 379–96, p. 385.

64 Bradbrook, 'The Politics of Pageantry' 106. This is a particularly good
example of the 'selective tradition' discussed by Raymond Williams,
Marxism and Literature.

65 R. Mackenny, *Traders and Tradesmen* (Beckenham, 1987), pp. 155–65,
esp. table 4.1.

66 Puget de la Serre, *Histoire de l'Entree de La Reigne Mere Dv Roy Tres-
Chrestien Dans La Grande Bretaigne* (London, 1639), sigs. F2^{r-v}.

67 MSC 3, 62 and 67 (1604) includes gowns and food for the poor, whilst
in 1610 they received direct charity (MSC 3, 79). The women who
cleaned the 'house' and washed the linen in 1604 may well have been
members of the poor (MSC 3, 66).

68 On the union and drama, see A. Patterson, *Censorship and Interpretation:
The Conditions of Writing and Reading in Early Modern England* (Madison,
Wis., 1984), pp. 58–73.

69 G. Botero, *A Treatise Concerning the Causes of the Magnificence of Cities*
(London, 1606), sig. B1^v.

70 Compare *Survey*, p. 484: 'And whereas commonwealths and kingdoms
cannot have ... any surer foundation than the love and goodwill of one
man towards another, that also is closely bred and maintained in cities,
where men by mutual society and companying together, do grow to
alliances, commonalities, and corporations.'

71 See Clode, *Early History*, I, pp. 275-318. The feast cost £11,061 5s 1d
(p. 307). On civic hospitality, see F. Heal, *Hospitality in Early Modern
England* (Oxford, 1990), and see also B. R. Masters, 'The Lord Mayor's
Household before 1600', in A. E. J. Hollander and W. Kellaway, eds.,
Studies in London History (London, 1970), pp. 97–112, on the growth of
feasting facilities.

72 For example, *Troia-Nova Triumphans* emphasises the honorary guild
members, sigs. C2^r–C3^r.

73 Thomas Middleton, *Honourable Entertainments (1621)*, ed. R. C. Bald

(Oxford, 1953) (hereafter *HE*); for Barkham entertainment, see *Works of Middleton*, VII, pp. 369–78.

74 The *Booke of Common Prayer* (London, 1603) insists on 'godly vnitie' as a pre-condition to communion (sig. M3^r). I owe this point to J. R. Mulryne.

75 J. P. Collier, ed., *Illustrations of Old English Literature*, 3 vols. (London, 1866), III, pp. 1–17; extracts are given in L. Manley, ed., *London In The Age of Shakespeare: An Anthology* (Beckenham, 1986), pp. 182–3.

76 Berlin, *Civic Ceremony*, and *Survey*, p. 476.

77 *Survey*, p. 151. For the sermon house at St Paul's (featured in a painting now at the Society of Antiquaries) see R. Somerville, 'St Paul's Cathedral Repairs; The Propaganda of Henry Farley', *London Topographical Record*, 25 (1988) 163–75.

78 E. H. Pearce, *Annals of Christ's Hospital* (London, 1901), pp. 217–27.

79 J. Stow, *A Survay of London*, ed. A. Munday (London, 1618), sig. Y2^r.

80 Roger Fenton, *A Sermon Preached at St Mary Spittle on Easter Tuesday 1613* (London, 1616), sig. A2^r.

81 Lancelot Andrewes, *A Sermon Preached at St Mary's Hospital, on the tenth of April, being Wednesday in Easter Week, 1588*, in Andrewes, *Works*, ed. Bliss and Wilson, Library of Anglo-Catholic Theology, 11 vols. (London, 1841–51), V, pp. 36–7, 40, 39, 17.

82 E. P. Thompson, 'The Moral Economy of the English Crowd in the Eighteenth Century', *Past and Present*, 50 (1971) 76–136.

83 See *Works of Middleton*, VII, pp. 369–78, p. 375.

84 Sayle, *Pageants*, pp. 60–1, and *Barges*, p. 3.

85 A. Munday, *Camp-Bell, or the Iron-Mongers' Faire Field* (London, 1609), sig. B4^r. The Ironmongers' Court Book for 3 November 1609 notes: 'Att this court Mr Anthonie Mondaye came into Courte and the obiections then made weare theise, that the children weare not instructed in their speeches ... that the Musick and singinge weare wantinge, the apparrell most of it old and borrowed' (MSC 3, 76).

86 I rely on J. G. Nichols, 'On the Amity Formed Between the Company of Fishmongers and Goldsmiths', *Archaeologia*, 30 (1859) 499–513.

87 J. H. P. Pafford, ed., *Chruso-thriambos* (London, 1962), pp. 26 and 35–6.

88 J. Pitcher, ed., *Francis Bacon: The Essays* (Harmondsworth, 1985), p. 215.

89 L. S. Marcus, 'City Metal and Country Mettle: The Occasion of Ben Jonson's *Golden Age Restored*', in Bergeron, ed. *Pageantry*, pp. 26–47, esp. p. 31.

90 M. Williams, 'Dramatic Technique in Thomas Middleton's Later Plays', unpublished D.Phil thesis, Oxford, 1990, pp. 126–7, 132.

91 *Calendar of State Papers (Domestic)* 120, no. 74, cited in Williams, 'Dramatic Technique', p. 132.

92 *Ibid.*

93 Stow, *Survay*, ed. Munday, p. 231. Stow, *A Survey of London*, ed. J. Strype, 2 vols. (London, 1720), I, p. 16, adds further details.

CHAPTER 7

The Reformation plays on the public stage

Julia Gasper

I

From 1602 to 1605, the period following the Essex rebellion, a spate of plays about the Reformation appeared in the public theatres of London. *Sir Thomas Wyatt*, by Dekker and Webster, was probably the first of these, although we know it only in a revised and pirated version of 1607. After Queen Elizabeth's death came Thomas Heywood's *If You Know Not Me You Know Nobody, or, The Troubles of Queen Elizabeth*, which was followed by a sequel, *If You Know Not Me You Know Nobody Part II*, whose conclusion features the Armada victory. Both were performed by the Queen's Men, possibly at the Red Bull or otherwise at the Curtain. The Prince's Men competed by offering Samuel Rowley's *When You See Me You Know Me*, concerned with the reign of Henry VIII, and Dekker's *The Whore of Babylon*, an allegory about Elizabeth's reign. Somewhat later, in 1613, came Shakespeare's and Fletcher's *King Henry VIII*.

Many of these plays have been regarded in a patronising, dismissive way by literary critics, and labelled as 'popular'; they are supposed to have catered to public taste in a commercial and therefore inartistic way.[1] But if this popularity is to be credited, it is the very factor which may attract the notice of the historian who wishes to read the plays as documents, and use them to address controversial historical issues. Not that there are any non-controversial issues of the late Tudor and early Stuart period: indeed, to attempt this kind of reading is to venture onto a minefield, and the undertaking is all the more perilous because the kind of evidence provided by drama is some of the hardest of all to interpret.

Most of the plays listed above have also been objected to on the grounds of their inaccuracy, yet there is no such thing as an accurate history play. Those which enjoy high cultural and artistic prestige,

particularly Shakespeare's, are as fictional as any others. The Jacobean plays on the Reformation are texts which cannot really be
classified as fiction or pure non-fiction. Again, should we regard the
authors as early historians, or as contemporaries participating personally in the religious–political issues of the Reformation period?
They seem to be a combination of the two, and this is a conundrum
before we even consider such questions as the influence of censorship, or whether it is possible to construct a picture of the audience's
beliefs and attitudes from the plays offered to them in the public
theatres. Who were the audience, and if a play was successful at the
box-office does that necessarily mean that they, and hence a majority of Londoners, agreed with what the play was saying – always
assuming that we ourselves can agree on what it is saying? With six
different plays, we might come up with six pictures, or we might
attempt a composite one. And did anybody in this period use the
stage for what we would call deliberate propaganda – even suppos-
ing that deliberation is the point?

To dwell too much on these assorted hazards might discourage us
from looking at the plays themselves at all, but they have received
some careful and sensitive consideration from recent critics, particularly Margot Heinemann and Judith Spikes. Heinemann has
written that Heywood's *If You Know Not Me You Know Nobody*
glorifies great merchants like Sir Thomas Gresham and rejoices in
the harmonious relationship between them and the crown.[2] Judith
Spikes has treated the plays as a group and chooses to emphasise
their common elements. Observing that all the Jacobean history
plays concern Tudor history, and that they all draw on John Foxe
for at least some of their source material, Spikes argues that they
form together a single, national myth, and that this myth, deriving
from Foxe, concerns England as an 'elect nation'.[3] By this term
Spikes means the theory that the whole of England was collectively
predestined, in the Calvinist sense, to salvation, and that God had a
special and unique role for England to play as Leader of the True
Church. This theory derived from Haller's study of Foxe. Providential history is one way of describing the plays, but whether Foxe
did conceive England to be an elect nation is now questioned by
many scholars, such as Katherine Robbins Firth and Richard
Bauckham.[4] And while the plays obviously do possess common
elements, they are far from being unanimous or consistent with each
other. It is truer to say that they offer a spectrum of views produced

by authors who were all attempting to mythologise and interpret the events of the Reformation for their Jacobean audience. The political harmony and optimism of the plays is easy to exaggerate too.

One of the most fundamental questions the dramatists had to grapple with was whether the English Reformation had been a popular movement or something imposed by royal decree on the majority of the subjects. This is a highly controversial issue among present-day historians, as Adams has discussed in his essay in this volume. Some historians, such as Christopher Haigh, argue that the Henrician Reformation was essentially an act of state, which involved the destruction of popular Catholicism.[5] This leads to the question of whether the English Reformation had reinforced or, as a popular movement, perhaps even undermined the power of the crown. What, anyway, was the Reformation? Was it the Henrician schism, or the reforms introduced over the next generation, in the reigns of Edward VI and Elizabeth? A tension between Protestantism and the demands of absolute monarchy is detectable in most of the plays, whatever stance they adopt.

Foxe's *Actes and Monuments* presents the English Reformation as a popular movement, one which had its roots in the religious dissent of Wycliffe and the Lollards and in an earlier True Church that had come to England even before Roman Catholicism. The followers of Wycliffe, many of whom were regarded by Foxe as martyrs, had been particularly numerous in the south-east and London where the theatres were.[6] But this view of events, disseminated by one of the most widely read books of its time, was not shared by King James. In *Basilicon Doron* James contrasted England with Scotland:

But the reformation of Religion in Scotland, being extraordinarily wrought by God, wherein many things were inordinately done by a populare tumult and rebellion ... and not proceeding from the Princes ordour, as it did in our neighbour country of England, as likewise in Denmarke, and sundry parts of Germanie; some fierie spirited men in the ministerie, gote such a guyding of the people at that time of confusion, as finding the guste of gouernment sweete, they begouth to fantasie to themselues, a Democratick form of gouernment...

and he warns Prince Henry against these 'Puritanes, very pestes in the Churche & commonweale'.[7] If King James found views such as Foxe's pestilential and democratic, it is strange that Foxe today has such a reputation as an absolutist. It is a pity that there are no plays from this period about the Scottish Reformation, but it was probably a subject too hot to handle.

In 1593 the Admiral's Men (precursors of the Prince's Men who performed *The Whore of Babylon* and *When You See Me You Know Me*) had put on Marlowe's *The Massacre at Paris*, a play in which the Catholic League displays unsurpassable treachery and brutality, and poses a threat to the power of the weak kings of France. Militant Protestants liked to portray Catholicism as a threat to the power of the crown: it suited their purposes. Whether militant Protestantism was also a threat to the crown's power was a stickier question. They did not like to profess it openly, but there is much literary evidence, sometimes of a subtle kind. It is very difficult to back-date the friction between Calvinism and absolutism; in fact it is doubtful whether there was ever much of a honeymoon between them. In the case of Foxe, the further his subject-matter is from home, the less careful he is to defend the authority of secular rulers. Not only did he canonise many common English folk who had been burnt as heretics or agitators under monarchs from Richard II to Henry VIII, but when relating the history of the religious wars in Bohemia he clearly takes the side of the Hussites, who went to war against their emperors and kings for the cause of religion.[8]

Calvin's teaching on 'Politicke Power' in the closing section of his *Institutes of the Christian Religion* (1536, expanded 1541 and 1560) is not a straightforward one; in fact it is remarkably inconsistent and contradictory. At the outset he says that there are 'two kindes of gouernment in man ... one which consisteth in the soule or in the inwarde man ... the other, which perteineth only to the ciuile and outwarde righteousnesse of maners'. Though innocent enough at first glance, this could be taken to mean that the governors of the civil and outward realm ought to have no jurisdiction over the inward man. He goes on to say that he seeks a middle way between 'on the one syde, mad and barbarous men [who] do furiously go about to ouerthrowe thys order stablished by God: and on the other side the flatterers of princes, aduancing their power without measure who stick not to set it against the empire of God himself. Unlesse both these mischefes be met withall, the purenesse of fayth shalbe lost.' And he offers the axiom: 'Spiritual libertie may very well agree with ciuile bondage', advice very pleasant to the ears of an absolute monarch.[9]

A little further on Calvin seems to be asserting the divine right of

rulers: 'whosoeuer be in place of magistrates ar named gods ...
therby is signified that they haue commandment from god, that they
are furnished with the authorities of god, & do altogether beare the
person of god, whose stede they do after a certaine maner supply'.
Strong stuff, and every line probably increased his life expectancy,
but by the term 'magistrate' Calvin did not necessarily mean a king.
On the next page he says:

> I wyl not deny that eyther the gouernmente of the chefest men, or a state
> tempered of it and common gouernmente farre excelleth all other ...
> bicause it most seldome chaunceth that kinges so temper them-selues, that
> their will neuer swarueth from that which is iuste and righte, againe that
> they be furnished with so great sharpnesse of iudgement and wisdome that
> euery one of them seeth so much as is sufficient. Therefore ... it is safer and
> more tolerable that many should haue the gouernment.

Yet he quickly adds, 'But if they would bryng thys kynde to themselues, to whom the Lord hath appointed another forme of gouer-
mente, so that therby they be moued to desire a change, the very
thinking therof shal not only be foolish and superstitious, but also
hurtful.'[10] This is a very provocative and unstable teaching: it is
telling people 'Such and such is good: now do the opposite.' And to
call something foolish and hurtful is not quite the same thing as
calling it wicked; it could imply that such rebellion is to be avoided
as futile more than anything else, a pessimistic view to be discerned
in Tyndale's *Obedience of a Christian Man* (1528) which reminds the
reader that the secular ruler 'beareth not a swearde for nought'.[11]
Yet it is possible to read even Tyndale's text as an attempt to attract
crowned heads to the cause of the Reformation, not a hard-and-fast
guide to Protestant political thought.

Tyndale had used the common argument that evil rulers were
sent by God to punish the sins of the people,[12] and Calvin includes
this but puts it in a curious fashion:

> we nede not much to labor to proue that a wycked kyng is the wrath of God
> upon the earth, forasmuche as I thynke that no man wyl say the contrary,
> and other wise there shuld be no more sayd of a kyng than of a comon
> robber that violently taketh away thy goods, and of an adulterer that
> defyleth thy bed, of a murtherer that seketh to kyll thee, wheras the
> Scripture reckeneth all such calamities among the curses of God.[13]

Considering that half the states of Europe were or had been, by
1560, involved in civil war or turmoil as the Reformation spread, the
assertion that 'no man wyl say the contrary' can only be ironic:

indeed, I suspect that the whole passage is ironic. It does not take a very minute biblical knowledge to observe that the Old Testament is full of examples of wicked rulers slain or deposed.

A couple of pages later Calvin says,

and here both his maruelous goodnesse, and power, and providence sheweth it self, for somtime of his seruants he raiseth up open reuengers and furnisheth them with his commaundment, to take vengeance of their uniust gouernment, and to deliuer his people manye wayes oppressed out of miserable distresse.

He cites the case of Moses, who delivered the Jews from Pharaoh (though Moses did not of course overthrow Pharaoh), then says that sometimes even assassins have, unwittingly, done the work of God:

when they were by the lawful calling of God sent to do such actes: in taking armure agaynst kynges, they did not violate that majesty which is planted in kinges by the ordinance of God: but being armed from heauen they subdued the lesser power with the greater: like as it is lawful for kinges to punish the Lordes vnder them.

Thus it may be the duty of magistrates to defy a monarch:

I affirme that if they wynke at kynges wilfully ragyng ouer and treadyng down the poore communaltie, their dissembling is not without wicked breach of faith, bicause they deceitfully betray the libertie of the people, whereof thei know themselues to be appointed protectors by the ordinance of God.[14]

This is a long way from what we found at the start of the chapter. And since he has said earlier that the duties of a magistrate include resorting to both war and execution if need be, by implication a magistrate is required to take arms against a tyrannical ruler.[15]

Calvin closes the chapter with a powerful directive:

And truely how unorderly were it, for the satisfying of men to runne into his displeasure for whom men themselues are obeyed: The Lord therfore is the kyng of kyngs ... If they commaunde anythyng against him, let it haue no place and let no accompt be made of it.

The highest maxim is 'that we ought to obey God rather than men'.[16] Rebellion sanctioned by religion was not rebellion: rebellion became obedience, obedience became rebellion.

In the next generation, the writings of Knox and Buchanan are well known. Those of John Poynet (or Ponet) are less often quoted, although Poynet went quite as far as his Scottish contemporaries in

advocating tyrannicide in defence of the True Church. These Protestant thinkers of the mid-century discarded Calvin's distinction
between the duties of a magistrate and those of lesser mortals.
Poynet's forthright work, *A Shorte Treatise of Politicke Power* (1556) is
of particular relevance to the Reformation plays, since according to
Stow's *Annales*, which was one of the sources for *Sir Thomas Wyatt*,
Poynet himself, who was then Bishop of Winchester, took an active
part in Wyatt's rebellion against Queen Mary, the subject of the
play.

Doctor Poinet and other, did counsell the said Wyat to march forwards and
keep his appointment, and to let the gun lie, which in no wise he could be
perswaded to do. Doctor Poinet therefore, considering how many of his
confederacie was stolne away from him, he began to perswade the captaine
Bret, and other his friends to shift for themselves, as he would do, and at
that very place where the gun did breake, he tooke his leave of his secret
friends, and said he would pray unto God for their good successe, and so
did depart, and went into Germany.[17]

It is a pity that Poynet does not appear in *Sir Thomas Wyatt*. There
are no sympathetic bishops in Webster's plays, and it may be that he
was omitted because the dramatists wished to give the play a more
Puritan, in the sense of anti-episcopal, slant.

But bishop or not, Poynet was a militant Protestant, and from his
exile in Strasburg he poured out his eloquence against the evil
doctrine that subjects must continue to obey rulers no matter how
heretical or corrupt:

why maie not they sende for their subiectes children, and cause them to be
killed, baked and geue it to their parentes in steade of other meat: and for a
second course bring into them, the heades, fete and handes, as king *Astiages*
did to *Harpagus*? All the papir of England wold not serue to set out the
mischiefes that might folowe, whan princes euil commandements should be
obeid and fulfilled.[18]

Among the examples of justified tyrannicide that he quotes are those
of Edward II and Richard II in England, several from classical
history and several more from the Old Testament; conspicuous
place is given to the case of Queen Athalia, the wicked and idola-
trous monarch who was slain by her household, after which Israel
'banished all idolatrie and false religion'.[19] The treatise was meant
to give moral support to Sir Henry Dudley's conspiracy to kill
Queen Mary, though of course its relevance is not confined to that

one occasion. The treatise concludes: 'Thou hast sufficient warning, God geue thee grace to considre it, and vse it.'[20] Yet in the first edition it was followed by an Exhortation to Englishmen, promising that if England will repent of her sins and 'be content to suffer all martirdome' then God will deliver her from tyrants.[21] This Exhort-ation was left out when Poynet's *Treatise* was twice reprinted in the reign of Charles I (1639 and 1642), but its presence in the original edition faces us with the problem of how far to compensate in our reading for the pressures under which Poynet, like Calvin, wrote. It is possible that Poynet appended the Exhortation as a safety measure, or it may be an indication that some Protestants were at a stage of development where they were able to believe both things at once. Perplexing as this may be, Poynet had taken part in Wyatt's rising, and the presence of this senior churchman, one-time chaplain to Cranmer and author of the doctrinal declaration of 1553 which led to Cranmer's imprisonment and eventual martyrdom, makes it hard to believe the claim of the historical Wyatt that his rebellion was unrelated to the cause of religion under the Catholic queen.

Where Poynet was less far-sighted than Calvin is that he does not envisage (even disapprovingly) replacing one system of government with another. The object of political action was only to replace one ruler with another, and this was the weakness of most English militant Protestant thinking for a long time. The prospect of consti-tutional change was far more distant and difficult even than rebel-lion, and for most of the time knuckling down was the most realistic solution. Besides, no Protestants wanted to alienate monarchs who, like Queen Elizabeth, were potential or actual allies of the True Church.

II

When we turn to the plays which Jacobean authors wrote about the Reformation we find many of the same issues, together with some of the tensions and contradictions displayed by Calvin and Poynet. *Sir Thomas Wyatt* is as important as any of the group, but as I have treated it in detail elsewhere[22] it should suffice to say here that it is a work which made ingenious use of the coincidental similarities between the rebellion of Sir Thomas Wyatt in 1554 and the Essex rebellion of 1601. Both rebellions were motivated by, among other factors, militant Protestant discontent: Queen Mary was of course a

Catholic, whose marriage to Philip of Spain caused alarm in a realm
which had been Protestant for a whole generation. Queen Elizabeth's policies in the post-Armada years were not sufficiently or
openly militant for the followers of the Earl of Essex, who disliked
the prospect of peace with Spain. Both rebellions were failures, and
to support Essex's cause was still regarded as highly seditious when
the play was first performed, so the dramatists had to treat the
subject in an indirect fashion. Wyatt in the play denies that he is a
traitor, and he has been a pillar of legality in the opening section,
but the attitude to his insurrection presented in the play is Calvinis-
tic: rebellion sanctioned by religion is not rebellion. Where the
interests of the True Church are pitted against the demands of a
monarch, rebellion becomes obedience and obedience becomes
rebellion. Essex was an important figure to militant Protestants in
England, but not quite important enough to persuade the populace
of London to support him against Queen Elizabeth.

In *Sir Thomas Wyatt* all social ranks are shown supporting the
Protestant cause, from Wyatt himself and the aristocratic Lady Jane
Grey, down to Captain Brett and his company of London soldiers.
Of all the Reformation plays, Samuel Rowley's *When You See Me You
Know Me* is the most overt in suggesting that the English Reformation had been a popular movement. Its version of history is a bold
one. It plunges *in medias res* by opening with King Henry VIII
already married to Jane Seymour, who is about to give birth to
Prince Edward. She dies in childbirth, and her place as queen is
taken by Katherine Parr, a staunch Lutheran, but there is no hint of
the Henrician schism with Rome until Prince Edward is a grown
boy. It is not until Henry embarks on his last war against France
that Cardinal Wolsey, who favours a French alliance, falls from
favour and is spurned by the King. This signals the eventual
triumph of the Protestants in the long power-struggle of the Reformation.

Rowley's King seems designed to illustrate why Calvin thought
that rule by one individual – monarchy – was unsafe and intoler-
able. Henry is a buffoon, possessing absolute power but usually
manipulated this way or that by the skill of his ministers and
courtiers. Bishop Gardiner in the play recalls 'how soone his Maiestie was wonne, / To scorne the Pope, and Romes religion, / When
Queene *Anne Bullen* wore the diadem.'[23] Anne Boleyn's influence
was not, in Rowley's version, enough to cause the break with Rome.

The action of the play is a contention between the adherents and the opponents of the Reformation for control of the King. The Protestants are led by Cranmer, Queen Katherine Parr and two bawdy jesters whose jibes and squibs against Wolsey represent popular anti-clerical feeling. The Catholics plot to have Katherine arrested on a treason charge, but the Protestants win, mainly because they have, with forethought, concentrated on gaining control of the young Prince Edward, the future king. His intervention with his father enables Katherine to plead with the King and acquit herself of the charge against her. It is Edward VI whose influence, in this account, is crucial, suggesting that the reforms in his reign, not the schism of 1553, constituted the true Reformation, and that it was gained not because of, but in spite of, the overbearing Henry. Yet the play displays a kind of naive Erastianism, with Henry acting the part of a hero and saviour setting to rights all the corruptions he discovers while visiting, incognito, the King's Bench gaol for one night.

The portrayals of Wolsey and Gardiner in this group of plays are fixed and somewhat predictable: Wolsey who dares to keep the King waiting, Gardiner conspiratorial and vindictive. Gardiner was, as Spikes has observed, the villain of all these Jacobean history plays, and their consistency in this respect suggests a broad consensus on the subject of Protestant martyrdom. Even the least militant were aroused to anger by seeing Protestants sent in such numbers to the block or the stake. The description of Gardiner offered in Poynet's *Treatise on Politicke Power* gives some idea of the kind of being established in popular memory and imagination:

This doctour had a swart colour, an hanging loke, frowning browes, eies an ynche within the head, a nose hooked like a bussarde, wyde nosetrilles like a horse, euer snuffing into the wynde, a sparowe mouthe, great pawes like the deuil, talauntes on his fete like a grype, two ynches longer than the naturall toes, and so tyed with sinowes, that he coulde not abyde to be touched, nor scarce suffre them to touche the stones.[24]

Not the warmest account that one Bishop of Winchester could give of another. The Jacobean companies would have had difficulty making him repulsive enough for popular taste in their stage portrayals.

Cranmer is shown in Rowley's play labouring to teach Protestant doctrines to Prince Edward – in particular that there is no need for Purgatory – but the Prince's whipping-boy, young Browne, seems to live in a perpetual Purgatory, being whipped whenever Edward prefers to play tennis instead of studying. The Prince with a twinge of conscience knights him, and Henry approvingly adds an income for young Browne of 'a Thousand Markes a yeere'.[25] Is this a pun, a joke? The naive Erastianism emerges from the way that Will Summers, the clown, who sides so boldly with Katherine Parr in taking the part of the poor against the Pope, can also join in the merry pranks of Ned Browne's knighthood. The puns and innuendos that accompany Henry's disguised sojourn in prison reveal that the audience was expected to find royal power romantic and thrilling. When the King is disguised his identity is a pleasurable secret for the audience. Secular authority retains its charisma, while ecclesiastical is under attack.

There is a possible irony available to us in the conclusion of *When You See Me*. King Henry, reunited with his Protestant Queen, trounces Wolsey and reverses the French alliance that Wolsey has so painstakingly built up. Instead, Henry allies himself with the Holy Roman Emperor and declares war on France, to the approval of Will Summers, who concludes the play cracking bawdy jokes with King, Queen and Emperor. Modern historians consider that this war against France starting in 1543, 'one of the drabbest and most inconsequential wars in English history', was highly significant in one respect, because in order to finance it Henry VIII sold off most of the church lands seized at the dissolution of the monasteries a few years before. This rash extravagance threw away wealth that could have established the English monarchy as an absolute power, able to rule without parliaments as the kings of France and Spain did for centuries to come. Because of Henry's rash act, his lack of capitalist acumen, future British monarchs would be unable to afford an army or a civil service without raising taxes from the gentry.[26] Will Summers may not know this, Rowley may not have known it, but we know it and so can regard Henry's triumph over Wolsey as a delusory one. No sooner is absolutism established in England than it has sown the seeds of its own downfall.

For sheer boldness in deploying historical material, Rowley is rivalled by Heywood, for in *If You Know Not Me You Know Nobody* Heywood, (who concentrates on Elizabeth and her sister Mary after the death of Edward) presents the young Princess Elizabeth as a quasi-martyr for the Protestant religion, struggling to preserve her spiritual liberty while kept in civil bondage by her Catholic sister. It

is a bold fiction because the historical Elizabeth had no inclination
to be a martyr and conformed to Roman Catholicism during Mary's
reign. Elizabeth's historical submission would suggest that the True
Church cannot be reconciled with absolutism, and that Calvinists
needed some more sophisticated solution to their political problems.
But Heywood is a first-half-of-the-chapter Calvinist, who still puts
his trust in princes, and presents the all-powerful monarch as the
refuge of the True Church. Since the monarchs in question are
hard-line Catholics this leads to what seems an extraordinary
paradox: Heywood depicts King Philip II of Spain as a noble and
attractive character, who protects the persecuted Elizabeth from her
sister – and of course her sister's evil minister, Bishop Gardiner.

Heywood's Elizabeth is, though intransigent over religion, a
resigned and compliant figure who submits without resistance or
anger to being imprisoned and humiliated by Mary. Elizabeth
shows none of the spirit of Sir Thomas Wyatt, and early in the play
denies involvement with Wyatt's rebellion, despite the fact that
Mary is shown breaking her promise to the Suffolk men who put her
on the throne on condition that she would allow them religious
freedom: 'Since, they, the limbs, the head would seek to sway, /
Before they gouerne, they shall learne t'obey.'[27] Gardiner orders the
upstarts to be placed in the pillory for three days, but although
Mary's perfidy offers a temptation to rebellion the heroine Elizabeth
remains a dutiful subject. Gardiner plots with the Constable of the
Tower to get Elizabeth executed, and still the possibility of death
does not deter her. As she passes the Tower, she sends her supporters
the message that she is going 'tanquam Ovis', as a sheep to the
slaughter, imitating the example of Christ and remaining obedient
unto death.[28] The pathos is amplified with curious comedy as rustics
garble the message, but it is a crucial decision. Elizabeth's submission is rewarded by Providence. Angels appear to her in a dream
defending her from friars, symbolising divine protection for the True
Church. Philip II resolves to take her part and persuades Mary to be
clement towards Elizabeth. Sir Thomas Gresham (oddly here shown
as an agent of the Spanish King) uncovers Gardiner's plot against
Elizabeth. Eventually Gardiner dies, then Cardinal Pole and finally
Mary herself. Elizabeth is left as Queen: before she governs, she has
learnt to obey.

How would the London audience have reacted to seeing King
Philip presented as an amiable character, indeed as a hero? While

Mary is, as a result of his intervention, receiving Elizabeth and
listening to her humble defence, Philip eavesdrops and exclaims,
'Mirror of vertue and bright Nature's pride. / Pity it had been such
beauty should have dide.'[29] He is compassionate, a tender husband,
and scrupulous in restraining his followers from taking any liberties
on English soil: one who does is promptly executed on Philip's
orders. This view, which is in part derived from Foxe, is an optimistic, providential one. Providence is protecting England from any
terrible harm. But it is a view that involves a distinct and unconceal-
able strain, and the play shows no actual martyrdoms, as that would
make its optimism harder to uphold.

III

It has sometimes been thought that *If You Know Not Me You Know
Nobody* and *Sir Thomas Wyatt* derive from a single play, but such an
idea is implausible because although the two plays do cover some of
the same ground, namely, the accession of Queen Mary, they are not
taking the same angle on events. *Sir Thomas Wyatt* is much more
militant: it presents the rebel as a tragic hero, who is betrayed first
by the monarch who owes him her throne, then by the men of
London who should have fought for him. Dekker and Webster do
not shrink from showing actual martyrdoms, Jane Grey's in particular, which is attended by no miraculous intervention of Providence. Poynet's *Treatise* refers to Jane Grey in a fashion very reminiscent of the play:

whan the innocent *Lady Iane* contrary to her will, yea by force, with teares
dropping downe her chekes, suffred her self to be called *Quene of Englande*:
yet see, bicause she consented to that which was not by ciuile iustice laufull,
she and her husbande for company suffred the paines of Traitours, bothe
headles buried in one pitte.[30]

In *Sir Thomas Wyatt* the commoners of England are vehement in
their hatred of Spanish rule, and Philip II is feared as the monarch
of the Inquisition: for Dekker and Webster to have presented him in
a favourable light would have been unthinkable. Sir Thomas Wyatt
himself is a magistrate – indeed a privy councillor – but only in that
respect can it be said that the tragedy conforms to second-half-of-
the-chapter Calvinism, rather than going with Poynet the whole way.

　In *If You Know Not Me You Know Nobody* there is certainly a very strong popular desire for the Reformation, evident in the behaviour of the low-ranking people, who are unanimous in their sympathy for Princess Elizabeth. But they show no more sign of rebellion than is evinced by the clown playing some rather foolish tricks on Sir Henry Beningfield, the Princess's gaoler.

The sequel to this play, *If You Know Not Me You Know Nobody Part II*, which was written and performed only a few months after Part I, is a terrible hotchpotch of a play, full of incomplete sub-plots and loose ends. We never discover whether John gets back the patrimony he thinks his uncle has cheated him of, nor do we ever find out whether Timothy, the hypocritical Puritan, has been saved from the gallows, or hanged: Hobson sets out in flying pursuit to have him reprieved, but neither of them is ever heard of again. Heywood's attempt to cram the maximum number of characters and incidents into one play is perhaps intended to show a cross-section of the commonwealth, but while it might have worked in a novel, there is simply no room for it in a play and the result is chaotic. There is a severe inconsistency, too, in the way that Philip II, so admirable in Part I, becomes a villain in the sequel, the adversary of England in the Armada battle. The hand of Providence is not very generous either to Sir Thomas Gresham, whose foundation of Gresham College and the Royal Exchange is celebrated in the play: his benevolence is followed by the loss of all his ships, and of £60,000 lent to the Barbary King. Whereas Part I was filled with certainty, Part II retreats from this certainty into a world that is harsh, puzzling and unknowable. In a sense this strong negative emphasis makes the play interesting.

Hobson, the comical city merchant of Part II, admits at an early point in the play that he got rich by exploiting the religious oscillations of the Tudor epoch:

> Am I worse because in *Edward*'s days,
> When Popery went downe, I did ingrosse
> Most of the beads that were within the kingdome,
> That when Queen *Mary* had renew'd that Church,
> They that would pray on beads were forc'd to me?
> I made them stretch their purse-strings, grew rich thereby;
> Beads were to me a good commodity.[31]

Doubtless the touch-paper for burning martyrs was a good commodity to somebody too, but it makes very uneasy humour, and Hobson's speech punctures and deflates the hagiography, and the ethics, of Part I. Is Hobson worse because of it? Not financially, at any rate: and it is made abundantly clear that the Armada victory in the last act is made possible only by the support of merchants like Hobson and Gresham. There was no distinction in Tudor times between merchant and royal navy. The defence of the realm relied entirely on the magnates of London and the other ports, who were expected to lend their ships as well as their funds. We witness Queen Elizabeth sending to Hobson for a loan quite early in the play (she needs to borrow money because of her father's improvidence), and later when she dines at the house of Gresham and knights him, the Queen herself meets Hobson. The blunt merchant assures her that her credit limit is, as far as he is concerned, boundless: 'When thou seest money with thy grace is scant, / For Twice fiue hundred pound thou shalt not want.'[32] This proves useful, as defence never comes cheap. Before Elizabeth governs, she must learn to pay. If Providence is guiding England, it is the kind of providence that lays up coins in hessian sacks, not the kind that sends bright dreams of angels.

It does not seem to occur to Heywood's merchants that they could ever refuse the crown a loan, or, more subtly, join together to put conditions on a loan or a subsidy. In a play by Dekker, *If This Be Not a Good Play the Devil Is in It* (written 1611), a city merchant called Bartervile does try to avoid giving the King a forced loan, but he is put to the most desperate stratagems in the process. Neither Dekker's nor Heywood's merchants seem aware, as yet, of the political power that might be theirs if they organised themselves to get it. They are certainly more realistic contenders for power than Rowley's clowns.

Prayer-beads are not Hobson's only source of pelf. We know that John accuses him of having embezzled a fortune – his nephew's patrimony – and even if that is false, we see that Hobson has rents and buildings on the Bankside, where Tawny-coat is found living in frightful poverty. His wife and children have been evicted and must go cold and hungry until he has paid off a debt of £20 by labouring for threepence a day:

> I haue this quarter by exceeding thrift,
> Bare clothing, and spare dyet, scrap'd together
> Fiue shillings in a purse, which I lay vp
> Towards your worships debt.[33]

At that rate it would take him twenty years of grinding hardship to pay off the debt. Heywood is not a very good capitalist, as there is no reference to paying interest, which would have made Tawny-coat's situation quite impossible. The grimness of this picture is increased by the fact that it is sandwiched between the scene showing Gresham's feast, where he drinks a toast to Queen Elizabeth containing a crushed pearl worth £1,500, and a later scene in which John riots in France, spending his money on a courtesan.

Tawny-coat's resignation to his plight is rewarded when Hobson's heart is melted enough to remit the debt, and we can see here the outline of the same kind of absolutist argument found in Part I, translated into economic terms. If the poor will submit, and be content to suffer martyrdom, then Providence will deliver them. But in Part II the doubts are more lingering. Can all the poor be as lucky as Tawny-coat? Doubtless Heywood intended Hobson's generosity here to be an example to other landlords. In *The Shoemaker's Holiday*, Dekker had cast doubt on whether wealth as great as Simon Eyre's could really be acquired completely innocently.[34] Heywood has similar misgivings, but goes one step further and makes it more disturbing by linking it with the Armada victory. Is that glorious triumph paid for by the misery and starvation of wretches like Tawny-coat? And if the English merchant Gresham is or was working for the Spanish King, the tarnishing process would be complete.

Shortly after Heywood's plays were performed, Dekker's *The Whore of Babylon* staged another version of the Armada battle, and the two make an interesting comparison. While Heywood's version is minutely circumstantial – for instance, listing all the ships that fought in the battle, and describing the exciting rescue of Sir Martin Frobisher – Dekker presents the battle, and the whole of Elizabeth's reign, in a framework of religious allegory. For Dekker, the Armada battle becomes not merely one between England and Spain, but between the Protestant True Church and the forces of Babylon; Roman Catholicism is the apocalyptic beast which must be faced and overcome. *The Whore of Babylon* is an apocalyptic comedy, which models its view of events on ideas from the Book of Revelation, which was regarded by many people as containing a prophetic history of the church. John Foxe, among others, had provided the lead which Dekker followed in this somewhat extraordinary work.[35]

To Dekker the Armada battle is a religious confrontation, but to
Heywood it is only a national victory. Heywood takes care to show
that some English Catholics, such as Sir Anthony Browne, fight in
the battle for England, and in fact Heywood exaggerated the
number of Browne's followers from 200, which he found in his
source, to 500.[36] Elizabeth is shown thanking Sir Anthony personally, mentioning his religion:

> For you, Sir *Anthony Browne*,
> Though your religion and recusancy
> Might, in these dangerous and suspicious times,
> Haue drawne your loyalty into suspect,
> Yet haue you herein amply clear'd yourself,
> By bringing vs fiue hundred men, well arm'd.[37]

A Catholic can still be a good Englishman. Heywood is trying to
avoid the kind of Protestant militancy typified by Dekker, a militancy that could border on fanaticism and challenge every other
source of authority.

Richard Bauckham has written, somewhat surprisingly, of 'the
type of allegorical history which we find confusing or irritating in
Christus Triumphans or Thomas Dekker's *The Whore of Babylon* (or, in
a different medium, Edmund Spenser's *The Faerie Queene*)'.[38] If
religious views are the stumbling-block, why should they seem any
more archaic or alien than the views on absolute monarchy detectable in many of Shakespeare's plays? While *The Whore of Babylon* is
not a very accessible work to most modern readers, its artistry and its
coherence have been greatly under-rated. It is certainly more coherent than Heywood's view of Elizabeth's reign. But *The Whore of
Babylon* is not altogether free from the tensions and contradictions
which beset this generation of religious–political thinkers. On the
surface it presents an idealised picture of Queen Elizabeth as
Titania, heroine of the True Church. But in places Dekker uses
devious means to imply that Queen Elizabeth was not actually
militant enough for his taste, and here the friction between his
religion and absolute monarchy is visible.[39] What Dekker is really
doing in *The Whore of Babylon* is not so much glorifying Elizabeth as
appropriating her as a figure of authority, and claiming her, posthumously, for the militant Protestant cause which she distrusted
during her historical reign.

Some Protestants, such as John Knox, had been hostile to the idea
of being governed by a woman, even if she was an ally of the True

Church. Heywood's Elizabeth finds it necessary to defend herself against anti-gynocratic prejudice:

> Haue you not read of braue *Zenobia*,
> An Easterne queene, who fac'd the Romaine legions,
> Euen in their pride and height of potency,
> And in the field incounter'd personally
> *Aurelianus Caesar?* Think in me
> Her spirit surviues, Queen of this western isle.[40]

Yet there is a kind of logical necessity for this if Heywood is keeping to the absolutist version of history (the version King James favoured), according to which the Henrician schism was the Reformation, for the Henrician schism was itself anti-gynocratic in motive and principle. Henry wanted a son, a male heir. The Elizabethan church and state upheld the schism, yet were gynocratic. So Elizabeth can never stop apologising for her own sex.

IV

All Is True, the title given to Shakespeare's and Fletcher's *King Henry VIII* at its first performance in 1613, may have been meant to suggest that it is less unhistorical than the Reformation plays of Rowley, Dekker or Heywood; nevertheless, signs of the authors' creative license are visible in it everywhere. Most modern editors of the play have agreed that it was written for the Palatine wedding celebrations which took place (belatedly) in February 1613. Foolhardy though it may be to challenge so many opinions, evidence for this court performance seems to me to be notably lacking.[41] R. A. Foakes, who first set out the theory in detail, suggested that there might have been a performance of *Henry VIII* at court on 16 February 1613, but we know from Chamberlain's letters and other records that the court actually watched a masque by Francis Beaumont on that evening.[42] And E. K. Chambers's *William Shakespeare: A Study of Facts and Problems* reprints the surviving record of payment to the King's Men for all the plays performed at the Palatine wedding: there were about twenty, but it does not include *Henry VIII*. Furthermore, *Henry VIII* is a play largely concerned with a divorce and, to make matters worse, a divorce in the British royal family in recent times. To perform such a play at a royal wedding would surely have been an offence against taste and decorum. It is far more likely to have been written for the Globe, where spectators on 29 June 1613 described it as a new play which had been performed only a couple of times before.[43]

This point is worth stressing since the determination of critics and editors to believe, in the face of all the evidence, that *Henry VIII* must have been aimed primarily at the Jacobean court indicates critical attitudes which are very prevalent: the concept of Shakespeare as a court writer, and the idea that the public stage was inferior, irrelevant, or a place of vulgar amusement. The latter idea is one often expressed by Shakespeare's contemporaries, but some Elizabethans, such as Dekker, praised the public theatres for the inclusiveness of their audience, and regarded this vulgarity as a virtue.[44] I think that Shakespeare was aiming at the widest possible audience, but whether the play could have appealed to Catholics – or whether any play on the Reformation could placate both Protestants and Catholics alike – is a very sticky question. There may be some who will resent it being grouped with the Reformation plays of Rowley, Dekker, Webster and Heywood, but, since it is another chronicle play on Tudor history, to omit it might be snobbish. It hardly needs saying that there are some respects in which *Henry VIII* is artistically superior to *When You See Me You Know Me*: for instance the speech of the Duke of Norfolk in the opening scene, which appears to be a panegyric of the court, but which reveals more and more scepticism, disgust and ridicule the more often we read it.[45] Rowley could not have written such an artful piece of time-release poetry (and nor, I think, could Fletcher, whose poetry in the last act has perhaps been over-praised). Nevertheless, there are insights to be gained by recognising that *Henry VIII* has a lot in common with *When You See Me*, and these insights may be more important than isolating particular passages for praise.[46]

The sturdy structure of Rowley's play, with its fourth-act Catholic plot against the Protestants, and its fifth-act rescue for the Protestants through the grace of the king, must have been very effective on stage and is emulated in *Henry VIII*. (I am of course making up the act divisions which were not there in early editions, but Rowley's play falls easily into them.) And the dream-vision of Queen Katherine in Act IV of *Henry VIII*, for which there is no chronicle source, has a marked resemblance to the dream-vision of Princess Elizabeth in *If You Know Not Me You Know Nobody*, Part I. Katherine, like Elizabeth, is a wronged princess kept in custody, resigned and pathetic in her endurance of her fate: Katherine actually has a maid called Patience to suit her Griselda role. The dream is a message from heaven bringing comfort and hope.

What is startling in the later play is that the heroine comforted by heaven is a Catholic, not a Protestant. This would have been most uncharacteristic of a militant Protestant account of events. In *Henry VIII* the dying Queen Katherine is presented as a virtual saint, and her vision promises that she will soon be in paradise. The wronged Queen, cast off so unjustly by King Henry, has attracted sympathy also in the scenes of the divorce court, and earlier she has shown herself to be a friend of the people, persuading the King to remove an oppressive tax – a fictional episode inserted by Shakespeare without chronicle source, to make Katherine more attractive.[47] So a blameless wife is cast off by a King who is really an embarrassing hypocrite, going on about his conscience in court when we have already seen him getting involved with Anne Boleyn, the prettiest woman at Wolsey's feast.

If Katherine is a sympathetic figure, she could all too easily become a symbol of Roman Catholicism, the old religion spurned, just as Heywood's fictive Elizabeth in *If You Know Not Me* is a symbol of the persecuted Protestant church. But *Henry VIII* is not open to any such simple interpretation, because of grave inconsistencies in the way that Katherine is made to behave. J. C. Maxwell has suggested that the first scene of Act III, in which Katherine receives the two cardinals, Wolsey and Campeius, and denounces them vehemently, is meant by the dramatists 'to divert possible obloquy from Henry'.[48] That could be part of its function, but there is more to it than that. Throughout the play, Katherine is consistently hostile to Wolsey. Before the question of the divorce arises, she denounces him for taxing the realm too harshly:

> These exactions,
> Whereof my sovereign would have note, they are
> Most pestilent to th'hearing; and to bear 'em
> The back is sacrifice to th'load. They say
> They are devised by you.[49]

When we come to the tense scene of the divorce commission, Katherine publicly explodes in anger at Wolsey, whom she calls her 'enemy' and 'most malicious foe', whose 'heart / Is crammed with arrogancy, spleen and pride.'[50] Then after her divorce, the two cardinals visit her, and advise her to trust and obey the king. Again

Katherine lashes out at both of them, castigating them for an entire scene. When they attempt to talk in Latin, she interrupts them:

> WOL.: Tanta est erga te mentis integritas, regina serenissima –
> KATH.: O, good my lord, no Latin;
>   I am not such a truant since my coming in,
>   As not to know the language I have lived in;
>   A strange tongue makes my cause more strange, suspicious . . .
>   Lord cardinal,
>   The willing'st sin I ever yet committed,
>   May be absolved in English.[51]

And she denounces them as 'cardinal sins and hollow hearts'.[52]

Holinshed attributed the divorce plan to Wolsey, rather than to Henry. But what could be less apt than for the representatives of Rome to take Henry's part against Katherine, or for the Catholic queen to attack the bishops of her own church, the church she clung to until death and in which she brought up her daughter? The problem here is not that it is fiction – of course it is fiction – but that it is a deeply incoherent fiction. Heywood's Elizabeth clinging to her Protestant faith despite threat and imprisonment is fictive, but it makes sense on its own terms. I fear (though I may be abused for saying it) that the presentation of Katherine in *Henry VIII* does not do that. She seems to be being used by the dramatists to voice popular Protestant hostility to Rome. It was the Protestants who disliked the Latin liturgy and preferred their native tongue. This is why, in the dream-vision of Elizabeth in *If You Know Not Me*, she goes to sleep with an English Bible in her hand. The English Bible was forbidden under Henry VIII and the liturgy remained in Latin until the reign of Edward VI.

Katherine's attacks on the cardinals can be compared to the anti-clerical outbursts of Will Summers in *When You See Me*: 'Would the King wood whip thee and all the Popes whelpes out of *England* once, for between yee, yee haue rackt and puld it so, we shall be all poore shortly, you haue had foure hundred threescore pound within this three yeare for smoake-pence.'[53] In Lollard fashion he is identifying Rome with exploitation and elitism, and while we may question whether Rome was the only possible culprit in these respects, his stance is an understandable one. Queen Katherine's stance in *Henry VIII* is divided and illogical, and it betrays a fundamental dislocation in the argument of the play.

At this point it might be objected that Shakespeare and Fletcher are more interested in Katherine as a woman, distressed and emotional, than in the political consistency of what she is saying. But this is not a very good defence. It is in danger of trivialising the play and reducing it to a soap-opera level. If they had just wanted an emotional scene, the authors could have made Katherine attack Cranmer, who actually divorced her and married Henry to Anne Boleyn. Any Shakespeare critic who tries to say that the historical details do not matter will have to extend that judgement to the benefit of Rowley, and many more writers.

There are various other explanations. One is the possibility that Shakespeare and Fletcher may have been trying to present Katherine as a crypto-Protestant. This category was quite important in Foxean thinking, and militant Protestants argued that there had been many pioneers of the True Church before the official Reformation. Such an attempt on the part of the dramatists would of course be daring, even by the standards of the Reformation plays of their contemporaries, but it would make the play internally consistent. Another possible explanation is the hypothesis that Fletcher took over and altered a play that Shakespeare left unfinished. The Shakespeare scenes do not use Foxe as their source, and signs in other plays could suggest that Shakespeare had little sympathy for the militant Protestant view of history. *King John* offers a very different view of that monarch from Foxe's hagiographical picture, and in *Henry IV* Falstaff, who was originally named Oldcastle, caused deep offence to those who regarded the historical Sir John Oldcastle as a martyr. In Foxe, there is a woodcut of Oldcastle dying a martyr. The descendants of Oldcastle commissioned the Admiral's Men to put on a counter-play defending them from what they felt was the insult of Shakespeare's portrayal.[54] On the other hand, Margot Heinemann has tried to ally Shakespeare with the Puritan side by arguing that in *King John* the presentation of the papal legate Pandulph as an unscrupulous plotter would have gratified popular anti-episcopal feeling, and she is on strong ground in asserting that the slant of Shakespeare's histories is on the whole Erastian.[55] Other critics argue that Shakespeare held aloof from the aggressive sectarianism of his era, and it is not really satisfactory to try to approach one play through generalisations about the others.

Least helpful and convincing are the remarks by Leonard Tennenhouse in his book *Power on Display*. Regarding *Henry VIII* as a Jacobean court play, Tennenhouse argues that Henry VIII's will which had, historically, excluded the descendants of Margaret Queen of Scotland from the English throne treated the crown as property and so clashed with the model of the realm as the mystical body of the monarch: this argument is central to his book. But James's exclusion had everything to do with his genealogy and not with the property law that excluded foreigners from inheriting land in England. Proof of this is found in the case of Arbella Stuart, James's cousin, who was also excluded by Henry VIII's will although she was born on English soil. Tennenhouse has a habit of overlooking women, as he refers to Katherine of Aragon as King Henry's 'unproductive mate': he is wrong, since Katherine did have a daughter. It is not she who is unproductive, but Henry and Tennenhouse, who are anti-feminist.[56]

Tennenhouse tries to impose on *Henry VIII* a political model according to which Wolsey represents 'populist energy' and the 'carnivalesque', which are harnessed and appropriated by the king. But the ready-made model simply does not fit: what is so populist or carnivalesque about Wolsey's high taxes, or his French alliance? *Henry VIII* resembles all the Jacobean Reformation plays in presenting the prelates of Rome as opposed to and hated by the common people. Furthermore, if we regard the play as a ritual of power, the result is failure, since the Henrician schism with Rome had the motive of giving Henry a son, a male heir. But the only visible result in the play is to bring him another daughter. Providence is gynocratic and Henry must like it or lump it. His display of absolute power has been absolutely futile. Tennenhouse ignores the issue of religion almost entirely, and this is one of the severe weaknesses of his book.

There is no doubt that the conclusion of *Henry VIII* is Erastian, and how we react to this depends on whether we regard Erastianism as a stage in political evolution, as progress, which is how Heinemann regards it. The Catholic faction brings charges of treason and heresy against Cranmer, but King Henry defends and protects him. ''Tis well there's one above 'em yet', says the king, eavesdropping on the council meeting, and his appearance at the vital moment provides a metaphor of the strong monarch solving the problems of the Reformation and defending the Protestant church from its enemies.[57] Cranmer produces the King's ring like a magic talisman protecting the True Church. But this sunny picture of an Erastian solution is only arrived at by skirting the whole issue of persecution, and this ultimately is the play's greatest weakness. It dilutes the political problems of the Reformation, problems of authority that sent Cranmer to the stake and Thomas Cromwell to the scaffold. Even in Henry's reign, the historical Cranmer clashed with him over such cruxes as the Six Articles. There is no hint of that in the play, where Henry is shown in harmony with Cranmer and Cromwell. The play gives the impression that there was a smooth transition from Henry's reign to that of Elizabeth.

Cranmer dominates the last scene, holding up the infant Elizabeth in his arms, symbol of an Anglican settlement. Elizabeth the expedient and Cranmer the martyr make an odd pair, but there is no hint in the play of the fate of Cranmer, when 'one above 'em yet', Queen Mary, decided to exert her government over the soul or inward man. Awkward bits like that are left to plays such as *Sir Thomas Wyatt*. The sticky question of Elizabeth's legitimacy is solved in *Henry VIII* by making her birth take place just after the death of Katherine of Aragon. Yet, if the Henrician schism with Rome is accepted in an absolutist fashion, there should be no problem to smooth away. Henry demanded a divorce and re-marriage, Cranmer granted it to him, therefore Elizabeth was legitimate. Some doubt about the extent of Henry's authority is implied by the play's tactful distortion.

V

The pattern that emerges from this heterogeneous and perplexed group of plays is one of a society which agreed to uphold 'thys order stablished by God', but which disagreed greatly as to what that order should be or how to maintain it. To search for a consistent model is often to falsify our reading. Protestantism could take refuge in the power of the crown or, when more militant, it could challenge the power of the crown. Conflict and uncertainty are visible everywhere, created by the fact that the Reformation was still in progress, and nobody could yet tell what its eventual impact on government and society would be. Among the plays discussed here, Dekker's *The Whore of Babylon* is the most consistent and lucid, but it was the least successful on stage. Was this because Dekker's brand of militant Protestantism was too extreme for a large section of the audience? Nevertheless, all the dramas are products of an era of doubt, conflict and dilemma. The dramatists moulded as well as catered for public opinion, rather as Eisenstein did with his film versions of the events of the Bolshevik revolution. On stage and in print they could direct the course of history and enjoy the sweet taste of government, so long as they received the suffrage of the playgoers, but in so doing they betrayed the tensions and contradictions of their own position.

NOTES

1 See, for instance, M. C. Bradbrook, *John Webster, Citizen and Dramatist* (London, 1980), p. 100, remarks on *The Whore of Babylon*.

2 *Puritanism and Theatre*, Past and Present Publications (Cambridge, 1980), p. 65.

3 See Judith Spikes, 'The Jacobean History Play and the Myth of the Elect Nation', *Renaissance Drama*, ns 8 (1977) 117–49. For the 'elect nation' theory, see William Haller, *Foxe's 'Book of Martyrs' and the Elect Nation* (London, 1963).

4 Bauckham, *Tudor Apocalypse*, The Courtenay Library of Reformation Classics, no. 8 (Oxford, 1978), pp. 86–7, quoting Firth and Olsen.

5 See Simon Adams in this volume, pp. 46–7 above.

6 Julia Briggs, *This Stage-Play World: English Literature and its Background 1580–1625* (Oxford, 1983), p. 73.

7 *The Basilicon Doron of King James VI*, ed. J. Craigie, Scottish Text Society, 3rd ser. vol. XVI (Edinburgh, 1944–50), pp. 75, 79.

8 *Actes and Monuments*, 1583 edition, vol. I, pp. 588–695.

9 Translated into English by T.N., printed by Richard Harrison, 2nd English edn (London, 1562), Book IV, chap. 20, fol. 491.

10 Calvin, *Institutes*, fol. 492, 493ᵛ.

11 Facsimile edn, Scolar Press (Menston, 1970), fol. xxix.

12 Tyndale, *Obedience*, fol. xlv.

13 Calvin, *Institutes*, fol. 499ᵛ.

14 *Ibid.*, fol. 501–501ᵛ.

15 *Ibid.*, fol. 495–495ᵛ.

16 *Ibid.*, fols. 501–2 (end of volume).

17 John Stow, (or Stowe), *Annales* (1600), p. 1,048. The tradition is accepted by C. H. Garrett, *The Marian Exiles* (London, 1938), p. 254, and by W. S. Hudson, *John Ponet 1516?–1556, Advocate of Limited Monarchy* (Chicago, 1942), pp. 63–5.

18 Facsimile of 1st edition, Scolar Press (Menston, 1970), sig. E vii verso.

19 *Ibid.*, sig. H ii.

20 *Ibid.*, sig. K verso.

21 *Ibid.*, sig. M iiiᵛ–M iv.

22 In my *The Dragon and the Dove: The Plays of Thomas Dekker*, Oxford English Monographs (Oxford, 1990), pp. 44–61.

23 Malone Society Reprints no. 90, ed. W. W. Greg (Oxford, 1952), sig. C.

24 Poynet, *Treatise*, sig. I iv.

25 Rowley, *When You See Me You Know Me*, sig. G 3 verso.

26 Perry Anderson, *Lineages of the Absolutist State* (London, 1974), pp. 124–5, 140–1.
27 Heywood, *Dramatic Works*, ed. John Pearson (London, 1874), vol. I, p. 196.
28 *Ibid.*, p. 223.
29 *Ibid.*, p. 236.
30 Poynet, *Treatise*, sig. D vii verso.
31 Heywood, *Dramatic Works*, vol. I, p. 266.
32 *Ibid.*, p. 318.
33 *Ibid.*, p. 305. If the interest rate was only 5 per cent, the debt would continue to mount as fast as Tawny-coat is paying it off. If the rate was any higher, he would get deeper and deeper into debt.
34 See my *The Dragon and the Dove*, p. 32.
35 *Ibid.*, chap. 3, contains a more detailed discussion of this play and its sources.
36 Pointed out by O. Rauchbauer, 'The Armada Scene in Thomas Heywood's *If You Know Not Me*', *Notes and Queries*, ns 24 (1977) 144.
37 Heywood, *Dramatic Works*, vol. I, p. 338.
38 Bauckham, *Tudor Apocalypse*, p. 76.
39 See *The Dragon and the Dove*, pp. 88–96.
40 Heywood, *Dramatic Works*, vol. I, p. 336.
41 *Henry VIII*, ed. R. A. Foakes, New Arden Shakespeare (London, 1957), pp. xxviii–xxxiii. Also *King Henry the Eighth*, ed. J. C. Maxwell, New Cambridge Shakespeare (Cambridge, 1962, rpt. 1969), p. x. Also *Henry VIII*, ed. A. R. Humphreys, Penguin Shakespeare (Harmondsworth, 1971, rpt. 1981), p. 12. The same dating is accepted by E. M. W. Tillyard in 'Why Did Shakespeare Write *Henry VIII?*, *Critical Quarterly*, 3 (1961) 22–7.
42 John Nichols, *Progresses of King James I* (Oxford, 1930), vol. II, p. 343.
43 L. P. Smith, ed., *Life and Letters of Sir Henry Wotton* (Oxford, 1907), vol. II, pp. 32–3. And Maija Jannson Cole, 'A New Account of the Burning of the Glove', *Shakespeare Quarterly*, 32 (1981) 352.
44 *The Gull's Hornbook*, ed. R. B. McKerrow, The King's Library, gen. ed. I. Gollancz (London, 1904), p. 49.
45 *Henry VIII*, I.i.13–38.
46 J. C. Maxwell's edition of the play, *King Henry the Eighth*, has examined many of the parallels between the two plays, and their common source material.
47 *Henry VIII*, I.ii.30–67. See also Maxwell, *King Henry*, notes, p. 135.
48 Maxwell, *King Henry*, p. xxxvi.
49 *Henry VIII*, I.ii.44–51.
50 *Ibid.*, II.iv.73–83, 107–10.
51 *Ibid.*, III.i.40–50.
52 *Ibid.*, III.i.104.
53 Rowley, *When You See Me*, sig. F iii verso.

54 Stanley Wells, *Shakespeare: An Illustrated Dictionary* (London, 1978), p. 126.
55 'Shakespeare als Dramatiker der Nachreformatorischer Zeit' (Shakespeare as a Post-Reformation Dramatist), *Shakespeare Jahrbuch*, 120 (1984) 55.
56 *Power on Display: The Politics of Shakespeare's Genres* (New York and London, 1986), pp. 75, 96.
57 *Henry VIII*, v.ii.27.

CHAPTER 8

Politics and dramatic form in early modern tragedy

Kathleen McLuskie

In a review of four recent productions of *Hamlet*, the theatre critic Michael Billington announced

a growing awareness that *Hamlet* is a profoundly political play: one that deals not just with a tortured individual soul but with the whole question of governance in society.[1]

Billington's opposition between 'a tortured individual soul' and the 'question of governance in society' crystallised a debate in academic circles among those who saw tragedy as embodying 'profound and ennobling truths about the human condition' and those who insisted on its analysis of the operations of power.[2] However hotly contested within the academy, the opposing interpretations were easily resolved. A dramatic focus on the suffering individual renders 'the whole question of governance in society' sufficiently generalised to apply both to the seventeenth century and today, and the political drama of the seventeenth century is admired for the extent to which it prefigures the political concerns of our own time.[3]

There is an important sense in which the cultural pre-occupations of the seventeenth century were prefigurings of our own. Dramatic representations of the anguished negotiations around the use and abuse of power, the accommodations of patriarchy to changing material conditions and the contest over 'value' in a new economic situation have evident resonances in our own time. Theatre performances and criticism which stressed these motifs have made the texts of Renaissance drama seem particularly available to a modern audience.[4] However, the very 'availability' of these plays as a locus for political criticism needs to be questioned.

The texts which are most commonly discussed and performed are materially 'available' in the form of accessible editions, because they are part of an established canon of 'Shakespearian drama'[5] and are thus granted a status removed from their original conditions of production. They can be read as *symptomatic* of the ideology of a moment in history[6] regardless of their representative status. They are available, too, because their concerns (whether political or moral) are expressed and dramatised by recognisable characters invoking a powerful emotional response. The setting of revenge tragedies in the courts of princes gives them a political resonance, but their focus on a meta-theatre of personal identity through which the thwarted revenger explores his relation to the oppressive institutions which thwart his revenge was the product of a particular dramatic form.

As Catherine Belsey has shown, the tragic drama of the 'tortured individual soul' owes everything to the development of soliloquy:

the soliloquy makes audible the personal voice ... the moral conflicts externalized in the moralities are internalized in the soliloquy and thus understood to be confined *within* the mind of the protagonist.[7]

This use of soliloquy creates characters who transcend their narrative function and, through their relationship with the audience, foster the illusion of a life outside the drama.

This complex relationship between role and individual, the subject who acts and speaks according to the decorum of artistic as well as moral demands, was of crucial importance in creating tragic characters who could lay a moment-to-moment claim on the audience's sympathy and attention. In the case of *Hamlet*, the metaphors of playing, and the rejection of simple models of decorum as a means of determining character and behaviour, intensify the play's mimetic power and give additional resonance to the tragic hero's generalisation of the revenger's dilemma into reflections on the nature of action and passion itself.

The self-dramatising hero was a particularly important characteristic of the self-conscious and reflexive drama produced by the playwrights who wrote for the boy companies at the turn of the seventeenth century. These dramatists inherited the politics of the stoic and classical tradition most clearly exemplified in Sidney's magisterial confidence that 'Tragedy maketh kings fear to be tyrants and tyrants to manifest their tyrannical humours'.[8] However, the form of their plays, as Reavley Gair has shown,[9] dramatised the question of acting and performance, in part as a showcase for all of the skills and styles which they had at their disposal. They used the metaphors of acting and performance, embedded in the trope of the *theatrum mundi*, to go beyond an existential concern for the problem of action into parody and burlesque of the conventions of revenge drama.[10] In doing so, they addressed their audience as an elite group, knowledgeable about theatre and capable of a sophisticated play with that knowledge.

In the boy-player tragedy, the nature and style of action and passion sometimes seemed to be more significant than the action and passion itself, even when the setting and narrative of the play gave particular political resonance to the question of style. In Chapman's *Bussy D'Ambois*, for example, the hero presents himself in his opening soliloquy as an oppositional figure with an acute sense of the corruption of the world. He nevertheless accepts a place at court where, in spite of his idealised hopes for honest advancement, he is outmanoeuvred by his political opponents and killed, on the pretext of revenge for adultery. The opening mode of the play seems simply emblematic in its contrast between *Bussy, poor* (1.i.1 s.d.), *Monsieur with two pages* (1.i.33 s.d.) and the corrupt and foppish steward, Maffe. However, this simple opposition between the virtuous poor outsider and the corruptly wealthy court is soon complicated. The imagery of Bussy's opening speech moves from the moral abstraction of Reward, Honour and Need to the language of artistry and performance. He compares great men and

> Unskilful statuaries, who suppose
> (In forging a Colossus) if they make him
> Straddle enough, strut, and look big, and gape
> Their work is goodly: (1.i.7–10)

and talks of the 'affected gravity of voice' in statesmen. The signs of unskilful actors have become the bywords for affected courtiers, with no need to invoke the metaphor of playing explicitly.[11]

When the politic Monsieur invites Bussy to court, his initial refusal is a refusal of the demeaning and hypocritical roles of 'strumpet', 'juggler' or 'dame schoolmistress' (1.i.86–90). However, when he does decide to go to court, 'for honest actions not for great', it is difficult for him to find a role. When he courts the Duchess of Guise and insults powerful courtiers, he seems merely boorish and reckless, for the court of intrigue is no context for his version of old-fashioned heroism either in behaviour or in dramatic style.

The exception comes in a scene when the King takes him into his protection by granting a pardon for having killed a courtier in a duel. The news of Bussy's action is delivered to the court by a Nuncius or messenger, in the style of heroic narrative, using similes to connect this quarrel with the wars of Greece and Troy. Like the player speech in *Hamlet* or Andrea's narrative in *The Spanish Trage-dy*,[12] this messenger speech connects a motive for heroism to a past world, dramatised in a different style, contrasting it with the surrounding world of the drama. In Bussy's case, moreover, the heroic narrative is not the story of a past action, or a contrast to the protagonist's present situation, but another performance. It explicitly places Bussy's action in a heroic framework in order that style should outweigh justice in the debate on the legality of murder between Monsieur and the King. Protected by Monsieur, Bussy is pardoned, but even in his role as the King's eagle, the eloquent spokesman for egalitarian values, he is no match for the courtier's politic skills. His eloquently angry denunciation of his patron's evil (iii.ii) is merely part of a formal flyting, a game of mutual frankness, and is greeted with sophisticated laughter.

Bussy's sense of moral absolutes is also compromised in his affair with Tamyra. The lovers represent their courtly adultery in high-flown language, and it involves midnight assignations, a secret passage to bring the lovers together, and an intermediary friar with occult powers. This curious mixture of styles dramatises the characters' moral uncertainty with reference to the more stable dramatic modes of earlier drama. Tamyra, like Faustus, asks the friar to raise a devil 'in some beauteous form / That with least terror I may brook his sight' (iv.ii.28–9), but when Behemoth appears he is almost petulant at the triviality of the quest (to spy on Monsieur and the Guise's plots) on which he is despatched. The hideously violent torture with which her husband revenges Tamyra's adultery is the palpable dramatic reality which renders the rest empty rhetoric, a searching for styles of action, and frameworks to give them reality, which no longer exist. The moral implications of the failure to find appropriate action are reflected on in Bussy's speech in which he regrets the

> Frail condition of strength, valour, virtue,
> In me like warning fire upon the top
> Of some steep beacon, on a steeper hill;
> Made to express it like a falling star
> Silently glanc'd – that like a thunderbolt
> Look'd to have stuck, and shook the firmament. *He dies.* (v.iii.188–93)

Chapman's experiments with tragic form, his fusing of the actions of heroism and sexual passion, can be seen as a radical critique of the formal resolution of conflict, undermining the providential view of world order or claims to authority of the Jacobean court. As such they have enormous appeal to modern 'political critics' for whom radical existential doubt is the premise for political opposition. However, as Raymond Williams has shown,[13] the tragic character, whose integrity of existence and whose suffering in the face of irremovable and inevitable evil was his primary claim to tragic status, was the paradigm figure of naturalism. It allowed the soliloquising revenger-hero to resolve the contradictions of contemporary politics within himself, sidestepping the messy problems of political relations and political action into a purity of personal integrity whose destruction carries enormous emotional appeal, but precisely denies engagement with the particularities of *realpolitik*.

II

The canon of revenge tragedy has tended to obscure the surrounding dramatic culture of the public theatres. Revenge plays were the product of a particular group of dramatists who quite explicitly distanced themselves from the popular traditions of theatre in the effort to write tragedies which would be worthy of the name. In his seminal discussion of tragedy, Sidney had found 'Our tragedies and comedies not without cause cried out against, observing rules neither of honest civility nor skilful poetry',[14] and in the introduction to the printed text of *Sejanus* Jonson regretted the pressure of a commercial theatre which made it impossible

in these our times, and to such auditors as commonly things are presented, to observe the old state and splendor of dramatic poems, with preservation of any popular delight.[15]

The contest for the attention of an elite audience is evident too in Webster's preface to the reader of the printed text of *The White Devil*. The play was first performed at the Red Bull, an amphitheatre in the north of the City which had a reputation for a rough and popular clientele. Webster complained about the conditions of the performance, but he did so in terms which claimed the attention of a more upmarket 'full and understanding auditory',[16] insisting on a knowledge of the classical tradition of tragic writing beyond the capacities of the 'uncapable multitude'.

Dekker and Heywood, by contrast, as jobbing professional dramatists, showed no such contempt for the dramatic traditions in which they worked. They addressed questions of politics through plays which were called tragedies, but whose *lack* of coherent tragic form showed them negotiating political questions which cannot be conceptualised in terms of a commitment to individual freedoms characteristic of political liberalism and opposition to the power of the state.

Heywood was explicit that his role as a popular dramatist was not to foster rebellion. In his *Apology for Actors* he recognised the cultural importance of the writer in maintaining rather than subverting order in the state. He insisted that plays were

to teach ... subiects true obedience to their king, to show people the untimely ends of such as have moved tumults, commotions and insurrections, to present them with the flourishing estate of such as live in obedience, exhorting them to obedience, dehorting them from all traiterous and felonious stratagems.[17]

Unlike Sidney, whose political theory of tragedy spoke confidently of its hope for influence on the monarch, Heywood recognised that he was dealing with the much more volatile element of the consumer population. The popular audience for his plays influenced both their dramatic form and the style of political opposition which they embraced.

Heywood's expression of loyalty is not in itself evidence of an absence of opposition, for opposition to the Jacobean court took a number of different and contradictory forms. The accession of James had put an end to manoeuverings around the question of the succession, but there remained an active concern with state policy in relation to questions of religion and foreign policy. David Riggs has shown that the new political situation after 1603 offered cultural alternatives:

the continuity between the new regime and the old, emphasising James's Protestantism, his English ancestry, and his readiness to participate in the national heritage of his new subjects, [or] the differences between Elizabeth and James, emphasising James's determination to make peace with European nations, his plans to unify England and Scotland, his imperial status as ruler of the British (and not simply English) people.[18]

As the new situation settled it became clear that James preferred the latter option, and both religious and political opposition settled around commitment to militant Protestant nationalism centring its hopes on Prince Henry.[19]

Heywood seems to have been closely involved in these political debates through his connection with the Earl of Worcester, the patron of his playing company and master of Queen Anne's household. His most explicit statement of his commitment to the Protestant nationalist group comes in his *Elegy* on the death of Prince Henry. The dedication to Worcester is emphatic about the importance of sustaining the young prince's memory:

since the heavens have given us this cause it is a duty to entertain the occasion and an unanswerable negligence to omit it.[20]

The suggestion that the elegy was more than a celebration of an individual is sustained in the poem itself. It was the occasion not only for praise of the dead prince but also for the suggestion that all was not well in the world which he had left behind. It begins with a series of rhetorical questions about whose fault the death could be and the answer finally comes down to 'our sinne'. Heywood avoids any precise account of the supposed sins by a mythological tale in which Pleasure leaves the world and her garment is taken on by Sorrow which 'deluded / The world with fading ioyes and transitory'. The allegory holds at bay any suggestion of precise political dissatisfaction, but the analogy with Astraea, the familiar mythological representative of Elizabeth, is a possible echo of such dissatisfaction. When Pleasure left the world, moreover,

> Honour fled, with it, it beares his tracke
> No Time, nor Age can stay or call him backe.   (sig. c20ᵛ)

The shift from Pleasure to Honour makes the political resonance more precise. Prince Henry's honour was connected with the political demands for a more actively anti-Catholic foreign policy and this notion of honour is made even more pointed in the succeeding stanza of praise for the prince:

> His Spirits were all active, made of fyre
> Which saue in travell can admit no rest
> High were his thoughts, yet still surmounting hy're
> His very motives Industry profest
> To be in Action was his sole desire
> And not to be so he did most detest.

In the final couplet, the poem tries to deflect any suggestion of implied critical comparison with King James by asserting

> To end his Praise and proue him past compare
> To all his Father's vertues he was heire.

To those alert to the political issues, however, the comparison may have been invidious rather than complimentary.

Mervyn James has shown how an opposition between Honour and Policy had more than moral resonances in the factional politics of the Elizabethan and Jacobean courts. In his analysis of the Essex rebellion, he points to the importance of the code of honour which rallied Essex's followers in their opposition to the 'oppressive and corrupting influence of an upstart and therefore unnatural regime' represented by the Cecilian faction which barred the natural elite of the nobility from the queen's person. Ideals of honour and the law of arms created the bond of faithfulness which attached his followers to Essex, but also acted as the focus for support from the citizens of London, who hoped for militant Protestantism from this flower of the nobility and gentry of England. Essex clearly hoped to rally the citizens to his cause by shouting as he made his way through Ludgate to the City 'that the realm was sold to the Spaniard'.[21]

In the event, the City did not rally to his support. For the citizens were more content to see Essex's opposition to the faction surrounding the queen as a symbolic locus of opposition, rather than as a military coup which they would support with force of arms. The rebellion itself, in spite of Essex's continued claim of allegiance to the queen was seen as a breach of civil order which could not be tolerated and certainly not supported.

Essex's symbolic role as a focus for oppositional values was paradoxically reinstated with his repentance and death:

A reaction in his favour set in, which promoted the survival both of his faction and of the radical attitudes (in a suitably modified form) and policies (like the anti-Spanish Protestant crusade) which had been characteristic of the Essex House circle.[22]

These negotiations around particular factional policy, the role of popular support and what Mervyn James describes as a 'culture of honour' seem also to inform the complexities of Dekker's and Heywood's dramatic production and make it appropriate to use the concept of an 'opposition drama'.

The connection between the politics of state and the politics of populism was made quite explicit in Heywood's dedication of his elegy on Prince Henry to the population at large:

> Why should I unto any private Peere
> Commend these sorrows for a Prince like deere
> To all sorts, Sexes Titles and Estates.

He even extends the dedication to the illiterate: 'thou that canst not read / Canst thou but heare?'

The audience which could not read but could hear was, of course, most readily available at the public theatres, for the locus of both Dekker's and Heywood's political action was the theatrical profession. As a result, the relationship between tragedy and politics had to be mediated through the institutions in which they worked, involving not only political ideology but also dramatic form. The contradictions of a political culture which was oppositional but also loyal, which claimed popular support but was principally concerned with aristocratic values, are dramatised in plays which lack narrative and generic coherence, and operate through a series of set pieces which call forth emotional and political responses, but which do not always achieve a consistent relationship between the two.

III

One of the most explicit treatments of political ideology is to be found in Dekker's collaborative play *The Famous History of Sir Thomas Wyatt* on the Wyatt rebellion, probably written in 1602 for Worcester's Men. Wyatt's rebellion in 1554, according to Antony Fletcher, 'came nearer than any other Tudor rebellion to toppling a monarch',[23] and in 1602 its subject of a disputed succession and aristocratic manipulation of the resistance to it had obvious immediate resonances.

The narrative does not work along a single trajectory focusing on the eponymous hero; it involves the double movement of Northumberland's rebellion, which precedes Wyatt's. The play opens with a direct discussion of problems of succession following the death of Edward VI. Suffolk plans to place his daughter Lady Jane Grey in the succession and is supported by Northumberland. Sir Thomas Wyatt is appealed to for his support but acts as a man of integrity, reminding them that he is a supporter of 'those Princely Maides' (I.i.30).[24] A machiavellian courtly manoeuvring is opposed to the simple concept of undisputed and rightful inheritance. Since Northumberland's plots are so easily foiled, this episode may seem a false start in the play (and with its multiple authorship, this is a serious possibility). Nevertheless, it generates scenes in which just the opposition between honour and politics can be dramatised, regardless of their role either in narrative coherence or in political movements.

In Act II scene ii, Northumberland is told that 'the lords have all revolted from your action' and he accepts the inevitable defeat. At no point has there been any sympathy for Northumberland, but the dramatisation of his defeat draws on the resources of the popular tradition for representing the fall of great men, and so complicates the lines of sympathy generated by the scene. The speeches are structured around the powerful symbolic opposition between two opposing heralds. In a last attempt to proclaim the right of Jane Grey, Northumberland calls for a Herald:

> *A Trumpet sounds, and no answere*
> *The Herald sounds a parlee, and none answers.*

As the sound of the trumpet dies away Ambrose enters to tell Northumberland of his defeat and he calls for a second Herald. On this occasion the Herald is answered by '*Within a shoute and a flourish*'. For Northampton this rejection of Lady Jane's claim is tantamount to a rupture in his very identity. He has told Ambrose,

> My selfe will now reuolt against my selfe   (II.ii.48)

and as the people respond to the proclamation he concedes

> Amen, I beare a part,
> I with my tongue, I doe not with my heart.   (II.ii.54–5)

The model for dramatising the fall of a great man is followed through to the end. He enquires ingenuously after his false friends, accepts his crime and hopes for mercy,

> when all soules
> Stand at the bar of Iustice, and hold vp
> Their new immortalized handes.   (II.ii.112–14)

The localised dramatic effect is pathetic rather than condemnatory.

The following scene in which Northumberland's fellow conspirator Suffolk meets his end is dramatised even more fully. In an autonomous sequence his servant Holmes betrays him with a Judas kiss and then kills himself in grief-stricken repentance. The speed of the sequence allows no dramatic elaboration and it is clearly simply lifted from an older morality tradition. But the dramatic form is further overlaid by the intervention of a clown who watches Holmes strangle himself, and then mockingly comments to the audience:

So, so, a very good ending, would all falce Seruants might drinke of the same sauce. (ii.ii.85–6)

The representation of different social orders together with the image of Judas offers contradictory allegorical readings, but the Clown's casual violence at the end presents a powerful image of the inevitable end of disorder:

Gold, you are first mine, you muste helpe to shift my selfe into some counterfeite suite of apparel, and then to London: If my olde Maister be hanged, why so: if not, why rusticke and lusticke: Yet before I goe, I doe not care if I throwe this Dog in a ditch: come away dissembler ... (ii.iii.84–90)

A similar complex negotiation between political and dramatic coherence is evident in the representation of Wyatt's own rebellion, which occupies the second half of the play. Like Essex, Dekker's Wyatt rebels in the name of nationalism and English honour. When Winchester proposes the Spanish match, he protests:

> Is shee a beggar, a forsaken Maide,
> That she hath neede of grace from forraine princes?   (ii.i.81–2)

and insists that Winchester's proceeding is 'policie deare Queene, no loue at all' (iii.i.136). His decision to rebel is taken as a direct consequence of the queen's commitment to the Spanish match, and the soliloquy in which the decision is taken works through the contradictory loyalties to sovereign and nation:

> And ere hee land in *England*, I will offer
> My loyall brest for him to treade vpon.
> Oh who so forward *Wyat* as thy selfe,
> To raise this troublesome Queene in this her Throane?
> *Philip* is a Spaniard, a proud Nation,
> Whome naturally our Countrie men abhorre.
> Assist me gratious heauens, and you shall see
> What hate I beare vnto their Slauerie.
> Ile into *Kent*, there muster vp my friendes
> To saue this Countrie, and this Realme defend.   (iii.i.157–66)

The historical Wyatt asserted at his trial 'before the Judge of all Judges, I never meant hurt against her highness person'.[25] By using the rhetoric of nationalism and freedom, Wyatt's soliloquy similarly obscures the issue of rebellion against the monarch. At this point in the play he is given considerable theatrical power, both in his soliloquy and in the rhetoric earlier in the scene. His theatrical power is matched by ideological power. Mary appears at her most autocratic in this scene as she prepares to restore the monasteries and dismisses Arundel's reminder of her oath with:

> But shall a Subiect force his Prince to sweare
> Contrarie to her conscience and the Law? (II.i.26–7)

The potentially powerful opposition between corrupted monarchy and the reluctant traitor is, however, not fully carried through in the drama. A residue of the queen's earlier characterisation as the royal victim remains in the reminder that the restoration of the monasteries is to be undertaken at the queen's personal expense. The catch phrase 'Better a poore Queene, then the Subiects poore' (III.i.17 and 34–5) is repeated in similar terms, blurring the outlines of sympathy which the narrative requires.

This tiny formal flaw in III.i. is, moreover, a feature of the play's construction as a whole. It can, of course, be attributed to textual problems, or to the play's multiple authorship, but it is also an indication of the political problems of negotiating aristocratic rights within monarchy, which generate the dramatic problems of clear lines of sympathy within consistent characterisation. The ambivalence of these scenes demonstrates the discursive complexity which an episodic popular dramaturgy affords. It reproduces certain conventions of representation which carry contradictory political resonances, as they negotiate the problems of aristocracy within monarchy and the limits of popular support.

Those limits are dramatised even more fully in the scenes of the rebellion itself. By eliminating Wyatt's fellow conspirators, Sir James Croft and Sir Peter Carew, Dekker kept the issues of the rebellion more clearly focused on the relations between different orders in society. Antony Fletcher, in his account of the historical rebellion, has suggested that

Only in Kent, where it was a rising of the gentry, was the issue sufficiently immediate and the leadership sufficiently capable to make success possible.[26]

The play, too, makes the rising of the commons a test of Wyatt's leadership. Before the gates of Rochester, he reiterates the anti-Spanish appeal, calling

> Hee that loues freedome and his Countrie, crie
> A *Wyat*: he that will not, with my heart
> Let him stand foorth, shake handes, and weele depart.   (IV.i.23–5)

The soldiers, of course, reply 'A *Wyat*, A *Wyat*, a *Wyat*!'. Northumberland's experience with the Herald is repeated and the emblem of royal power is now defeated by the cries of Wyatt's supporters.

However, popular support was not unambiguously an advantage to a rebellious aristocrat and the dramatic form again modulates the sympathies. In Act IV scene ii Bret, one of Norfolk's followers, converts his regiment to Wyatt's cause. He does so by invoking anti-Spanish feeling in a bawdy comic set piece, using a tantalising question-and-answer routine with his lowlife followers.

> BRET: And wherefore is *Wyat* vp?
> CLOWN: Because he cannot keepe his bed.
> BRET: No, *Wyat* is vp to keepe the Spaniards down, to keepe
>   King *Phillip* out, whose comming in will giue the Land
>   such a Phillip, twill make it reele agen.
> CLOWN: A would it were come to that, a would, wee wold
>   leaue off Philips and fall to Hot-cockles.
> BRET: *Philip* is a Spaniard, and what is a Spaniard?
> CLOWN: A Spaniard is no Englishman that I knowe.
> BRET: Right, a Spaniard is a Camocho, a Callimanco, nay
>   which is worse, a Dondego, and what is a Dondego?
> CLOWN: A Dondego is a kinde of Spanish Stockfish, or poore
>   Iohn.
> BRET: No, a Dondego is a desperate Viliago, a very
>   Castilian, God blesse vs ... A Spaniard is cald so,
>   because hee's a Spaniard: his yard is but a span.
> CLOWN: That's the reason our Englishwomen loue them not.
> BRET: Right, for he caries not the Englishmans yard about
>   him, if you deale with him looke for hard measure: if
>   you giue an inch hee'le take an ell: if he giue an ell,
>   youle take an inch.   (IV.ii.42–66)

The comic vitality of his performance is attractive, as is the narrative support for Wyatt. However, the politics of his speech locate his version of nationalism with lowlife anti-alien riots rather than the honourable nationalism of his leader. The dangers as well as the strengths of popular support are economically dramatised, but the force of the dramatisation holds the two in an uneasy equilibrium. The balance shifts only at the end when Bret invokes 'policy':

Therefore my fine, spruce, dapper, finicall fellowes, if you are now, as you
haue alwaies bin, counted politique Londiners, to fly to the stronger side,
leaue *Arundell*, leaue *Norfolke*, and loue *Bret*. (IV.ii.66–9)

Wyatt's ultimate defeat takes place off-stage after he has been
abandoned by his soldiers, and the finale grows in pathos as Wyatt's
end is accompanied by the pathetic end of the innocent victims,
Lady Grey and her lover Guilford. Sympathy for Wyatt is mediated
through his final soliloquy in which, once again, generalised notions
of 'periured Counsellors' and 'innovators' are set against the honour
embodied in Wyatt's desire 'to keepe Spaniards from the land'.

In these final sequences, Wyatt comes closest to a tragic figure
(the lessons of Richard II and Henry VI are evident), since the
tragic devices of soliloquy and contemplative irony are in play.
However, the overall political impact of the play does not oppose the
stoic individual to the corrupt and repressive monarch, for this is a
politics of negotiation among contradictory alternatives, aware of
the *realpolitik* of competing hierarchies and the establishment of
legitimate authority rather than the liberal opposition of the individual and the state.

IV

A further complication in the relations between rebellious subjects
and the state is dramatised in Heywood's image of rebellion in
Edward IV.[27] A lengthy sequence at the beginning of the play
presents Falconbridge's attack on the City of London supported by
rebels from Essex and Kent. Its theatrical shape is provided by a
number of 'sieges to the tiring house', interspersed, in familiar
history play fashion, by parleys and confrontations between the
rebels and the good citizens of London. By these dramatic means
Falconbridge's attack is presented as invasion by a foreign power,
and his claim that he acts in King Henry's right is given little
dramatic weight. It shows rather 'the untimely ends of such as have
moved tumults', but within that overall opposition to rebellion there
are a number of contradictions which suggest a more complex
relationship to the political currents of Heywood's time.

Within the framework of opposition to rebellion against the King,
the play's dramatisation allows other sympathies to emerge. When
the news of rebellion first breaks, King Edward is given a completely
conventional response:

Well, let this *Phaeton*, that is mounted thus,
Look he sit surely, or, by *England's George*,
Ile breake his necke. This is no new euasion;
I surely thought that one day I should see
That bastard Falcon take his wings to mount
Into our eagle-aerie. Methought I saw
Black discontent sit euer on his browe
And now I see I calculated well.   (Scene i)

In the event, Edward plays little part in the plot of the rebellion.
Rather, opposition is couched in terms of competing claims to
monarchy, rather than a conflict between rebels and rightful king.
Falconbridge claims that he is undertaking rebellion on behalf of
'True-hearted English', disenfranchised by 'the sad yoke of Yorkish
servitude'. This rhetoric is further used to distance Falconbridge's
attempt in the name of 'ancient libertie' from the rebellions of

Tyler, *Cade* and *Straw*
Bluebeard, and other of that rascal rout
Basely like tinkers or such muddy slaues
For mending measures or the price of corne,
Or for some common in the wield of Kent
Thats by some greedy cormorant enclos'd.   (Scene ii)

Falconbridge's distinction between political rebellion and rebellion for economic reasons is clear enough, but the rhetoric of his
speech creates a certain confusion. The line 'that's by some greedy
cormorant enclosed' is conventional rhetorical padding, but it
allows the possibility of at least a measure of sympathy for the rural
poor who are his followers. This rhetorical confusion suggests the
possibility of *political* complexity which is even more evident in the
dramatic presentation of the rascal rout itself.

The representation of the rebels draws on the tradition of comic
lowlife performance familiar from Shakespeare's presentation of
Jack Cade or the anonymous play of Jack Straw.[28] Spicing, Smoke
and Chub the chandler of Chepstow comically echo Falconbridge's
words, and their readiness to fight and threaten have enormous
potential for ad-libbing popular performance. This association with
popular rebellion complicates the political implications and perhaps
undermines the seriousness of Falconbridge's claim, but it enhances
its theatrical impact and echoes other motifs from contemporary
political culture. Roger Manning has noted that in the popular
rebellions of early modern England 'the participants often displayed

a remarkable degree of legal sophistication'.[29] Falconbridge is clear
that his rebellion is within the law:

> Our quarell, like ourself, is honourable,
> The law our warrant.   (Scene ii)

But the legality of his claim is trivialised by the ragged low life
interventions:

> SMOKE: I, I, the law is on our side.
> CHUB: I, the law is in our hands.   (Scene ii)

One of the principal debates among social historians of early
modern rebellion is the extent to which popular disturbances can be
described as political. Roger Manning suggests that before the
mid-seventeenth century,

anti-enclosure riots may be regarded as displaying primitive or pre-politi-
cal behaviour ... their motives are devoid of political consciousness and
their writings or utterances do not employ a political vocabulary.

Nevertheless he notes the way in which 'aristocratic manipulation or
gentry factionalism complicate the picture'.[30] Though the Falconbridge coup is led by a politically motivated aristocrat, the play
presents the rabble's motives in economic rather than political
terms. They view London as a source of booty:

> You know *Cheapside*: there are the mercers shops.
> Where we will measure veluet by the pikes,
> And silkes and satins by the street's whole bredth:
> We'le take the tankards from the conduit-cocks
> To fill with ipocras and drinke carouse,
> Where chains of gold and plate shall be as plenty
> As wooden dishes in the wild of Kent ...
>
> No sooner in *London* will wee be
> But the bakers for you, the brewers for mee.
> *Birchin lane* shall suite vs.
> The costermongers fruite vs
> The poulters send vs in fowl,
> And butchers meate without controul:
> And euer when we suppe or dine
> The vintners freely bring us in wine.
> In [if] anybody aske who shall pay,
> Cut off his head and send him away.   (Scene ii)

This doggerel invokes a familiar image of economic disorder, but it is
also a carnivalesque fantasy of conspicuous consumption. Spicing
has lined the rebels up on the stage and invited them to share the

vision of London's plenty. The scene has an ambiguous dramatic impact as both a celebration of London's plenty and an attack on London and the values of an urban culture on guard against depredations both from rural invasion and from disorder initiated by the disadvantaged urban poor.

Manning describes how 'Between 1581 and 1602, the city was disturbed by no fewer than 35 outbreaks of disorder'.[31] The response of London's ruling orders was partly to guard against economic hardship by importing and distributing food, and partly to enact repressive measures against vagrants and immigrants into the city. Falconbridge's supporters represent both kinds of threat to civic order, for although they are supposed to be from Essex and Kent, they are also described as

> those desperate, idle, swaggering mates,
> That haunt the suburbes in the time of peace,
> And raise vp ale-house brawls in the streete.   (Scene v)

This description comes in a flyting between Spicing and a pair of apprentices who are keen to take part in heroically defending the city. By setting apprentice against rebel, citizen against suburban, the text minimises the potential for equating populism with rebellion and drives a wedge between different elements within popular culture which is given symbolic physical form in the

> *very fierie assault on all sides, wherein the prentices doe great*
> *seruice.*   (Scene v, s.d.)

This alignment of apprentices with the ruling elite of the Lord Mayor glosses over the historical conflict between apprentices and the city authorities which lay behind much late-Elizabethan civil unrest. Just as Falconbridge rested his claim on history, so the Lord Mayor and the apprentices are allied through their heroic history of allegiance to the crown. When Falconbridge accuses the citizens of treachery towards Henry VI, Shore retorts

> My lord *Maior* bears his sword in *his* defence,
> That put the sword into the arms of *London*,
> Made the lord Maiors for euer after knights,
> *Richard*, depos'd by *Henry Bolingbroke*,
> From whom the house of *Yorke* doth claime their right. (Scene iv)

The Lord Mayor too reminds the citizens of the occasion for that honour when Walworth killed the rebel Jack Straw and the apprentices themselves place their resistance to Falconbridge as part of a history reported by the Chronicles of England.

Popular narratives of heroic apprentices often provided the sources for Heywood's version of popular drama, but this play deals very gingerly with the dangerous contradictions of popular politics. The City, the apprentices and the crown are marshalled in support of the ideology of rightful monarchy. The allegiance works symbolically in the theatrical psychomachia of the alarums and excursions, but the overdetermined insistence of the speeches, the array of ideologically fraught reference and imagery, suggest tensions in the political understanding which are far from completely resolved.

Part of the lack of resolution comes, of course, from the play's rag-bag structure, which attaches the 'merie pastime of the Tanner of Tamworth' and a full-blown domestic tragedy of Jane Shore, the King's citizen mistress, onto the story of the rebellion which threatened Edward's reign. Each of these plots, however, deals with relations between the monarch and the populace; they raise questions about the source of authority and the corruption of power, though they are always held within the conventions of popular dramaturgy as a source of pathos and comedy and excitement which complicates the explicitly articulated political position.

In Henslowe's diary entries these two plays are referred to by the names of the protagonists of their subsidiary plots. *Edward IV* is called 'Jane Shore' and *Sir Thomas Wyatt* either 'lady Jane' or 'The overthrow of the rebels'. The narratives which provide excitement and pathos are extracted from their surrounding actions and indeed could be reassembled in different form, as is suggested by Heywood's use of material in *If You Know Not Me You Know Nobody*, which may have come from his contribution to *Sir Thomas Wyatt*.[32] For the popular dramatists of the public theatres, contemporary political issues and recent history were grist to the cultural mill of dramatic production. The negotiations of their politics can be located in the courtly opposition of honour to policy which nonetheless could be combined with a defence of the legitimate authority of City and state. Their representation, however, depended on the popular dramatic forms which could move from sympathy for the fallen individual to atavistic nationalism to the celebration of populist misrule. The resulting plays have only sporadic emotional and intellectual power and their politics do not easily transfer to the modern age. However, they do provide some indication of the complex richness of the political culture of early modern drama.

NOTES

1 'Prince's Progress', *The Guardian*, 21 November 1989, p. 38.
2 The debate over political readings of tragedy is usefully summarised in Jonathan Dollimore's introduction to the reissue of J. W. Lever, *The Tragedy of State* (London, 1971; reissued 1987 with an introduction by Jonathan Dollimore). The controversy is re-awakened in *The London Review of Books*, 15 March 1990.
3 In the introduction to *The Tragedy of State*, J. W. Lever found in the works of the great Jacobean tragedians a prefiguring of the opposition to the state and the commitment to individual freedoms characteristic of the long tradition of liberal politics.
4 For a discussion of politically inflected productions by the Royal Shakespeare Company see Ralph Berry, *Changing Styles in Shakespeare* (London, 1981). See also Alan Sinfield, 'Royal Shakespeare: Theatre and the Making of Ideology' in Alan Sinfield and Jonathan Dollimore, eds. *Political Shakespeare, New Essays in Cultural Materialism* (Manchester, 1985), pp. 158–81.
5 The debate over the ideology of canon formation is discussed in Gary Taylor, *Reinventing Shakespeare* (London, 1989) and in Terry Hawkes, *The Shakespeherian Rag* (London, 1984).
6 The problems of historical readings based only on canonical texts is discussed in James Holstun, 'Ranting at the New Historicism', *English Literary Renaissance* (1989) 189–225.
7 Catherine Belsey, *The Subject of Tragedy: Identity and Difference in Renaissance Drama* (London, 1985), p. 43.
8 Philip Sidney, *The Defense of Poesie* in *Literary Criticism from Plato to Dryden*, ed. Allan H. Gilbert (1967), p. 432.
9 See Marston, *Antonio and Mellida*, ed. Reavley Gair (Manchester, 1978), Introduction, pp. 27–39.
10 The suggestion that boy players were engaged in parody rather than failed comedy was made by R. A. Foakes, 'Tragedy of the Children's Theatres after 1600: A Challenge to the Adult Stage' in D. Galloway, ed., *Elizabethan Theatre*, v (1970) 37–59.
11 George Chapman, *Bussy D'Ambois*, ed. Nicholas Brooke (London, 1964).
12 See *Hamlet*, I.ii.440–85 and *The Spanish Tragedy*, i.i.
13 See Raymond Williams, *Modern Tragedy* (London, 1966). See also the discussion in his *Politics and Letters* (London, 1979), pp. 211–13.
14 Sidney, *The Defense of Poesie*, p. 449.
15 Ben Jonson, *Sejanus*, ed. Jonas Barish (New Haven, 1965) p. 26. The relationship between discussions of popular and elite culture and the change from patronage to commerce in early modern dramatic production is discussed in Kathleen McLuskie, 'The Poet's Royal Exchange: Patronage and Commerce in Early Modern Drama', *The Yearbook of English Studies*, 21 (1991).

16 John Webster, *The White Devil*, ed. John Russell Brown (London, 1960), pp. 2–4.

17 Thomas Heywood, *Apology for Actors* in G. E. Bentley, *The Seventeenth Century Stage* (Chicago, 1968), p. 16.

18 David Riggs, *Ben Jonson: A Life* (Cambridge, Mass. and London, 1989), p. 47.

19 See Ronnie Mulryne's essay in this volume, pp. 13–14.

20 Thomas Heywood, *Elegy* (London, 1613), dedication.

21 Mervyn James, 'At a Crossroads of the Political Culture: the Essex Revolt, 1601' in *Society, Politics and Culture: Studies in Early Modern England* (Cambridge, 1986), pp. 416–65.

22 *Ibid.*, p. 461.

23 Antony Fletcher, *Tudor Rebellions* (London, 1973), p. 90.

24 *The Dramatic Works of Thomas Dekker*, ed. Fredson Bowers (Cambridge, 1962), vol. I.

25 Fletcher, *Tudor Rebellions*, p. 81.

26 *Ibid.*, p. 85.

27 Thomas Heywood, *The Dramatic Works*, vol. I (reissued, 1964 by Russell and Russell . . . from the edition of 1874). There is no act, scene or line numbering in this edition. The scene numbers given have been added to assist identification of the quoted passages.

28 The intersection of political concepts and dramatic form in the representation of popular rebellion is discussed in Kathleen McLuskie, ''Tis but a Woman's Jar': Family and Kinship in Elizabethan Domestic Drama', *Literature and History*, 8 (1983) 228–39.

29 Roger B. Manning, *Village Revolts: Social Protest and Popular Disturbance in England 1509–1640* (Oxford, 1988).

30 *Ibid.*, p. 2.

31 *Ibid*, p. 187.

32 A. M. Clark, *Thomas Heywood: Playwright and Miscellanist* (Oxford, 1931), pp. 216–17, discusses the probable relationship between *Edward IV*, *Sir Thomas Wyatt* and Heywood's *If You Know Not Me You Know Nobody*.

CHAPTER 9

Drama and opinion in the 1620s: Middleton and Massinger

Margot Heinemann

> You complain
> You serve one lord, but your lord serves a thousand,
> Besides his passions, that are his worst masters;
> You must humour him, and he is bound to sooth
> Every grim sir above him: if he frown,
> For the least neglect you fear to lose your place;
> But if, and with all slavish observation,
> From the minion's self, to the groom of his close-stool,
> He hourly seeks not favour, he is sure
> To be eased of his office, though perhaps he bought it.
> Nay, more; that high disposer of all such
> That are subordinate to him, serves and fears
> The fury of the many-headed monster,
> The giddy multitude: and as a horse
> Is still a horse, for all his golden trappings,
> So your men of purchased titles, at their best, are
> But serving-men in rich liveries.
> (Page to court servants, in Massinger's *The Unnatural Combat*,
> III.ii.117–33; *c.* 1626)

In considering the relations between theatre and government in the 1620s, it seems useful to begin with the plays of the exceptional 1623-4 season, and to re-establish the argument for their importance in articulating and reinforcing something like a popular public opinion, critical of the policy of the crown, at what can now be seen as a turning-point in relations between the government and the nation.

It is generally agreed that the particularly radical surviving plays of this season (and especially *A Game at Chess*) could be staged at all only because of exceptionally sharp divisions at the top, which temporarily softened the censorship. But this does not mean that they were simply a freak, a 'once-off' phenomenon. On the contrary,

237

they provide a rare insight into what many people might have liked to see in the theatre at other times, if they had not been prevented by the fear of repression. The ways of seeing and thinking which these plays embody and fuel are indeed part of a much longer post-Reformation crisis of authority, in which the theatres help to form the 'mentalities' to which they will later appeal, not only at court and among the political elites but more widely among London citizen audiences.

The 1623–4 plays cannot be reduced (as some scholars have recently suggested) simply to part of an opportunistic propaganda campaign by Prince Charles and Buckingham in support of their new 'war party'. Intense dramatic and literary protest against the policy of the crown had begun much earlier, and was to continue after the stance of prince and duke had again changed. Moreover, much of the evidence for their direct instigation of these plays is unconvincing and strained. Nor should we interpret the plays merely in terms of the victory of one faction at court over another. Some factions, such as those of the Earls of Pembroke and South-ampton, were consistent for many years in their support of a 'forward' foreign policy and some did represent consistent ideo-logical stances and attract supporters accordingly.[1] Moreover, at times the dramatists appear to have stirred up popular disrespect for hierarchy and the actualities of court life, in a way that went far beyond what any court patrons, even the most anti-Spanish, would have wished in normal times, and with far-reaching long-term consequences for the loyalties and allegiances of London people.

How far, then, is it appropriate to speak of 'opposition drama' at this period? Clearly, there was no single polarised parliamentary or national opposition with a coherent policy as we understand it today, and taken in that sense the term is misleading. Rather, in a society under increasing strain and tension, there were shifting divisions of opinion and questioning among different groups and interests concerning the nature and use of power, in relation to a variety of political, religious, constitutional and social issues. We can agree that none of these groupings (whether defined in terms of court and country, City and patrician, Puritan and Arminian, Dutch and Spanish or local and national) was arguing for radical alteration or overthrow of the existing political system, much less for civil war. Nevertheless, on specific issues serious opposition and demands for reform were widespread and continuous, and the

drama often articulated and reinforced these feelings, making ideological conflicts over prerogative and property, local justice and
foreign policy visible and understandable for those outside as well as
within the 'political nation'.

It has been argued by some (though not all) new historicist critics
that early Stuart drama necessarily serves to uphold the dominant
ideology, the power-relations and institutions within which the
theatre exists, and that any social or political criticism is on balance
'contained', functioning as a safety-valve rather than a motor of
change. This is not something which can be proved or disproved.
Yet it does seem that some plays not only appealed to the anxieties
and grievances of audiences, but on occasions – as in 1623–4, and
again in 1625–6 when parliament was moving to impeach Buckingham – by so doing helped to form and stimulate a mood of resistance
to the policies of the crown. In this respect the influence of the
drama has analogies with that of churches and preachers, at least in
London where the theatres were most active.[2] Above all, it gave
people – including the unprivileged and non-literate – images and
languages to think with, and enabled them to feel that their personal
anxieties and resentments were widely shared. In this sense plays
might help to demystify royal power, to desanctify prerogative and
the rule of over-mighty favourites, and thus to impede the drift
towards absolutism.

Failure to take full account of pervasive censorship and self-
censorship has tended to mask real ideological and political conflicts
underlying the drama of the 1620s. The 'consensus' in the fraction of
the plays which has come down to us is itself largely a product of that
censorship. Censorship and self-censorship must also be partly
responsible for the disappearance of so many of the plays, including
what were probably some of the most controversial. Even if they
reached the stage, companies and playwrights may often have been
unwilling to take the further risk of publication. Among plays which
have been completely lost, but may have been directly concerned
with topical conflicts, are *A Match and No Match* (Samuel Rowley),
The Hungarian Lion, The Spanish Viceroy, The Spanish Contract, Massinger's *The Judge* and *The Tyrant, The Plantation of Virginia* and
several history plays by Robert Davenport. There may be more of
which not even the titles have survived. Massinger, for instance,
published two of his unaided plays in 1622–4, then none for the next
five years, resuming in 1629 when the death of Buckingham may

have made texts like *The Roman Actor*, *A New Way to Pay Old Debts*, *The Unnatural Combat* and *The Maid of Honour* seem less risky.

If there is relatively little political criticism or subversion in the drama from 1620 to later 1623, this is scarcely evidence of 'consensus' in society. After the King's Men got into trouble over the topical *Sir John Van Olden Barnavelt* (Fletcher and Massinger, 1619) – which was first banned, then staged in a heavily censored form – the dramatists did not again appeal to the intense interest in European politics by direct documentary staging of contemporary events. Indeed, from 1620 to 1623 the clamp-down of royal censorship under James's proclamation would have made it impossible to do so. In the 'evil time' Fletcher retreated to flippant comedy and tragicomedy; Massinger, perhaps with a stronger political interest, devised fable-plays with topical allusions which could be construed as political allegory if one so chose; and there was a wave of anti-tyrant plays at outdoor playhouses like the Red Bull – Dekker and Massinger's *Virgin Martyr*, Massinger's *Duke of Milan* and Gervase Markham's *Herod and Marianne*.

MASSINGER, MIDDLETON AND THE YEARS 1623–4

The theatrical and political climate changed rapidly when Charles and Buckingham returned from Spain without the Infanta. They can scarcely be said to have *initiated* a propaganda campaign against the Spanish alliance, but their change of stance gave a new freedom and respectability to the anti-Spanish cause. Whereas much of the polemical material of 1620–3 (notably the satirical pamphlets of Thomas Scott) had been illicit, smuggled in from abroad, much more could not be openly produced in England and legally distributed, even dramatised. Many of the anti-popery, anti-Spanish tracts that poured from the presses in 1624 had already been preached as sermons, privately circulated and even printed at some time over the previous ten years. It was the changed political atmosphere, with the heir to the throne apparently joining the existing popular movement, that now favoured their publication on a wider scale.[3]

The change in atmosphere is evident if one compares Massinger's *The Maid of Honour*[4] (probably of 1621–2) with his *The Bondman*, performed at court in December 1623, 'the Prince only being there'. Both are political plays, making obvious parallels between a fictitious Sicilian (or Syracusan) state and the military situation of

England in the early 1620s. Moral ambiguities, however, surround the burning issue of war and peace in *The Maid of Honour*, where king and favourite behave ignobly, misusing power and prerogative for selfish ends, but where the cause of Frederick, the aptly named ally they desert, is not fully just either. There is no such ambivalence, in contrast, about *The Bondman*, in which the case for a bold foreign and military policy is directly and powerfully dramatised. Syracuse is in danger of invasion because the aristocracy have forgotten how to fight, and the council, formerly made up of men who have served their country in war and peace,

> is now filled
> With green heads, that determine of the state
> Over their cups, or when their sated lusts
> Afford them leisure; or supplied by those
> Who, rising from base arts and sordid thrift,
> Are eminent for their wealth, not for their wisdom.
>
> (1.iii.185–90)

The state is saved by the noble general Timoleon, who arrives from campaigning abroad (as it might be in the friendly Netherlands) to take command of its defence. Scorning the idea of a conscript or mercenary army,[5] he calls on the young nobility to follow him to war, and on the rich to part with their money to finance it. He is unequivocally a hero for the times, whose victorious courage and skill might well suggest to the audience a parallel either with Prince Maurice, leader of the Dutch Protestant forces against Spain, or with English commanders experienced in the European wars, like Sir Horace Vere, recently returned after fighting in the Palatinate to join the Council of War. The model is not individual but typical – Southampton, Essex, Willoughby or Fairfax could all serve to provide a contrast with the hesitations and self-deception of James's government as the anti-Spanish groupings saw it.[6]

Such an exceptionally bold and risky play as *A Game at Chess* – unlike any other of the Jacobean period in its representation of royalty and its iconoclastic treatment of 'mysteries of state' – could certainly not have been staged at all without the change in stance by Buckingham and Prince Charles and their urgent wish to break the Spanish match. The division between them and the king, and the temporary alliance it brought about between Buckingham and Lord Chamberlain Pembroke,[7] his former opponent, allowed the play to be passed by the Master of the Revels, Sir Henry Herbert, – a kinsman of Pembroke's, very recently enabled to purchase that office through the earl's personal influence.[8] For the time being the political censorship was softened. However, to see the piece either as an uncritical celebration of new-found unity, or simply as part of an opportunist propaganda campaign by prince and duke for their new 'war party', is to miss the main point about what the play actually is and does, and underrate its importance in tapping deep currents of popular feeling.

By focusing and sharpening fears of a Spanish takeover in Britain, and exposing alleged Spanish and Catholic machinations to that end, *A Game at Chess* would indeed have helped the so-called 'patriot coalition' towards the aim of breaking the Spanish treaties and war with Spain. The dramatisation of Buckingham's and Charles's trip to Madrid as a bold venture undertaken on purpose to discover and expose Spain's double-dealing would have been especially useful to Buckingham and Charles at this point, since the duke was anxious for this somewhat selective and romanticised account to be widely disseminated before the Earl of Bristol returned with a less flattering version.[9]

The audiences who packed the Globe certainly came to celebrate their relief that the Spanish marriage project appeared to have failed and the supposed Spanish and popish plotters were in retreat. However, in more self-consciously political circles, the 'patriot coalition' constructed by Buckingham was not a full enthusiastic consensus, but an uneasy pragmatic alliance between men who were prepared to come together to resist the Spanish marriage and attempt to pressurise James into war with Spain, but who had very different outlooks and over the years had come deeply to distrust one another.[10] The distrust was expressed even in 1624 in the unwillingness of parliament to grant open-ended subsidies for a war that had not been declared and might never be; and in the efforts of MPs to tie the use of the money to the war they wanted, directly against Spain, in alliance with the Dutch republicans and fought largely at sea, rather than to the financing of mercenary armies in a land war for the Palatinate. Moreover, as the French marriage negotiations developed under Buckingham's direction, later in 1624, he excluded from them (and even from information about them) those councillors most committed to the Protestant cause, who might object to the concessions proposed for the English Catholics. The 'patriot coalition' was already being disrupted by its own contradictions.

Hence a drama such as *A Game at Chess*, rousing and reinforcing feeling against popish plots and Catholic penetration of the court, was potentially dangerous to Charles and Buckingham, in that it might limit their freedom of manoeuvre later (though they may well have lacked the foresight to perceive this). They were being lionised and made popular *on condition* that they pressed ahead with the anti-Spanish, anti-popery line. Meanwhile, the long-term support-ers of such a policy could see demonstrated in the theatre their own strength among the 'people'.

Thus, while some aspects of the play had immediate propaganda value for Buckingham and Charles, this should not lead us to miss the obvious central impact of *A Game at Chess* as a whole on public opinion. The main image of the political situation in 1622–3 pre-sented to the cross-class Protestant audience was clear-cut and alarming, confirming popular fears and the warnings of the preachers and pamphleteers till recently repressed. England is shown as a victim of Jesuit plotting to undermine its military and political security and bring it under the 'universal monarchy' of the papacy and Spain. Moreover, the king (however respectfully pre-sented) is shown as failing to expose and resist these plots in good time because he has been duped by the influence of the witty and plausible Spanish ambassador Gondomar, who has succeeded in establishing a network of secret agents at court, in the government and especially among court ladies. However one interprets the details of the allegory concerning the attempted seduction of the White Queen's Pawn by the Jesuit black pieces, the stage impression would still be of unsuspecting great ladies cajoled by skilful Jesuit con-men, exploiting their religious credulity, into transferring their loyalty from the White House (England) to the Black House (Spain).

The emphasis on Catholic converts as spies, and especially the focus on the susceptibility of women, makes it most unlikely that Buckingham can have been a main instigator of the play, at least in its final form, for the obvious contemporary application the audi-ence was likely to make was to his own family. The conversion to Rome of his mother, the old Countess of Buckingham, had been a public sensation two years before, and it was known that the Duke himself, whose recently married wife was a crypto-Catholic and whose father-in-law Rutland was a prominent Catholic peer, had been contemplating the same course. All this was recalled, early in

1624, by the belated publication of a series of disputations between the leading Jesuit John Fisher[11] and divines of the Church of England, held in 1622 at the king's request in the countess's presence, and intended to persuade the lady – and more importantly her son – to renounce Rome. Some of these disputations James himself attended. The book had been ready but banned from publication since 1622, but in the changed political situation it was personally read and sanctioned by the king in November 1623.[12] This very recent report (one section of it written by William Laud, who had since become the duke's chaplain), or another version by Daniel Featly, chaplain to archbishop Abbot, may well have formed part of Middleton's sources for the Jesuit plot to take over England – the very centre of his play.[13]

It had been widely rumoured in 1622–3 that both James and Charles might be persuaded to convert to Catholicism for the sake of the Spanish match. Indeed, Dr Francis White, Dean of Carlisle, one of the divines officially appointed to put the Protestant case against Fisher, was so alarmed that during the Twelfth Night services at St Paul's (January 1623) he led the congregation in a prayer that God 'preserve the King and Prince from any that go about to change their religion' (for which he was reprimanded and confined to his house). In the event the old countess remained a Catholic, but to the king's relief Buckingham decided not to convert. However, his Catholic associations were not forgotten, and were revived as a source of widespread distrust soon after the play was performed.

The efforts of some scholars to impose on *A Game at Chess* interpretations and complexities which no audience could conceivably have picked up in the theatre may reflect unwillingness to face the most obvious meaning, which drew almost one-tenth of the population of London to see the play during its nine-day run. For modern liberal readers, it can be difficult to accept that the mature Middleton, at the period when he was writing *The Changeling* and *Women Beware Women*, could also have produced what they see as a crudely biased, bigoted attack on the Catholic church in England. This is a real difficulty. It requires a considerable effort of historical imagination to understand what anti-popery may have meant for English Protestants in the seventeenth century, when political issues were discussed and fought over largely in religious terms, and when it had patriotic, rationalist and sometimes (though not necessarily) popular democratic connotations. Moreover, the idea of a political and military Catholic plot to change the religion and dominate England was then by no means absurd: people looked back to the Armada and the Gunpowder Plot, while later the Popish plot on which Pym built much of his attack on Charles I had (as Caroline Hibbard has shown) a solid foundation of fact.[14]

Popery is exposed in the play not so much in terms of doctrine (predestination and transubstantiation are never mentioned), but rather as a superstitious, anti-rational, anti-patriotic religion establishing Jesuitical power over the individual believer, who is thus recruited as an obedient agent in plotting and spying to bring England under the universal monarchy of the pope or the King of Spain. The thrust is political and anti-clerical rather than theological. Confession serves as a means of blackmail. There is continual stress on the fabrication of 'miracles', with examples listed or shown (moving images, conjuring with mirrors), to induce awed obedience to the priest and his manipulations. All in all, the play dramatises the militant Protestant fear of popery as an anti-religion of Antichrist and the organiser of a 'fifth column' in war. The response of those who flocked to see it makes it clear that such fears of conspiracy went far beyond a small fanatical Puritan minority.

A GAME AT CHESS AND THE PAMPHLETEERS

Although anti-court satire is by no means its central point, the tone of *A Game at Chess* throughout is radical and populist. Incidental sidelights on the way offices and preferments are handed out at court, with heavy bribes to those (like Gondomar) believed to have influence, play to a cheerful cynicism in the audience about that institution, which scarcely reinforces a 'deference culture'. Black Knight shamelessly boasts:

> The court has held the City by the horns
> Whilst I have milked her. (III.i.108–9)

Corruption in the inner sanctum, the bedchamber, promises him the opportunity to plant agents there as well as to enrich himself:

> Sirrah, I have sold the groom-o'-the-stool six times,
> And received money of six several ladies
> Ambitious to take place of baronets' wives;
> To three old mummy-matrons I have promised
> The mothership o' the maids ... (IV.ii.42–6)

Meanwhile the Church of England dignities and benefices conferred by the King himself on the turncoat Fat Bishop (De Dominis, who was also a noted propagandist for royal absolutism) imply a comic comment on the venal and pluralist ecclesiastical set-up at home:

> FAT BISHOP: I am persuaded that this flesh would fill
> The biggest chair ecclesiastical
> If it were put to trial ...
> There's but two lazy beggarly preferments
> In the White Kingdom, and I have got 'em both.　　(III.i.9–16)

There is indeed every indication that, while respectful to the firmly Calvinist and anti-Spanish Archbishop Abbot, the play follows Thomas Scott's pamphlets, its main source, in its political and religious radicalism, going well beyond what its noble patrons would normally have countenanced.

The various mildly mocking references to Buckingham have to be understood in this context. No one would suggest that the play is primarily an attack on the duke by a rival faction. His change to an anti-Spanish line had to be welcomed as crucial by any supporter of the Protestant or imperial cause. Nevertheless, the assumption that in mid-1624 his former opponents and the whole theatre public saw him as a hero and saviour, and forgot their earlier suspicions, is not supported by the facts. In particular Thomas Scott, whose pamphlet *Vox Regis* (1624) has been cited as evidence that even the duke's most severe critics had now gone over to 'fulsome praise', in reality offers cautious and even ironic commendation of Buckingham as having (thank God) recently mended his ways. In the course of this commendation Scott reminds the reader of all the original reasons for distrusting the favourite, and hopes that they have now been overcome. The hatred with which he was regarded till recently is emphasised:

How many curses did fill his sails going towards Spain? ... But now how many blessings and prayers attend him from these same hearts and mouths ... We saw his power with His Majesty and the Prince, we knew who was his wife, who was his mother; and all we could then see of him made us suspect, and tremble the more, the more we saw it.

Hopefully the duke (as he told Parliament) has now 'learned to abhor the idolatries of Rome, and to love the true Church better', as a result of his experience in Spain. The praise is made strictly conditional on this conversion:

Go forward, great Duke, and prosper, whilst thou dost nothing but what may justify thee, and what thou may'st justify before all the world.

Although Scott, like his patroness the Queen of Bohemia, is bound publicly to welcome Buckingham's change of heart, he clearly does not wish to create illusions. Indeed he seems at times to be hedging his bets against a possible further change.

This seems close to the politics of *A Game at Chess* itself. Buckingham is shown as doing valuable service in breaking with Spain, but there are sufficient references to his weaknesses to suggest that the theatre people and their regular patrons had not completely reversed their earlier suspicions, and neither had much of the audience. The allusions to the duke's social climbing, his vanity about his physical appearance, and his taste for lechery (especially homosexual lechery) are no briefer than those that got Jonson into trouble with James over *Eastward Ho*, (as R. C. Bald pointed out in his great edition of 1929).

The case of *Vox Coeli*, listed by Bald as one likely source for *A Game at Chess*, is instructive here. This irreverent satirical tract, dated 1624 and published anonymously 'from Elisium', showed six former royals, from Henry VIII to Elizabeth I, discussing the case for an anti-Spanish war, with the usual fierce attacks on Catholic plotters and some disrespect for James's hesitations. The Puritan author, John Reynolds, was tutor to Basil Feilding, son of Buckingham's sister, Lady Denbigh. He was accompanying Feilding in Kensington's train in France during the negotiations for the marriage with Henrietta Maria, when in July 1624 he was suddenly 'forced back' to England with his pupil, arrested ostensibly for writing *Vox Coeli* and *Votivae Angliae*, and kept in prison for more than two years. The reason may not have been just the censorship charge, for no other pamphleteer was so severely treated. The real cause was probably the fact that Reynolds had got to know and disapproved of the concessions to English Catholics that the French were demanding, and had written as much in June to his employers the Denbighs, expressing his hope that James would never consent.[15] Reynolds unwisely used the diplomatic messenger to send his letter; a month later came his extradition and arrest. It looks as if someone feared a leak of sensitive material damaging to the negotiations, on which secrecy was vital to the duke's new policy, and the long imprisonment served not only to punish Reynolds but to keep him out of circulation till the marriage was safely over. At all events, though

Feilding was Buckingham's nephew, the all-powerful duke does not seem to have protected the young man's tutor. It is interesting that Feilding himself, though a courtier and ambassador under Charles I, when the Civil War broke out joined the parliament side and became one of its leading commanders and later a member of Cromwell's government. His Villiers mother found this defiance of the family's attitude inexplicable, but perhaps we need not.[16] At all events, the episode suggests that the players of *A Game at Chess* were unlikely to be protected by the duke in August 1624.

MASSINGER'S *THE UNNATURAL COMBAT*
AND THE LATER 1620S

A Game at Chess and *The Duchess of Suffolk* mark the last point in time when the popular theatres could celebrate the achievements of the 'blessed revolution' and the patriot coalition. The volunteer force of 6,000 men sent to reinforce the English troops already fighting with the Dutch armies, in the late summer of 1624, attracted a great deal of support (much like that given to Timoleon in *The Bondman*). Its four colonels were all known and tried supporters of the 'Protestant cause' – the Earls of Southampton, Oxford and Essex, and Lord Willoughby. The grandmother of the last of these, Catherine Bertie, a royal exile under Mary and a Puritan patroness under Elizabeth, was the heroine of *The Duchess of Suffolk*, staged at the Fortune around the time when the expedition was leaving. Recruits flocked to serve as officers under these commanders.

There was no such enthusiasm for Mansfeld's expedition to the Palatinate, financed by the diversion to the mercenary general (without any consultation with parliament) of the subsidies MPs had been persuaded to vote for war with Spain. Men had to be pressed, and deserted wherever they could before embarking. The whole operation (in conflict with the strategy the Commons had envisaged) was grossly mismanaged militarily and diplomatically, and proved a disastrous failure, most of the luckless soldiers dying of starvation or fever before any campaign had even begun. The pamphleteer Tom Tell-Troth had argued that the preservation of 'the religion' and of English interests ought not to be entrusted to a general who was in it only for the money, and might easily give up or change sides. The event seemed to bear him out. It was the first of a series of humiliating British military reverses: Cadiz and Ile de Rhé were to follow. By 1628 MPs were thoroughly disillusioned with the war, reluctant to discuss it or make adequate provision for it. But this did not reflect a reaction against war itself so much as the experience of a war which from the outset had gone very badly.[17]

The political unease, insecurity and fear of absolutism in the later 1620s[18] is expressed, for example, in the series of classical anti-tyrant plays powerfully analysed by Martin Butler, notably Massinger's *The Roman Actor* and Thomas May's *Julia Agrippina*.[19] Despite the renewed censorship, which obliged dramatists to present their political themes obliquely, many of Massinger's other surviving plays of the later Buckingham years likewise articulate the frustration and anger not only of the MPs and peers who were trying to impeach the duke, but of much wider circles in the London audience. Massinger from this time seems to have looked for patronage and support not only to the Pembroke family, but also to dissident gentry and MPs prominent (and sometimes penalised) for resistance to the forced loan and unparliamentary taxation.[20] Among Massinger's long-time friends, Henry Parker and John Selden were outstanding as critics of the trend towards absolutism and over-use of the royal prerogative. If the terms 'country' and 'court', increasingly used in politics at this time, are taken to refer not to a place or an office, but to a set of attitudes, an ideology, Massinger seems to have aligned himself for most of his career with 'country' values, whereas Middleton was more closely associated with the City.[21]

Given the explosive political climate of the later 1620s and the revived censorship, open dramatisation of Protestant and Puritan fears would have been quite impossible. By the process that has been called 'the hermeneutics of censorship',[22] Massinger alludes to but does not consistently develop the suggestion that England's ills, including failure in war, result from undisclosed wickedness, irreligion and corruption in the highest places. At the same time the situation and evil character concerned is made sufficiently unlike the political analogue to refute any charge of direct subversion.

Following the failed expedition to Cadiz, and again after the humiliating defeat at the Ile de Rhé, the public became aware of the mounting crisis of government, not just through parliamentary debates (never very widely reported), but through rioting in the streets,[23] and imprisonment of the government's political opponents (including some London merchants) for refusing to pay unparliamentary taxes such as the forced loan. In spite of proclamations forbidding veterans to come 'in troops' about their grievances, London from 1625 to 1628 was repeatedly filled with masses of turbulent sailors and soldiers demanding their pay, holding meetings and breaking officials' windows. One such group in August 1626 held up Buckingham's coach by seizing the horses' reins; another later smashed the coach to pieces, and the duke's chamber at Whitehall was forcibly invaded as he sat at dinner by six captains, who had served in Ireland, demanding their pay. Another group, led by Sir Harry Ley, in February 1626 directly petitioned the king on behalf of all the captains returning from Cadiz, 'beseeching his Majesty, because their reputation was slain for want of their salary to pay their debts, that he should dispose of their lives as he pleased'. Some of the lords, interpreting this as taxing the king with tyranny, demanded who was the penman: they answered 'All, all!'[24] These events provide the context for plays like *Dick of Devonshire*, Dekker's *Wonder of a Kingdom*, and Massinger's *The Unnatural Combat*, and probably for others which have not survived.

The *Unnatural Combat* is directly linked with the Cadiz fiasco and its aftermath, both by internal evidence and by Massinger's dedication of the first printed edition (1639) to Sir Anthony St Leger, a Kentish gentleman whose cousin, Sir William St Leger,[25] had served prominently on the Cadiz expedition, had personally come to the Earl of Essex's assistance in the fighting, and was highly critical of Wimbledon, the commander appointed by Buckingham. On the fleet's return St Leger was left at Plymouth in charge of a mass of half-starved soldiers and sailors, on whose behalf he wrote repeatedly and urgently to Buckingham asking for their pay, since they had not even clothes to stand up in. St Leger was also present at an angry clash in the council between Essex and Buckingham as to who was to blame for the mismanagement, Buckingham continuing to defend his incompetent client. Massinger was personally known to the St Leger family (Sir Warham, Anthony's father, had already been his patron), and the more topical aspects of the play may well be based on some kind of first-hand account.

The political theme of *The Unnatural Combat* is expressed more directly and boldly in the (largely separate) secondary action, which seems to be entirely Massinger's own invention. The human interest here centres on Belgarde, a brave captain returning hungry and ragged from the wars, who is refused his pay by the governor of Marseilles, Beaufort, until the state has enough money from prizes to afford it – very much the authorities; reasoning after the Cadiz expedition had failed to capture the Spanish treasure fleet. He is allowed to eat at the governor's table to tide him over, but is later turned away by the steward because of his disreputable clothes. Having promised to return in his 'richest suit', Belgarde re-enters in armour with a case of carbines, to demand justice for the fighting men from the governor and lords. He draws a bitter contrast between the easy wealth of banqueting courtiers and city magnates and the poverty and hardships of the men who provide it for them. The imagery extends beyond the particular case of the unpaid soldiers to include all the overseas voyagers whose trade and plunder help to enrich court and city. He concludes with an open threat:

> Let it not then
> In after ages, to your shame be spoken
> That you with no relenting eyes look on
> Our wants that feed your plenty: or consume
> In prodigal and wanton gifts on drones
> The kingdom's treasure, yet detain from us
> The debt that with the hazard of our lives
> We have made you stand engaged for; or force us
> Against all civil government, in armour
> To require that, which with all willingness
> Should be tendered ere demanded. (III.iii.96–106)

Under duress (and perhaps also from a sense of shame) Beaufort concedes that all the troops shall be paid, including their arrears, and personally lays down 500 crowns towards a subscription for Belgarde himself, to which the other nobles contribute by emptying their purses. Belgarde, however, receives the money with cynical satisfaction rather than gratitude. In his view, it is his pistols that have done the persuading.

Even though the scene is emblematic rather than documentary, it seems to allude directly to the sailors' petitioning the king, as well as the captains breaking in on Buckingham's dinner. Belgarde is not sentimentalised as a perfect warrior – he is already in debt to the bawds, and if he got his back pay says crudely he might use it to open a brothel. Nevertheless he is sympathetically presented. His angry outburst, like those of Timoleon in *The Bondman* though more violently, speaks for the real indignation of the popular audience and the moral obligation of the 'natural rulers'. And it may well be this sharpness of tone that led to the play being performed only at the popular outdoor Globe, rather than repeated for a gentle audience at the Blackfriars.

Given the date for the play as 1626, it seems likely that the main action too invites a political interpretation. The protagonist, Malefort, is certainly nothing like a portrait of Buckingham – if he were the play could not possibly have been staged. Nevertheless the alterations and additions Massinger made to his sources strongly suggest analogies which the audience at that moment would be likely to draw.[26]

The original classical Declamation on which Massinger based his story tells of a general's son who fled to the enemy and later sent out a challenge to his father.[27] Massinger, however, made the general an Admiral, and his son a deserter to the pirates against whom the Admiral is supposed to protect the Marseilles fleet; there are no pirates in the original story. As Massinger's editors, P. Edwards and C. Gibson, say, 'it is probable that contemporary raids on the English coast by Barbary corsairs prompted the change from a military to a naval setting'.[28] But in the context of 1625–6 this change gave the play sharp political implications. For Buckingham, who had recently obtained by purchase the two offices of greatest naval importance, as Lord High Admiral and Warden of the Cinque Ports, was under heavy attack in parliament in 1625 and 1626, both for the Cadiz disaster and for alleged inaction in protecting English shipping against the pirates, who were making it dangerous for ships even to move from one English port to another. He was publicly accused not only of incompetence, but of being in collusion with the pirates and even of drawing a commission on their profits, very much as Malefort is in the play when it is revealed that his renegade son is now a pirate captain. Malefort is saved from condemnation only by a challenge from his son to single combat, to avenge an unnamed but hideous wrong. They fight and the son is killed; the pirate danger ceases and Malefort seems to be vindicated.

The second part of the play turns on his obsessive incestuous passion for his daughter, betrothed to the governor's son. To save her from his own terrifying lust Malefort gives her into the protection of a false friend, Montreville, with orders to keep her away from him: Montreville thereupon rapes her himself, while the enraged and raving Malefort tries in vain to storm his fortress and rescue her. A sequence of nightmarish ghostly visions of remorse reveals the origins of these crimes. Long ago Malefort had murdered his first wife (mother to the son he killed) in order to marry Montreville's mistress (later the mother of his violated daughter). As the spectres of his victims vanish, the Admiral is finally struck down and killed by a flash of lightning – the belated verdict of heaven – and the honest buff-jerkined soldier Belgarde takes command of the fortress, a conclusion satisfying the audience's sense of justice in more ways than one.

The play could no doubt be taken on one level either as exaggerated sensational fantasy in the Fletcherian manner or as a personal psychological study of incest and violence (an interpretation favoured by some modern critics). If there were any trouble with the authorities, playwright and players could argue that it was intended to be no more than that. However, it seems unlikely that the first audience in the popular playhouse would receive it in that politically innocuous way, given the emphatic naval parallels, the tension among the people, and the rioting sailors and soldiers in London streets. Malefort in the final spectral unmasking ceases to have much consistency as a character and is rapidly convicted of a wide variety of crimes, most of them hole-and-corner actions unconnected with incest or indeed with the patriarchal violence he has shown so far in the play. They include poisoning his first wife, seducing his second by charms and sorcery, breaking oaths, and changing his religion like 'a nose of wax' for his own advantage. All this does not add up to a coherent psychological 'character'. Rather, it enlarges Malefort into a symbolic figure of immeasurable evil, a type and tool of Antichrist whom the ineffective governor and council have failed to expose or control. At the same time it adds more parallels with the accusations being made against the favourite, both in the impeachment debates and in innumerable lampoons and anonymous ballads made against him in the last three years of his life.

'Unnatural' sex serves as an obvious link between drama and life. In *The Unnatural Combat*, Malefort's incestuous passion acts as moral equivalent for the homosexual affection which was widely believed (though not openly mentioned) to bind both James and Charles to the favourite. Basically the political hostility to the duke was founded on rational charges of ambition, nepotism, tyranny and incompetence. But mere incompetence and greed provided more convincing motivation, both in the drama and in politics, with the addition of sheer evil and irreligion. Cataline, whose life as summarised in Jonson's play may have served as a pattern for Malefort's, is represented there not only as a traitor but as a monster of every kind of personal wickedness – a devil-politician. The demonisation of Buckingham in popular perception followed a similar course.[29]

At a moment of panic fear of invasion and popish plots, horrors equivalent to those perpetrated by Malefort were attributed by rumour to the favourite and widely believed. The man whose meteoric rise, 'single counsel' and monopoly of the highest offices was thought to endanger the Protestant religion, and the military and naval strength, the very sovereignty of England, was credited also, in the many songs, ballads and poems circulated about him, with murdering King James and the Duke of Hamilton (and in some lampoons the Earls of Southampton and Oxford as well). He was alleged to dabble in the black arts, and with the help of his popish mother and his private astrologer Dr Lambe (beaten to death by a riotous London crowd in 1627) to have used charms and sorcery to bewitch both James and Charles into unnatural devotion to him and alienate them from their people. It was not only the broadside ballads and underground news-sheets that spread such accusations; the attacks in the parliament of 1625 (when Buckingham was first named as the 'grievance of grievances') and the impeachment charges in 1626 followed in part a similar sensational pattern. Unless one was prepared to blame the king himself for the naval débâcle, the rioting, the unparliamentary taxes and the imprisonment and deprivation of those refusing to pay them, the failures to aid the Protestant cause in Europe, and the growing toleration of Catholics at home, all these had to be laid at Buckingham's door, and were often explained in terms of wicked counsel and religious apostasy rather than political misjudgement.

In the theatre Malefort could serve as a symbolic focus for the kind of hatred and fear increasingly directed towards the duke and his clients as the centre of danger and disaster in the state. The intensity of this popular feeling was shown by the extraordinary public reaction to Buckingham's assassination by the discontented soldier Felton in 1628. The authorities dared not give the king's principal minister a daytime state funeral for fear of hostile demonstrations, and he had to be buried at night under armed guard. To this revulsion in public opinion the drama, alongside the anti-popish sermons and the newsletters and printed attacks, had contributed its share.

THE POPULAR THEATRES AND THE LATER 1620S

We know little of how all this turbulence registered in the down-market theatres, since so much of their repertory has been lost. But the central clash between fighters and governors is echoed in Dekker's *Wonder of a Kingdom* a little later.[30] The ragged soldier neglected by the rich was a traditional figure in earlier drama, from *Alarum for London* to Dekker's own *If It Be Not a Good Play* (1615); what is new here is the aggressive violence with which he now demands his rights.

The Cadiz disaster is again the subject of an unprinted manu-script play, *Dick of Devonshire* (probably by Heywood) closely based on a current real-life pamphlet of 1626 by a Devon soldier, Richard Pyke, narrating his exploits in the campaign, and afterwards as a prisoner of war in Spain.[31] Most of it is simple adventure stuff, boasting of Pyke's astonishing prowess with sword and quarter-staff. Pyke himself, who dedicated his tract to the king, would hardly want to spoil his chance of reward by criticising the expedition or its leaders (though his account does rather pointedly favour Essex over the other commanders). The playwright-adapter, however, gave the story a topical political edge by writing into the first act a long dialogue between two Devonshire merchants, explaining the relig-ious grounds for the war. They recall with pride Drake's victories over Spain in Elizabethan times, the vast wealth gained by the English from his privateering conquests, and finally the glorious defeat of the Armada. All of this stands in implied contrast to the miserable showing of the latest expedition, whose misguided strategy is mocked in the play even by the Spaniards. The whole play (dated precisely on internal evidence to 1626) thus becomes an argument for the 'blue-water' strategy of a diversionary sea war in the Indies against the Spanish treasure fleet. Thomas Heywood, as Bullen suggested, seems politically and stylistically the most likely author, the sea-fight story and the energetic verse being much in the line of *The Fair Maid of the West*: but whether or when the play was staged we have no means of knowing.

A NEW WAY TO PAY OLD DEBTS AND THE ATTACK ON BUCKINGHAM

A New Way to Pay Old Debts should not be seen as simply one more comedy about the clash between old gentry and new commercial wealth (a pattern familiar in Jonson, Middleton and Fletcher). It includes that conflict, but is nevertheless a different *kind* of drama, which in its contemporary context had a much sharper political thrust. What is presented with disturbing force in *A New Way* is nothing less than the threatened disintegration of the existing social and administrative system in the country – a relatively stable system like that headed by the Pembroke family in Massinger's native Wiltshire – as the traditional framework of law and order. The right to license alehouses, nominate JPs, present parsons to livings or retain private chaplains were all aspects of the authority of landed families, such as those Massinger's father had served and in whose ambience he had grown up. All these are menaced by the ambitious and power-seeking Sir Giles Overreach, who aspires by financial and legal trickery and violence to take over the influence of the old country families (represented in the play by the warrior-aristocrat Lord Lovel and the rich widow Lady Allworth), and appoint his bribed cronies as JPs so that he can prey on hardworking thrifty farmers as well as spendthrift heirs.

Although the plot is largely borrowed from Middleton's earlier City comedy *A Trick to Catch the Old One*, the situation is not (as there) treated as lightly humorous, nor is the attack on corrupt JPs (as in Middleton's *Phoenix* a generation earlier) irreverently funny. Too much is at stake for that. The rhetoric of Overreach's great speeches is that of the anti-tyrant play rather than the comic self-exposure of Middleton's merchants or Jonson's usurers; and when his schemes are thwarted by the plotting of the gentry characters his final explosion into madness makes a frightening as well as a reassuring ending.

The name of the cormorant-villain, Sir Giles Overreach, was clearly intended to alert the audience to analogies with the notorious Sir Giles Mompesson, impeached in 1621 over his monopolies and patents. True, by 1625–6 (the likeliest date for the play) the name had become proverbial, signifying all the abuses permitted in James's reign. But the association here with Mompesson is more specific. To minimise the connection of the play with the Mompesson case (on the grounds that it was no longer topical, or that Overreach the usurer cannot be an exact portrait of Mompesson the courtier and MP) is to obscure the coherent shape and political meaning that *New Way* certainly had for its contemporary audience.

That audience knew well enough that the original Sir Giles had not been a City moneylender or merchant, but a courtier-client and remote kinsman of Buckingham, grossly abusing the patents obtained through him, and associated in several of them with the duke's relatives.[32] Sir Giles was indeed, in Conrad Russell's phrase, 'the tip of the iceberg';[33] behind him lay the Villiers family and behind them the duke himself, as parliament knew when it attacked and impeached Mompesson in 1621. In the event Buckingham wisely cut his losses by disclaiming responsibility for the patentees' misuse of their powers, while parliament refrained from pressing charges against his brother. Nevertheless the case was a landmark. The name Sir Giles remained symbolic not only of privilege and corruption in high places, but also of the power and rightful function of king and parliament in rooting out and punishing such abuses as the contemporary broadside showed.[34] The accusation of using his power to enrich members of his own family surfaced again as one of the charges against Buckingham in the parliaments of 1625 and 1626. Mompesson was still attempting to enforce his alehouse patent in 1623, and (more to the point for the main attack directed against Buckingham in 1625), the duke's relatives and creatures were so influential that even the exposures of 1621 did not seriously harm them. Sir Edward Villiers, who shared the gold and silver thread monopoly, was still drawing profits from successor companies farming the duties on gold and silver wire in 1624, and when parliament dissolved a later company with which he associated, he had to be compensated for his loss by an annuity of £1,000.

By 1625 'Sir Giles' could thus stand for all those who profited from the favourite's power, in particular the Villiers clan and its hangers-on, feared and resented not only by the rival Herbert connection, Massinger's patrons, but also by important City interests led by the Goldsmiths' Company and the Lord Mayor and Aldermen of London.[35] The fact that Massinger makes his Sir Giles a City financier, rather than a courtier-client, seems like a necessary concession to caution, saving the play from total suppression. Moreover, it was in line with the aristocratic status-based values of the Herberts and their like, which were anti-absolutist but certainly not dangerously egalitarian.

The parallel explains much that would otherwise be puzzling about *A New Way*. Although Overreach is said to 'come from the City', he is deliberately characterised as *unlike* the usual stereotyped merchant or usurer of City comedy. Furnace the cook explicitly underlines the difference:

> To have a usurer that starves himself . . .
> To grow rich, and then purchase, is too common:
> But this Sir Giles feeds high, keeps many servants,
> Who must at his command do any outrage;
> Rich in his habit, vast in his expenses;
> Yet he to admiration still increases
> In wealth, and lordships.   (II.ii.106–14)

In lifestyle and personal arrogance Overreach behaves not like a bourgeois miser or penny-pinching trader, but rather like the proudest, most selfish and ungovernable of the gentry he has married into and preys on – a maverick courtier and gentleman without any restraining sense of 'country' or religious values or obligation to a local community. The satirically mocked upwardly mobile businessmen in Jonson's or Middleton's plays get enough wealth to buy into the country gentry by unfair trading or petty loan-sharking, and their ambitions are relatively modest – a pretty estate in Essex for Middleton's Quomodo, an officer's place for Gilthead's son and heir in Jonson's *The Devil is an Ass*. Overreach is personally and socially a quite different kind of figure, who has boundless aggressive ambitions to out-top all the old-established families. The role is, moreover, one of intense demonic violence which made it one of *the* star parts for emotional actors over the next 250 years – a tyrant's part, the stylised essence of heartless avarice and ruthless domination, rather than the detached observation of a particular social climber. In contemporary terms it provided an emotional equivalent, conscious or unconscious, for the mounting fear and hatred directed against the all-powerful favourite and his clients.

How closely Overreach as a character does or does not personally resemble the original Sir Giles is beside the point. For he is not a portrait or caricature, but the hyperbolic embodiment of avarice and ambition threatening a relatively settled traditional social fabric based on law, and the violence with which he does this confirms his historical origins. Mompesson had got rich not by thrift, or venturing, or even, like Shylock, by financing ventures, but through monopolies and protection rackets which he managed by fraud and force. Indeed, he was said to have threatened to fill all the prisons if necessary to enforce his gold and silver thread monopoly. Overreach, like Mompesson, dwells with pleasure on his power to imprison and to 'frighten men out of their estates'. On his first entrance he threatens his nephew Wellborn, whom he has beggared:

> If ever thou presume to own me more,
> I'll have thee caged and whipped. (i.iii.41–2)

The ruined Lady Downfall, compelled by want to be a servant to his daughter, lives under this threat:

> I took her up in an old tamin gown
> (Even starved for want of twopenny chops), to serve thee,
> And if I understand she but repines
> To do thee any duty, though ne'er so servile,
> I'll pack her to her knight, where I have lodged him,
> Into the counter, and there let them howl together. (iii.ii.43–8)

His hired hack Justice Greedy does the dirty work on the bench, against his own conscience, 'to the utter ruin / Of the poor farmer' (ii.i.7–8). But Sir Giles does not choose to be a JP himself, because he does not wish to be publicly accountable. 'In being out of office I am out of danger' (ii.i.14). His method is not mere financial trickery, but includes gang raids and legal fraud. Thus when Master Frugal refuses to sell his lands which Overreach covets:

> I'll therefore buy some cottage near his manor,
> Which done, I'll make my men break ope his fences,
> Ride o'er his standing corn, and in the night
> Set fire on his barns, or break his cattle's legs:
> These trespasses draw on suits, and suits expenses
> Which I can spare, but will soon beggar him ...
> Then, with the favour of my man of law,
> I will pretend some title: want will force him
> To put it to arbitrement. (ii.i.34–46)

The longest purse is bound to win at law. The racketeering process is all too like the lawsuits raised by Mompesson's own patent for discovering concealed crown lands.[36]

For good measure, the scandal of alehouse licences, a matter of bitter resentment to JPs in the Commons, also figures prominently in the play, notably in its opening scene – highlighting the link the audience was expected to make with the Villiers monopolies. Rascally Tim Tapwell, who openly runs his alehouse as a brothel and a depot for receiving stolen goods, is nevertheless allowed to hold his licence (supplied through Justice Greedy) on condition he obeys Sir Giles's orders, which include turning out of doors the prodigal heir Wellborn, who originally gave him the money to start in business. Ironically, Tapwell is now all set to rise from parish scavenger to overseer of the poor – a comment on the way standards of local government at the grassroots are eroded by the patentees. But as soon as Wellborn appears rich again and in favour with Overreach, Greedy immediately colludes with him to take away Tapwell's licence and close down the alehouse.

Overreach's obsessive desire to raise his family status by marrying his daughter into the nobility is another trait recalling the charges made in 1626 against Buckingham, who notoriously used his power to pressurise clients into advantageous marriages with his kindred. Overreach is, of course, a social upstart, who regards it as part of his revenge on 'true gentry' to make his daughter right honourable and the wife of a peer. However, even Buckingham himself, originally a mere knight's younger son (never mind his needier relatives) would have appeared to 'true gentry' like Pembroke and Arundel almost as much an upstart as Overreach does to 'the popular Lord Lovell, the minion of the people's love'.

By the time the play was put on, the 'natural rulers' in the country were threatened with a loss of their authority in another and more alarming way. The king and the favourite, failing to get parliament to finance wars without controlling policy, increasingly resorted to 'new counsels', to non-parliamentary taxation and forced loans, and those of the gentry who refused to pay or to organise the collection of what they saw as illegal, unconstitutional taxes were being removed by the government from their offices as JPs or lord-lieutenants, seventy-six of them being imprisoned or pressed for foreign service. Several of Massinger's patrons were involved in resistance to the policy, among them Sir Francis Foljambe, Sir Robert Wiseman, Philip Lord Stanhope, possibly the Knyvett family. His lawyer friends Henry Parker and John Selden were also concerned in such issues, which led directly to the attempted impeachment of Buckingham and the Commons' passing of the Petition of Right. The acutely status-conscious nobility and gentry in *A New Way* are similarly menaced not by a new, financially more vital and viable economic and social mode (a 'rising bourgeoisie'), but by a gangster with high-level political protection, representative not of City enterprise but of the most parasitic aspects of the old regime. City interests represented in parliament had joined with hostile peers and 'country' gentry to attack and expose Mompesson, as similar forces were about to attack Buckingham himself around the time when the play was staged. That the duke was the executor but not necessarily the main author of unpopular policies had not yet become clear to public opinion, which was still unwilling to blame the king himself for the drift towards absolutism, and made his evil counsellors – or the evil counsel of a single man, the real-life analogue of Overreach – responsible for it all.

The 1620s, indeed, saw the rise of something like an informed and articulate public opinion – or opinions – developing far beyond the 'natural rulers' in court and parliament. In the mounting tensions between the government and its critics the media of communication expanded rapidly. In spite of tight restrictions on domestic newspapers and parliamentary reporting, 'corantoes' of foreign news were imported from Europe; a network of news-collectors supplied the privately commissioned newsletters; a mass of pamphlets and 'separates' appeared, often illegally published and distributed; and all these provided attractive though risky material for the popular preachers and the commercial theatres. Although traditionalists were deeply worried about mysteries of state being thrown open to the 'giddy multitude' (an unease shared by leading dramatists like Ben Jonson), there was a growing sense of a new force in politics to be conciliated, manipulated or silenced. Even the increasingly fierce Laudian censorship of the later 1630s could hamper and obscure, but never wholly extinguish, the representation of political and ideological conflicts in the public theatres.

NOTES

1 See J. P. Sommerville, *Politics and Ideology in England 1603–1640* (1986), pp. 234–5.
2 On the public rhetoric of politics see Christopher Hill, 'Political Discourse in Seventeenth Century England', in *Politics and People in Revolutionary England*, ed. C. Jones, M. Nevitt and S. Roberts (London, 1986), and R. P. Cust, 'News and Politics in Early Seventeenth Century England', *Past and Present*, 112 (1986).
3 Jerzy Limon, *Dangerous Matter* (Cambridge, 1986), p. 121, argues that these publications were issued in line with the prince's new policy, and lists sixteen works published over the six months from December 1623 specifically showing the struggle of the true Protestant churches against

Rome as the struggle of Christ against Antichrist, in 'what appears to have been an ideological campaign of the war party'. However, many of these were from authors who had been publishing similar views for years. Thus Samuel Hieron's *Sermons* were the work of a well-known nonconforming preacher who died in 1617 and was patronised by Pembroke. Two of the books, by Daniel Featley and Francis White, were versions of the debates between the Jesuit Fisher and bishops of the Anglican Church, compiled in 1622 but held up for publication until King James sanctioned White's book in 1623. Anthony Wotton, author of *Run from Rome*, had been one of the 2nd Earl of Essex's Puritan chaplains in the 1590s, and had been deprived for nonconformity as long ago as 1604. Of the books listed by Limon, one (*A Gag for the Pope*) is dedicated to Pembroke, two to parliament, and three more are by authors who at some time dedicated to Pembroke (Featley, James Wadsworth and Hieron). None was dedicated to Prince Charles or Buckingham. There is thus no evidence for an 'ideological campaign of the war party' orchestrated by Buckingham and Prince Charles, as far as these tracts are concerned.

4 See the study of *The Maid of Honour* by Annabel Patterson in *Censorship and Interpretation* (Madison, Wis., 1984), pp. 79–84.

5 The emphasis on Timoleon's refusal to entrust defence to mercenary or conscript armies makes it impossible that the audience was meant to identify him with the mercenary general Mansfeld, later favoured by James and Buckingham, as Jerzy Limon strains to suggest (*Dangerous Matter*, pp. 62–88). Mansfeld did not arrive in England to seek this employment till April 1624, six months after *The Bondman* was first performed; nor did his personal character in any way resemble Timoleon's.

6 I have written at greater length about *The Bondman* in *Puritanism and Theatre* (Cambridge, 1980), pp. 213–17, and in my chapter on political drama in A. Braunmuller and M. Hattaway (eds.), *The Cambridge Companion to Renaissance Drama* (Cambridge, 1990).

7 For the 3rd Earl of Pembroke's 'distinctive political position', see J. P. Sommerville, *Politics and Ideology*, p. 234.

8 The seller was Sir John Astley, a client of Buckingham's.

9 Thomas Coghill valuably pointed out the political importance of the 'Relation', given by the Duke of Buckingham to parliament in February 1624, as a hitherto unnoticed source for the end of the play: 'Thomas Middleton and the Court, 1624: *A Game of Chess* in Context', *Huntington Library Quarterly*, 48 (1984) 273–88.

10 This accords with the view taken by Roger Lockyer, *Buckingham: the Life and Political Career of George Villiers, 1592–1628* (London, 1981).

11 He had reportedly converted the countess and some 130 others to Rome.

12 Francis White, *A reply to Jesuit Fisher's answer to certain questions propounded*

by His Majesty (1624). An Answer to Mr Fisher's relation of a Third Conference between a certain B. (as he styles him) and himself.... Which is here given by R.B., chaplain to the Bishop that was employed in the Conference (London, 1624). Daniel Featly, *The Romish Fisher caught in his own net* (London, 1624).

13 Jane Sherman, 'The Pawns' Allegory in Middleton's Game at Chess', *Review of English Studies*, 29, no. 114 (1978) 145–59, and Trevor Howard-Hill, the play's latest editor, have sought to neutralise the obvious anti-popish prejudice of the play. Identification of the White Queen's pawn with the Spanish Infanta, or with Prince Charles (as some scholars have proposed), runs directly contrary to the text and its central chess-metaphor.

14 See Peter Lake, 'Anti-Popery: the structure of a Prejudice', in R. Cust and A. Hughes, eds., *Conflict in Early Stuart England* (London, 1989), and Caroline Hibbard, *Charles I and the Popish Plot* (Chapel Hill, 1983). Not only had laws against recusants been relaxed in 1622–3, but, while volunteers for Frederick's forces had been cut, the Catholic Lord Vaux was permitted to raise a regiment to fight with the Spanish army of Flanders in the Palatinate; and even in the summer of 1624 he was permitted to reinforce these with 1,000 men, just when the officially backed volunteer force under Southampton was leaving to join the Dutch Republican armies fighting the Spaniards. It was not surprising if the Globe audience believed in secret popish influence in high places, subverting the will of parliament for war with Spain.

15 Reynolds's letter to Lord Denbigh is among the Newnham Paddox MSS of the Denbigh family, now in the Warwick Record Office, and is printed in *Royalist Father and Roundhead Son* by Cecilia, Countess of Denbigh (London, 1915), p. 30.

16 *Puritanism and Theatre*, chap. 10.

17 Cust and Hughes, *Conflict in Early Stuart England*, pp. 29–30.

18 See the lucid factual summary in Derek Hirst, *Authority and Conflict, England 1603–1658* (London, 1986), chap. 5, pp. 136–59.

19 Martin Butler, 'Romans in Britain: *The Roman Actor* and the Early Stuart Classical Play', in Douglas Howard, ed., *Philip Massinger* (Cambridge, 1985). See especially the editor's Introduction and chap. 6 by Christopher Thompson.

20 A theme to which he returned in the 1620s in *The Emperor of the East* (1631) and the lost play, *The King and the Subject* (1638). Patrons and associates of Massinger who were prominent as loan resisters included Sir Francis Foljambe, a Yorkshire MP who was punished for it, and whose relative Thomas Bellingham also received a Massinger dedication; Sir Robert Wiseman; members of the Knyvett and Stanhope families. Philip Lord Stanhope was removed from county offices on this account, but it was his wife Lady Catherine, daughter of the Puritan Sir Francis Hastings, who had received Massinger's dedication. The Earl

of Oxford was another leading refuser. Long after his death and Massinger's, *The City Madam* was dedicated to the Lady Ann, Countess of Oxford by the printer, Andrew Pennycuick. A fuller survey would probably reveal more such cases. See Richard Cust, *The Forced Loan and English Politics, 1626–1628* (1987).

21 The modern use of the terms 'court' and 'country' has been contested by some scholars (notably Kevin Sharpe), on the grounds that all groups shared a common ideal of 'courtliness'. Too many, however, saw the *actual* court as failing to live up to this ideal and becoming the source of much that was wrong in the body politic. The chapter quotation (on p. 237) from Massinger testifies to this. For a discussion of the meanings given by contemporaries to these terms, see Cust and Hughes, *Conflict in Early Stuart England*, pp. 19–22 and *passim*.

22 The phrase is invented and defined by Annabel Patterson in her suggestive *Censorship and Interpretation*.

23 For official documents relating to these riots see Thomas Birch, ed., *The Court and Times of Charles I* (London, 1848), I. A summary of these and other sources is in Keith Lindley, 'Riot Prevention and Control in Early Stuart London', *Transactions of the Royal Historical Society*, XXXIII (1983) 109–26.

24 *The Court and Times of Charles I*, I, p. 193.

25 For William St Leger's letters to Buckingham see *ibid.*, *passim*. For his opposition to Wimbledon's strategy, see S. R. Gardiner, *History of England 1603–1642* (London, 1905), vol. VI, p. 16.

26 R. S. Telfer in his critical edition (Princeton, 1932) favoured 1626, confirming for other reasons the date I have deduced from the close parallel between Belgarde's armed entry and the invasions of Whitehall by rioting soldiers and sailors during that year.

27 Edwards and Gibson identify the sources as (1) two story sketches from the Declamations then attributed to Quintilian, MS CCCXVIII (for the father–son story) and CCLXXIX (for the incest story). (2) The criminal career of Catiline as summarised in the Prologue to Jonson's play of that name.

28 Introduction to *The Unnatural Combat*, in *Plays and Poems of Philip Massinger* ed. P. Edwards and C. Gibson (Oxford, 1976).

29 A selection from this material is given in *Poems, Songs etc. relating to George Villiers Duke of Buckingham* ed. F. W. Fairchild (London, 1850).

30 Licensed by Herbert 1631, in Dekker's lifetime; printed 1636. The date of first performance is uncertain.

31 The attribution is by A. H. Bullen, who edited the play from the Egerton MS. *Old English Plays*, 4 vols., 1882–5.

32 Buckingham's half-brother Sir Edward Villiers was his partner in the gold and silver thread monopoly, while his brother Kit Villiers shared in the profits from the alehouse patents.

33 C. Russell, *Parliaments and English Politics 1621–1624* (Oxford, 1979), pp. 102–5.

34 *Description of Sir Giles Mompesson, Knight*, 1620, reprinted in R. H. Ball, *The Amazing Career of Sir Giles Overreach*, 1939.

35 The Goldsmiths' Company, staunchly supported by the Lord Mayor and Aldermen, were among the most powerful opponents of the gold and silver thread monopoly. A prominent leader of the company was Sir Hugh Myddleton, civil engineer and City benefactor, brother of the Puritan Lord Mayor Sir Thomas Myddleton, who was also a patron of Thomas Middleton the dramatist.

36 The Committee of the Lords that investigated the lands patent was chaired by the Earl of Southampton (Shakespeare's former patron), who was in trouble and interrogated later in 1621, among other things for discussing the case outside the House and getting private information from MPs about it. He was reputed to be the leader of those who wished to use this parliament to attack Buckingham himself (Russell, *Parliaments and English Politics*, p. 105).

Index